Hannah G. Solomon

Papers of the Jewish Women's Congress

Held at Chicago, September 4, 5, 6 and 7, 1893

Hannah G. Solomon

Papers of the Jewish Women's Congress
Held at Chicago, September 4, 5, 6 and 7, 1893

ISBN/EAN: 9783743311381

Manufactured in Europe, USA, Canada, Australia, Japa

Cover: Foto ©ninafisch / pixelio.de

Manufactured and distributed by brebook publishing software (www.brebook.com)

Hannah G. Solomon

Papers of the Jewish Women's Congress

INTRODUCTION.

When the World's Fair Congress Auxiliary was organized, it was determined that, among the other congresses, a Parliament of Religions should be held. The Parliament consisted of a General Parliament of all religions and of denominational Congresses. The General Committee on Religious Parliament was composed of two branches, one the men's, the other the women's committee. It consisted of representatives of every denomination, appointed by Mr. C. C. Bonney, president of the Auxiliary, and Mrs. Charles Henrotin, vice-president of the woman's branch. By virtue of this appointment, they became the chairmen of their respective denominational committees, with power to make up the committee. At the first meeting of the Jewish Women's Committee, it was decided to work along the lines adopted by the other committees. The Committee also decided to collect and publish the traditional melodies of the Jews as a souvenir of the occasion. In order to arouse the interest in the Jewish Congress and the souvenir, notices were issued to all Jewish publications, inviting the co-operation of all persons interested.

Circular letters were sent to the larger cities, asking Jewish women to hold mass meetings to elect delegates. This measure was more successful than had been anticipated, twenty-nine cities being represented by ninety-three delegates. An extensive correspondence was carried on with Jewish men and women of this country and England, no less than two thousand letters having been written and received by the members of the Committee.

The Programme Committee obtained subjects for papers from many sources, also names of women to write them. It was no easy task to arrange the programme and choose the essayists. It was found that every section of the country could be represented, and the committee, in every instance, was fortunate in its choice of essayists. Two representatives were chosen to present papers in the General Parliament. The Committee was equally fortunate in interesting the Rev. Wm. Sparger, of New York, and the Rev. Alois Kaiser, of Baltimore, in the work necessary for the souvenir. These gentlemen gave their services without compensation, and owing to their able efforts, as well as to those of the conscientious publisher, Mr. L. Rubovits, the Jewish Women's Congress has a souvenir of which it may justly be proud. Dr. Cyrus Adler kindly consented to write the introduction.

The Congress itself was a great success, arousing the interest of Jews and Christians alike. The room originally intended for the sessions was found inadequate to hold the audience, and the larger room chosen was at all times too small. At the Wednesday evening session, it was necessary to hold an overflow-meeting, the overflow completely filling another large hall. The meeting was, in every respect, satisfactory. The question of religious persecution was thoroughly discussed, in the manner and spirit hoped for by the Committee. The discussion was noteworthy, because Jews, Catholics and Protestants were animated by the same desire to battle in the cause of liberty of conscience. The influence of the Congress is, however, not to be measured by the size of its audiences, nor by the merits of its papers. Its chief result is that it brought together, from all parts of the country, East, West and South, women interested in their religion, following similar lines of work, and sympathetic in ways of thought, and was instrumental in cementing friendships between them. Its outcome is a National Organization, and its use was to prove to the world that Israel's women, like women of other faiths, are interested in all that tends to bring men nearer together in every movement affecting the welfare of mankind.

HANNAH G. SOLOMON, Chairman.

PROGRAMME.

Monday, September 4, 10 a. m.

PRAYER, ... RAY FRANK, *Oakland, Cal.*
ADDRESS, ... ELLEN M. HENROTIN,
    Vice-President of the World's Congress Auxiliary.
ADDRESS, ... HANNAH G. SOLOMON, *Chairman.*
POEM, "White Day of Peace," . . . MIRIAM DEL BANCO.
PAPER, "Jewish Women of Biblical and Mediæval Times,"
    LOUISE MANNHEIMER, *Cincinnati, Ohio.*
PAPER, "Jewish Women of Modern Days,"
    HELEN KAHN WEIL, *Kansas City, Mo.*
DISCUSSION, . . { HENRIETTA G. FRANK, *Chicago, Ill.*
    DR. K. KOHLER, *New York.*
    DR. E. G. HIRSCH, *Chicago, Ill.*

Tuesday, September 5, 9.30 a. m.

PAPER, "Woman in the Synagogue," . RAY FRANK, *Oakland, Cal.*
DISCUSSION, ... DR. I. S. MOSES, *Chicago, Ill.*
PAPER, "Influence of the Discovery of America on the Jews,"
    PAULINE H. ROSENBERG, *Allegheny, Pa.*
DISCUSSION, . . { ESTHER WITKOWSKI, *Chicago, Ill.*
    MARY NEWBURY ADAMS, *Dubuque, Iowa.*

Tuesday, September 5, 2.30 p. m.

PAPER, "Women as Wage-Workers, with Special Reference
    to Directing Immigrants," JULIA RICHMAN, *New York.*
DISCUSSION, . . . { SADIE G. LEOPOLD, *Chicago, Ill.*
    JESSIE BROSS LLOYD, *Chicago, Ill.*
PAPER, "Influence of the Jewish Religion in the Home,"
    MARY M. COHEN, *Philadelphia, Pa.*
DISCUSSION, . . . { JULIA I. FELSENTHAL, *Chicago, Ill.*
    ISABELLA BEECHER HOOKER.
    ADA CHAPMAN, *Dallas, Texas.*

Wednesday, September 6, 9.30 a. m.

POEM, "Israel to the World in Greeting," . CORA WILBURN,
    Marshfield, Mass.
PAPER, "Charity as Taught by the Mosaic Code,"
    EVA L. STERN, *New York.*

PAPER, "Woman's Place in Charitable Work; What it is, and What it should be," CARRIE S. BENJAMIN, *Denver, Col.*

DISCUSSION, ... { GOLDIE BAMBER, *Boston, Mass.*
{ R. W. NAVRA, *New Orleans, La.*

WEDNESDAY, September 6, 8.30 p. m.

ADDRESS, ... CHAIRMAN.
PRESENTATION OF HYMN BOOK, . . . EMMA FRANK.
PAPER, "Mission Work Among the Unenlightened Jews,"
MINNIE D. LOUIS, *New York.*
DISCUSSION, ... REBEKAH KOHUT, *New York.*
PAPER, "How can Nations be Influenced to Protest or even Interfere in Cases of Persecution," LAURA JACOBSON, *St. Louis, Mo.*

DISCUSSION, . { LILLIE HIRSHFIELD, *New York.*
{ ARCHBISHOP IRELAND, *St. Paul, Minn.*
{ WILLIAM ONAHAN, *Chicago, Ill.*
{ PROF. CHAS. ZEUBLIN, *Chicago, Ill.*
{ THE REV. JENKINS LLOYD JONES, *Chicago, Ill.*
{ DR. E. G. HIRSCH, *Chicago, Ill.*
{ THE REV. IDA G. HULTIN, *Chicago, Ill.*

THURSDAY, September 7, 9.30 a. m.

REPORTS, ...
PAPER, "Organization," . . SADIE AMERICAN, *Chicago, Ill.*
BUSINESS MEETING, ...

PAPERS read before the Religious Parliament under the Auspices of the Committee of the Jewish Women's Congress.

SEPTEMBER 16.

PAPER, "The Outlook of Judaism," JOSEPHINE LAZARUS, *New York.*

SEPTEMBER 21.

PAPER, "What Judaism has done for Woman,"
HENRIETTA SZOLD, *Baltimore, Md.*

MONDAY, SEPTEMBER 4, 1893, 10 A. M.

PRAYER.

RAY FRANK, OAKLAND, CAL.

Almighty God, Creator and Ruler of the universe, through Whose justice and mercy this first convention of Jewish women has been permitted to assemble, accept our thanks, and hearken, O Lord, to our prayer.

In times past, when storms of cruel persecution drove us toward the reefs of adversity, seemingly overwhelmed by misfortune, we had faith in Thee and Thy works, ever trusting and believing that Thou ordainest all things well. Because of this faith, we feel that Thou hast, in the course of events, caused this glorious congress to convene, that it may give expression to that which shall spread broadcast a knowledge of Thee and Thy deeds.

Grant, then, Thy blessing upon those assembled, and upon the object of their meeting. May the peculiar circumstances, which have brought together, under one roof, both Catholic and Jew, who, for centuries, have been seeking to serve Thee, though in different ways, be a promise of future peace. Grant, we beseech Thee, that this convention may be productive of that which is in accordance with Thy will.

Bless, O Lord, this our country and the President thereof, and all the people of the land. May love and peace be the heritage of men, to remain with them forever. *Amen.*

ADDRESS.

ELLEN M. HENROTIN, CHICAGO, ILL.

In Chicago, to-day, in this young, so-called "materialistic World-City," the representatives of the religion which has had the greatest influence over the creeds of modern civilization are gathered together. If a glorious past can insure a glorious future, then this parliament of Jewish women is moving on to a great triumph.

To what other race of women has it been given to inspire the spiritual ideals, not alone of its own people, but of the entire civilized world? To them, the arts and literature have turned for inspiration, until the type of character and of beauty of the Jewess is cosmopolitan, and surrounded with a halo of mysterious beauty, and now the spirit of association has come to them—the greatest modern factor, "working for righteousness." Dr. Stevenson, in her address to the General Federation of Women's Clubs, said that the "Brotherhood of man can only come through the Sisterhood of Woman"—a profound truth, and every day that sisterhood is enlarging, and is permeating society.

The great number assembled in response to the call of the committee testifies to the universality of sentiment on this point among Jewish women. That this meeting may result in a national organization is my earnest desire.

I have the pleasure of introducing, as the permanent presiding officer of the Congress, Mrs. Hannah Solomon, to whose courage, energy and devotion the success of this Congress will be due.

ADDRESS.

HANNAH G. SOLOMON, Chairman.

It is my pleasant duty, as chairman of the local committee, to extend to you all a hearty welcome to our city and to our Congress, the first Jewish Women's Congress. It was with some misgiving that I accepted a position on the general committee on Parliament of Religions, realizing that it was a new departure for the Jewish woman to occupy herself with matters pertaining to religion. But I felt that in the Parliament of Religions, where women of all creeds were represented, the Jewish woman should have a place. I was fortunate enough to secure a committee thoroughly in sympathy with me, all its members believing that, on an occasion on which women and men of all creeds are realizing that the ties that bind us are stronger than the differences that separate, that when the world is giving to Israel the liberty, long withheld, of taking its place among all religions, to teach the truths it holds, for the benefit of man and the glory of the Creator, the place of the Jewish woman should not be vacant. I need not say that the work has been great, and it is with pleasure that I look back upon the harmonious, efficient work of the committee. The only fault I might find is the too great enthusiasm shown and the confidence with which I was honored, causing me "to rush, where angels feared to tread." I am sure that the committee will always look back upon our work for the Congress with much pleasure, the *sang froid* with which we treated Roberts' rules resulting in tatters of parliamentary law which we shall treasure as trophies. And to the women of other cities, as well as of our own, who so earnestly seconded our efforts, I extend our sincere thanks. To the women of the general committee on Religious Parliament, representing all sects and creeds, our appreciation is due for the interest they have always felt in our work. Could the good-will entertained for each other by the members of the general committee be disseminated in the entire world, there would be no need of a Parliament of Religions; for each was desirous not merely to be just, but generous, in her treatment of others. I hope the same spirit may characterize all the congresses. To the women at the head of the Exposition, all women owe homage. The President and the Vice-President of the Woman's Branch of the Auxiliary must ever pose as goddesses of liberty for the women of our century, the one in material, the other in spiritual things, gaining for all women the full privilege of exercising their talents and capabilities. Our papers are not intended to startle the world as literary efforts, but we wish seriously to consider problems that are to be solved, in order to help along the great work of bringing men nearer together, to be co-workers in a world requiring the best efforts of all.

In our "Souvenir," a collection of the traditional songs of our people, we pay our tribute to the work and worth of those of our faith who have lived and suffered, making it possible for us to have our faith in this land of liberty. We pay our tribute to the traditions of the past, which were dear to our forefathers, who, however oppressed and unhappy, sang these songs. They were their staff and their stay. From the Ghetto they resounded, they raised them to a spiritual plane which no walls could encompass. Chanting the prayers and singing the songs uplifted them, so that they forgot their misery. And we in this land of liberty and prosperity, in this Columbian era, should not forget the deeper tones struck in days of adversity. We have not merely tried to publish a book, but we wished to preserve our traditions. Living, as we do, in this renegade city, belonging to radical congregations, thoroughly in sympathy with all endeavors to break down barriers, we are loyal to our faith, to our history and to the traditions of our families. In this sense, as a tribute to the past, we give our book to our co-religionists.

To those who are not of our faith, to many of whom we are bound by ties of love and friendship, as strong as those of faith, we bid a hearty welcome, and invite them to take part in our discussions and be frank with us. Perhaps, in this wise, we may overcome some of the inherited prejudices unfavorable to us, and if we cannot gain sympathy, we may at least command respect. To our delegates, we extend a special greeting. We expected to arouse interest, but the response has exceeded our fondest expectations.

And let us, above all things, remember that we are children of many mothers, that we have different points of view, different methods of reasoning. Let us be just to each other, give to each one the same patient hearing that we ask for ourselves. Let those of us who have orthodox views, believe that the radical views may be as sincere as our own; those of us who are radical, believe the others just as honest as ourselves, so that harmony and peace may mark our going as our coming.

WHITE DAY OF PEACE.

Miriam Del Banco, Chicago, Ill.

Heard ye the golden bells of peace that angels softly sway,
When, on the skies of progress, dawns the rose of freedom's day?
Heard ye the winds—the sweet, soft winds—that, through the scented air,
Swept o'er our boundless prairies like a whispered voice in prayer?
O, heard ye not above the waves that swell time's rushing tide,
A voice that to the ages like a silver clarion cried:
"White day of peace! by Toleration crowned and glorified!"

O day divine.! no industry alone thy kiss may claim,
No single art or science bear the impress of thy name,
No order trail its garlands through the splendor of thy hours,
No nation wave its banners 'mid thy sunshine and thy flowers;
All mankind—all the sons of earth thy countless ranks increase;
Their lips proclaim, in ringing tones whose echoes ne'er shall cease,
A congress of religions—God's great festival of peace.

But why, 'mid all this gleam and glow, shines the Menorah's fire?
Why throb through every festal strain the notes of David's lyre?
Why from the silken scroll resounds the tinkling silver bell?
Why gather with rejoicings loud the sons of Israel?
The quaint old Hebrew blessings of their fathers everywhere
Seem mingled with Joy's dimpled laugh and Gratitude's low prayer,
And blend like murmured music on the flower-laden air.

Four centuries look back upon a time when sunny Spain
Tore from her heart the bleeding child of misery and pain;
Rent tie and tendril from the graves and altars of his sires;
His sacred home, his golden fields laid low in smouldering fires;
Then, turning on the hated Jew with torture-racking hand,
She hunted him from hill and vale and silver-gleaming strand;
And—"sorrow's crown of sorrow"—robbed him of his fatherland!

Then floated over earth once more that cry of mortal pain
Whose mem'ry steals not only from the scented vales of Spain;
From Russia's steppes, from Bucharest, from England's daisied sod,
That cry of tortured Israel has swept aloft to God;
And now it trailed its pain upon the ocean's silver crest,
And e'en the dark-blue waters spoke of tumult and unrest,
Yet drifted toward the pearly gates that bar the sunset west.

Ah, gazing from some lonely deck, up through the silent air,
Unconscious of the answer to his supplicating prayer,
The weary exile heeded not as, toward the western sky,
Three white-winged ships—God's messengers—went slowly sailing by;
Sailed toward the line where sunset veils of gold and violet
Concealed an infant world that dreamed in dewy verdure yet,
Ere broke that dawning freedom's day whose sun has never set.

O bright New World, within thine arms the wanderer found rest;
The scourged and outlawed one revived, clasped to thy throbbing breast,
Clasped to thy heart, where hope's white bloom, picked fresh from freedom's sod,
Bore on its breath the exile's prayer of gratitude to God.
With thee, his manhood's sacred rights he dared once more to claim,
With thee, he dared once more to breathe Jehovah's holy name,
To hold aloft the lamp of truth, and feed its living flame.

And thus, of all who in the light of thy protection dwell,
None clings to thee with deeper love than grateful Israel;
The heart from which the first grand cry for freedom sprang to life,
And thrilled the world, beats close to thine, in days of peace and strife;
Its pure devotion to thy cause no stain, no blemish mars;
And though he bears or may not bear the soldier's honored scars,
None than the Jew more loyally defends thy stripes and stars.

For thee he strives each day to prove man's brotherhood to man,
For thee he seeks the scholar's fame, the crown of artisan;
The prophet's wisdom, David's gift, Spinoza's thought sublime,
And Heine's art and Mendelssohn's, through Israel, are thine;
Yea, every heart its tribute brings, its love forevermore;—
None can forget the voice whose call once thrilled from shore to shore:
"Ye outcast, scourged and weary ones, lo, enter at my door!"

And therefore in this gleam and glow shines the Menorah's fire
While echo through each festal strain the notes of David's lyre;
Sweet Nature lifts her floral horn the notes of peace to swell
That float from every happy heart in grateful Israel.
The hilltops are aglow with light; and hark, from far away,
Float dreamily the chimes of bells that unseen angels sway;
'Tis Toleration's jubilee—her white-robed festal day!

JEWISH WOMEN OF BIBLICAL AND OF MEDIÆVAL TIMES.

Louise Mannheimer, Cincinnati, O.

To be called upon to speak in these halls, where the giants in the realm of learning assemble from week to week to give their best thoughts to the world, brings to my mind the words of the men whom Moses sent to spy out the promised land. They said: "We saw there giants, the sons of Anak, and we were in our own eyes as grasshoppers, and so were we in their eyes." But Caleb and Joshua were not afraid, for they trusted in the Lord. So even I will not be afraid, and put my trust in the Eternal.

The history of the women of the Bible, like all historical writings, can be approached in three ways; either one accepts all the data unhesitatingly, with childlike faith, or by extensive reading and comparing of original texts, one strives to arrive at critical conclusions as to the facts, or by reading and re-reading the Bible, time and again, with earnest and absorbing zeal, one acquires the ability to grasp the deeper underlying meaning of the outward forms and to trace the psychological causes of the acts and deeds.

Very few women are in the happy position to have the required opportunities or even the necessary time for the studies which alone can enable one to arrive at independent, critical conclusions, while, on the other hand, it is pre-eminently woman who, when she does read the Bible, reads it, as it were, with her heart.

This it is which enables her to recognize the presence of the Eternal in the still small voice of history, to find the guiding hand of Jehovah in every historical event, as well as in the events in the life of each individual. She feels the pangs which are the source of tears to desolate Zion, and Zion's joy brings a happy smile to her face.

Through this deep sympathy, she is enabled to trace to their very sources the manifestations of the hidden emotions and energies of soul and mind, and to enlarge the scant but suggestive material which the Scriptures supply in regard to the history of "The Women of the Bible."

As a clear brook reflects the objects on its banks, without enhancing their beauty or obliterating their defects, so does the Bible delineate the recorded characters without exaggerating their virtues or concealing their shortcomings.

The Women of the Bible! what graceful forms, imbued with all that is good and noble, surrounded by the wonderful beauty of Oriental scenery, rise at these words before our mind, out of the gray mist of the hoary past!

In the multitude of types of maidenly loveliness, womanly beauty and matronly dignity, there are three groups which especially claim our attention and admiration.

These are not ideals, standing high above the level of human nature, to whom we can only look up with reverential awe, as if they were beings of a higher order who are beyond our comprehension—by no means.

We need but look into our own hearts to understand their impulses; we must but heed the longings of our own souls to comprehend their aspirations.

The three prominent groups among the women of the Bible, of whom this paper can give but a short sketch on account of the limited time, are, the Mothers in Israel, the Prophetesses in Israel, and the women who solved the problem of the proper sphere of woman's activity in Israel at this early historical time.

The Mothers in Israel! There is no title of honor which through all the generations of the adherents of Mosaic Law was more revered than this sweet, blessed name of "mother" and justly so, for what watchful care, what tender devotion, what self-sacrificing love are expressed in the name by which Sarah, Rebecca and Rachel are distinguished!

Sarah, the Bible shows us at once, in her womanly dignity, the faithful friend and companion of her husband Abraham, in whose soul dawned the great light of the world, the conception of the one and only God. The perfect confidence Abraham puts in Sarah on all occasions proves that she must have had a clear understanding of his great mission.

A promise of great blessing and an abundance of earthly possessions is hers, still she remains modest and active, for lo! three strangers pass, and Abraham desires them to partake of his hospitality. He does not call his young men, nor the hand-maids, but he calls Sarah, the princess, the honored mistress of the house, and *she* kneads the dough, and *she* bakes the cakes. What a grand lesson in this simple narrative!

We can trace Sarah's kind and motherly disposition in her solicitude for Lot. We find written: "And Sarah sent Eliezer to inquire after the welfare of Lot."* Lot had separated himself from Abraham, in whose house he had been brought up like a son; he did not send to inquire after the welfare of his foster-parents, nor did Abraham show, by any outward sign, that he

---
* Dr. B. Beer "Leben Abrahams."

missed Lot, but Sarah felt more than the others the separation, for her heart hungered for the love of a child.

After years of unwavering faith, the long deferred hope was realized. Isaac, the promised of God, had been given them, and now behold the God-fearing parents endeavor to prove themselves worthy of the happiness the Eternal has granted them.

Wide open are the portals of their house to the poor and the needy; those that hunger partake of food, and the needy ones are supplied with the necessaries of life. If any of the grateful ones wish to thank them, they answer: "Thank the Eternal who created all things; all we receive belongs to Him."

The first moral lesson to humanity was given by Abraham and Sarah. To feed the hungry, to give raiment to the needy, to speak kindly to the unfortunate, to act justly toward all mankind, and to be grateful to the Eternal—this is what Abraham taught to his household, and what Sarah put into practice.

Rebecca at the well, in childlike simplicity and charming kindness filling the trough for the camels, after having quenched the thirst of the stranger, what an attractive picture! Just as attractive as when, on seeing her future husband in the field, she alights from the camel in gentle deference, and covers herself with her veil in modest dignity. Rebecca combines all the sweet traits which arise from a generous heart, whose quick impulses are balanced by an understanding mind.

In the house of Abraham she learned to believe and trust in the Eternal, and so firm and strong grew her faith that she is the first woman in Israel of whom it is written: "In her distress she asked the Lord, and the Lord answered her."

An earnest and trusting prayer is sure to be answered even to-day as of yore, but where the prayers are only *recited*, it is done so euphoniously that our ear is filled with the euphony of the sounds, and cannot hear anything else. Rebecca's one failing, her partiality to her younger son, bore the seed of bitter fruit for herself. By the endeavor to secure Esau's blessing for Jacob, she drove her favorite son from her presence for years.

Children are variously gifted; parents should discern that it is not in the child's power to have one gift rather than another, less to the taste of the father or the mother perhaps. To lead their different inclinations in the proper direction, and bestow an equal amount of affection on each child, these are the sacred duties devolving upon parents.

Rachel, the shepherdess, in all the blooming beauty of youth, approaching the well where Jacob met her, will always be an object of admiration, though Leah, the less favored with outward charms, had a gentler and more devoted disposition. Leah eagerly and fully accepted the one and only God, of whose wonderful power and merciful love Jacob told them, but in Rachel there was still lingering an inclination toward the idols in her father's house, until the firm conviction of Jacob kindled the pure light of monotheism also in her soul. However, with all her shortcomings, Rachel must have been very lovable to be able to win such deep, unwavering affection as we find so touchingly described in Genesis xxix. 20, "And Jacob served for Rachel seven years; and they seemed to him but a few days through the love he had to her."

The most pronounced characteristics of the "Mothers in Israel" are their devotion to the duties of home and the deep and tender love for their children.

The next group claiming our attention is the group of prophetesses in Israel.

In times of great events it is that the spirit of the Lord moves, as it were, on the wings of a mighty but voiceless storm. Responsive souls are touched by the waves of the heaving commotion—others hear nothing, and feel nothing.

Miriam was the first among the women in Israel, whose responsive soul was moved by the breath of the Lord. With timbrel in hand, she led forth the women at the shore of the Red Sea, and sang the song of triumph, " Sing ye to the Lord, for He hath triumphed gloriously ; the horse and his rider hath He thrown into the sea."

Even as a child, Miriam must have been uncommonly thoughtful, or her mother would not have sent her to watch over the infant Moses. Patiently did she wait till she saw her little brother safe in the arms of Pharaoh's daughter.

With what intelligence did she act to secure the privilege of the care of the child for her mother!

Surely, these were the germs from which grew the rich blossoms of the gifts of her womanhood.

What a pity that one chilling gust of unsuppressed envy caused these rich blossoms to wither and droop!

Miriam grew jealous; she, the faithful companion of Moses' early youth, could not endure the thought that on account of Zipporah, the Ethiopian, she had to be content with a smaller share of her brother's affection.

" And Miriam and Aaron spake against Moses, because of the Ethiopian woman he had married."

Great as was this transgression of Miriam, so was also her punishment; she became leprous. The good deeds of her childhood, however, were not forgotten. She had patiently waited and watched over Moses on the shore of the Nile, now the whole camp of Israel waited for her until she was healed.

The growing intellectual and spiritual development of the women in Israel is well marked in Miriam, but with Deborah this development reaches a glorious culmination. Prophet, judge, leader in battle, poet and sacred singer, where in history do we see all these various offices filled by one individual, by a woman? And who was Deborah? Was she a princess, or the descendant of a high-priest, or the daughter of a man of high standing, and so a woman of authority? By no means, she was but the daughter of lowly parents and the wife of Lapidoth, a man not distinguished by position or wealth.

To hold the responsible position of judge, Deborah must have combined natural talents with untiring perseverance to cultivate and perfect them for the service of God, $i.\ e.$, for the advancement of her fellow-beings. Deborah's husband had perfect confidence in her, for he knew that the Eternal was with her.

And Deborah prophesied to Barak that he would be victorious, still he was wanting in courage to go without her into the battle, so she was forced to leave for the first time her quiet home in order to secure the victory.

Her prophecy was fulfilled to the very word; the victory was given to the Jewish people by the Lord, and brought them the clear consciousness that they were the people of the Eternal, the witnesses of the one and only God.

After the enemy is overthrown, Deborah bursts into a song of triumph in strains which only the psalmists and prophets have equaled in inspiration and beauty, still she does not claim any other title than: "Deborah, a Mother in Israel."

Several hundred years later there arose another prophetess in Israel. Hilkia, the high-priest, while repairing and cleansing the sadly neglected house of the Lord, found the forgotten Book of the Law. When the contents of the book were made known to Josiah, the king, it aroused him to the full comprehension of the people's transgressions and their ingratitude toward the Eternal. In his consternation and grief, he rent his clothes, and sent to inquire of the Lord for him and for the people. And to whom did his high officers go to inquire? Not to the young prophet Jeremiah, not to Zephaniah, but to the prophetess Huldah. Her reputation for superior wisdom and profound knowledge of the Law must have been well established. And *where* did the high officers go to seek her? According to the explanation of Jonathan, they found her *in the College.* "Huldah, the prophetess, she was the wife of Shallum, the son of the keeper of the garments, and she dwelled in the College." What an abundance of conclusions can be derived from this statement!

There were, then, no restrictive regulations at that time to exclude women from colleges among the Israelites, and women, even married women, were thirsty enough after the limpid waters flowing from the source of Zion, to take advantage of the opportunity offered to them.

There is, then, even in those remote times a precedent for the liberal views of the Hebrew Union College. Huldah came not forward of her own accord. We do not hear of her before nor after the king sends to her, for with all the exquisite gifts of prophecy and profound knowledge, she still retains the true womanly modesty of a Mother in Israel.

And now let us turn our attention to a group of energetic women, who, by their example, showed how to solve, with quiet dignity, the problem of the proper sphere of woman's activity.

The five daughters of Zelophchad, a descendant of Menasseh, pleaded personally their rights of inheritance before Moses and before Eliezer, the priest, and before the princes and the whole congregation at the door of the tabernacle. They said, "Why should the name of our father be done away from the midst of his family because he has no son? Give unto us a possession among the brothers of our father." And they were answered, "The daughters of Zelophchad speak rightly, they shall indeed have a possession among the brothers of their father, and the inheritance of their father shall pass unto them."

With remarkable independence did Abigail act when David sent his men to obtain food for himself and his warriors of the rich but mean Nabal, the unworthy husband of Abigail, and he refused the request. One of the servants of the household narrates the occurrence to Abigail in order to warn her of David's wrath.

With quick judgment does she comprehend at once the situation; not a moment does she hesitate, or stop to ask advice, but orders at once two hundred loaves, two bottles of wine, five sheep ready dressed, five measures of parched corn, a hundred clusters of raisins and two hundred cakes of figs to be conveyed to David. She herself accompanies the servants, and by her wisdom succeeds in calming David's wrath and preventing him from shedding blood. We see here the absolute authority woman could exercise in a Jewish household, even three thousand years ago, by her self-possession and dignity, even under the most trying circumstances.

Another incident which shows that energy well directed is the talisman that will secure success alike to woman and to man, is the event at the return of the gentle Shunammite from the land of the Philistines; she had gone there by the advice of Elisha, the prophet, during the famine in Judæa. On her return she finds her house and land confiscated. She does not ask the prophet to plead her case before the king; which Elisha would certainly have done, but she goes *herself* before Jehoram, and asks modestly, but firmly for redress, and obtains it fully and at once.

So we find woman in the full enjoyment of equality of rights in Israel, even to the extent of the highest office in the land, the office of ruler.

Alexander Jannæus, King of Judæa, when he felt his end approaching, called his wife Alexandra, and gave her such counsel as would secure her the kingdom.

He must have had the perfect conviction that her sex would prove no hindrance to her occupancy of the throne, and that she would be equal to the task, and so she was indeed. In a short time she had secured the homage of the warriors of the nation, whom she led on to victory. She reigned for nine years, during which time she maintained peace by energy and prudent counsel. Alexandra displayed the ability of a woman to rule a nation; other women proved themselves equally capable to be leaders in the realm of mind.

The book of Mosaic laws, found in the time of King Josiah, contained the precept that women should be admitted to listen to the public reading and expounding of the Law, and such good use was made by them of this privilege, that in Talmudic times there flourished many a woman whose authority in the expounding of the Law was acknowledged even by the rabbis. Beruria, the learned and pious wife of Rabbi Meir, acquired great renown. In Bagdad, the daughter of Rabbi Samuel ben Ali gave public lectures, as did also Miriam Shapira, the ancestress of the renowned Luria family. Graetz, in his "History of the Jews," speaks highly of the Talmudic knowledge of Paula dei Mansi, the wife of Jechiel; she copied commentaries on the Bible so beautifully that her writing is still admired.

Jewish women in all spheres of life held an honored position by their pure devotion to the sacred duties of the family, by their rich and well-perfected gifts of intellect and by their self-directed energy, but above all by their steadfast clinging to the belief in the one and only God.

Even women of other nations, when the pure laws of Jewish religion were made known to them, acknowledged their unsurpassed loftiness, and willingly adhered to them. Helena, the pious queen of Adiabene, is a noble example of these women; Ifra, the mother of the Persian king Shaber II, was strongly attached to Judaism without formally accepting it. The deep respect she felt for Jewish teachings, she showed by rich presents to their teachers. The same facts are recorded of Empress Judith, wife of the Frankish Emperor, Ludwig the Pious. A prelate of the court who wished to gain favor with her, dedicated to her his writings about the books of Esther and Judith, in which he compared her to these two Jewish heroines. Jews were freely admitted to the court, and to show her high appreciation and respect for them, she bestowed on them costly presents.

If we look for the most prominent trait among Jewish women of biblical and mediæval times, we shall find maiden and mother, prophetess and queen alike distinguished by perfect trust in the Eternal. In their distress they turn to Him, in perplexity they ask His counsel, and joy and happiness they accept gratefully as gifts from His hand. How few of us know the blessing of this ever-present faith! If we could but take the time to follow closely the intricate windings of our own lives, we would by their very events be safely led through the labyrinth of doubt and indifference to that Holy of Holies, a perfect trust in the Eternal, such as the Mothers of Israel possessed.

JEWISH WOMEN OF MODERN DAYS.

Helen Kahn Weil, Kansas City, Mo.

Show me a great man—I will show you a great mother! Show me a great race—I will show you an unending line of great mothers!

In the chronicles of time, whose synonym is eternity, Israel and Greece stand out as the two great nations of the world. Each of these peoples had its special mission to humanity—one, the teaching of eternal beauty, the other, the propaganda of the one great God, Who is both spirit and beauty.

In the annals of Greece, we read of Tyrtæus, the singer, whose inspiring song aroused the Spartans to battle when all other means had failed; in the tablets of Israel, we read of the prophetess and poetess, Deborah, who sat under the palm tree, chanting martial hymns, whose theme was the glory of Jehovah, the one true God.

Beauty is masculine! Spirit is feminine! Never is there an idea but has its obverse and reverse sides. The thought of Plato making the perfect being both male and female is not a discord. The earth, what would it be without this duality, which gives us the essence as well as the substance of creation? I believe it was James Freeman Clarke who used to pray to "Our Father and mother which are in Heaven," and if the great and good God maketh man in His own image, and if he is but a microcosm of his Creator, then surely the venerable divine was not amiss in his teachings.

Possibly, it may savor a little of heresy, this utterance of mine, that Israel pre-eminently endures, a symbol of woman's regenerative power. But proofs are not wanting to attest this assertion.

The greatest law-giver who ever drew breath owed the possibility of his career to woman. Pharaoh's daughter, who found the little Moses in his wave-rocked cradle, and nourished him as the fulcrum of her own being; Miriam, the houri-eyed, sweet-voiced sister, whose triumphant songs inspired the wavering tribes of Israel to follow their chosen leader through the unknown dangers of the trackless desert, are incarnations of this truth. Ever as the centuries grew apace, and the purpose of Israel waxed more and more manifest, did this verity assert itself. All through the Old Testament, at the most crucial times, it is a Deborah, a Judith, an Esther, upon whom the fate of their people revolves, and in more modern days, the discerning eye of Clio still awards this salient place to the women of Israel.

In Spain, where the descendants of the House of David were given sufficient breathing time to devote themselves anew to the study of philosophy and poetry, there were women philosophers and poets, and afterward, when the direful day of expulsion came, it was the mothers, wives and sisters of these ill-fated refugees who bore them up in their time of trouble.

In the awful roll of Jewish martyrs, woman does not stand a whit behind her brother, in her willingness to suffer loss of home, fortune and life for the sake of her holy religion. The tales told of these delicately nurtured women deliberately turning their backs upon the abodes that had sheltered their families for so many generations, clasping their weeping little ones to their breasts, and encouraging their husbands through their valorous examples, are a legion.

One of the most exquisite of the Old Testament idyls finds its repetition over and over again in these days. Many are the faithful Ruths who say in dauntless voices, "Entreat me not to leave thee, or to return from following after thee: for whither thou goest, I will go, and where thou lodgest, I will lodge."

In the sixteenth century, it was in Italy that the Jew was permitted to lead the most unmolested existence. The Hebrews who had inhabited the Italic peninsula previous to the Spanish dispersion were a rather mediocre class, but the influx of the polished Sephardim brethren, filled with memories of Hebrew and Arabic lore, infused new life into their sleepy existence.

Sitting on the shores of the Grand Canal at Venice, the foam-crested Mediterranean dashing its spray against her face, a Spanish Jewess would tell an Italian sister stories of the beautiful country from which she had just wandered. Extracts from Maimonides' "Guide for the Perplexed" would be interspersed with echoes from Ibn Gabirol, Moses ben Esra and Jehuda ben Halevi—"May my tongue cleave unto my mouth, and may my right hand wither, do I e'er forget thee, O Jerusalem!"

To the sad-eyed woman who chanted Halevi's song, the word Jerusalem bore a double meaning: it meant Palestine, the home of her forefathers, and it meant Spain, her own and her children's birthplace. And so, over the length and breadth of Europe, did these wandering people carry the tale of their culture and their past glory with them, and as there is no seed, be it never so wind-blown, but finds, sooner or later, some fruitful soil which receives it, and nourishes it, so did the thought which these homeless strangers carried with them find its mission, and do its good.

Graetz says that the Italian Jews of the sixteenth century were a people of few natural resources, that their literature was meagre, and that their achievements were few and far between. What little they did produce was due mostly to the Spanish Jews, who had taken up their homes amidst them. Nearly every prominent character at this period bears a Spanish name.

Among the few notable women of the sixteenth century, Benvenida Abravanel takes leading rank. Her husband was the son of him who vainly tendered his entire fortune to Ferdinand and Isabella, in order that the impending edict against his people might be repealed. From this sire, Samuel Abravanel inherited the remarkable financial gifts that enabled him speedily to reconstruct the family fortunes. He and his wife deserve to be called the Moses and Judith Montefiore of their period. Thus sings a poet of the day his praises: "Samuel Abravanel merits the triple crown. He is great and wise in the Law, great in nobility of character and great in the possession of riches." To the name of his patron, Samuel Usque might have joined, without fear of incurring censure for extravagance, that of his patroness, the beautiful and gifted Benvenida.

Don Pedro, Viceroy of Naples, held her in such high esteem, he chose her to be the intimate companion and adviser to his daughter, Leonora, who afterward became the wife of Cosimo di Medici. Through a long life, this princess continued to remember her Jewish friend, addressing to her letters, whose spirit was the very incarnation of tender, filial devotion.

When Charles V., crowned with the laurel gained by his African victories, was passing through Naples, it was his intention to expel the Jews from that city, but Benvenida, supported by the entreaties of her young charge, succeeded in deterring him from fulfilling his cruel purpose.

The Abravanel mansion was a popular *rendezvous*, where cultivated Christians, as well as Jews, loved to assemble. Chronicle tells us of one John Albert Widmanstadt, a pupil of Reuchlin, and a man of encyclopædic learning, taking up his abode there to further his advancement in Hebrew studies. At this distant time, it is rather difficult to realize the impediments besetting such intentions. Incited by Luther, Erasmus and Reuchlin, the learned world was just beginning anew to interest itself in the Scriptural tongue, and as the Jews were thus far almost the only custodians of the sacred language, a barrier between themselves and the Christians was withdrawn, when such intercourse was necessitated.

Contemporaneously with Benvenida Abravanel flourished a woman of Portuguese Neo-Christian extraction, whose serenity of soul, amiability of character and courageous steadfastness of purpose in prosperity, as well as adversity, constitute her one of the greatest female benefactors of her race. This was Donna Gracia Mendes. She was married to the principal member of a noted banking house, the extent of whose business relations with Charles V., Francis I. and other sovereigns enabled it to achieve a European reputation.

Like many of her people, forced by a cruel decree to subscribe to a faith which was only an intolerable simulation, Donna Gracia longed with pious fervor to be enabled once again to repeat untrammeled the confession of her fathers: "Hear, O Israel, the Lord, our God, the Lord is One!"

After the death of her husband, prompted by this desire, strengthened no doubt by fresh edicts of persecution against the Neo-Christians, accompanied by the one remaining pledge of her marriage, her daughter Reyna, she sought refuge with her husband's kindred at Antwerp. From this ephemeral vantage-ground, she and her wealthy brother-in-law spent fortune upon fortune in endeavoring to rescue from torture and the stake those of their unhappy co-religionists who were still under the fell dominion of the fanatical John of Portugal.

Notwithstanding the prominent position maintained by her family at Antwerp, where a nephew stood high at court, Donna Gracia was not content. In Flanders, which was still under the Austrian-Spanish *régime*, an open relapse to Judaism meant almost certain death, but until 1546, when the decease of her kinsman promoted her to the position of chief of the banking firm, she found a removal from Antwerp impossible.

Even then did fickle fortune continue to circumvent her, for hardly had Diego closed his eyes, when the insatiable greed of Charles V. prompted him to lay covetous hands upon the Mendes estate. The only excuse for so unwarrantable an action was the omnipresent charge of defection from the Holy Roman Church.

For two years did Donna Gracia combat the inquisitorial hydra, and even at the expiration of this long period, she was not permitted to depart from the country without surrendering a considerable portion of her worldly goods.

Once arrived at Venice, whence she had hoped speedily to embark for Turkey, new troubles awaited her. Her own sister, envious of her superior position, charged her with secret adherence to Judaism. The designed transfer of her estates to Turkey was also revealed. The Venetian authorities, always jealous of the Porte, were loath to permit such great riches to pass into the hands of the enemy. Donna Gracia was, therefore, thrown into prison, where she languished for many months, until she was released at the solicitation of Sultan Suleiman, who dispatched an especial envoy to Venice to effect this purpose.

After a sojourn of some years at Ferrara, where, for its devotion to polite learning, her own little court bore no mean comparison with that of Ercole D'Este, accompanied by her suite, consisting of some five hundred persons, she embarked for the Orient.

Having reached Constantinople, all dissimulation was thrown to the winds, and she stood before the world a self-acknowledged and self-respecting daughter of Israel. Here she witnessed the consummation of the long-delayed nuptials of her daughter Reyna, and her favorite nephew Joseph. As Prince and Princess of Naxos, favored by the Sultan and feared by his people, fate had an exalted destiny in store for this young couple.

The name of Donna Gracia and that of her daughter find frequent repetition in the literature of the period. Many are the books inscribed to them, and many are the songs sung in their praise. One of the first Hebrew printing presses erected in Turkey, was constructed by Reyna, Princess of Naxos, for the purpose of issuing a new and much needed edition of the Talmud.

A marked contrast to that of the two preceding characters, is the career of Esther Kierá, physician and politician at the court of Sultan Murad III. Acknowledged favorite of the queen of his harem, she employed her powers of statecraft for the elevation or abasement of princes. The mighty potentates of Europe, who, in their native lands, were grinding her own people into the very dust, were often forced to sue the favor of this Jewish woman, in order that the recognition of the Sultan might be obtained.

It was not to be expected that so much authority concentrated in the hands of one person would long remain unassailed. The blood of Esther and her three sons staining the marble entrance to the palace of the grand vizier was the forfeit paid by herself and her offspring for their exalted fortunes.

Toward the beginning of the seventeenth century, the condition of the European Jews grew more and more intolerable. The Catholic reactionists, with the Jesuits at their head, were everywhere waging a relentless battle against light and learning. In Turkey, where for fifty years the Jews had maintained such honorable positions, a new spirit of persecution had set in. The Thirty Years' War dancing its Dance of Death through Germany, and the Cossack massacres in Poland, threatened an almost vandalic annihilation of all higher civilization.

In this wholesale immolation, the Jew, ever the fated target for all changing political conditions, was again the first victim. Even his religious ritual is said to have suffered from this sad state of affairs, for we are told that the synagogical services were utterly incomprehensible to the female members of the congregation. The German Jewess, seated apart in the latticed woman's gallery, had to trust entirely to tradition and intuition, would she understand the import of the ceremonies of her faith.

Whither? and Whence? were again the queries of the Wandering Jew. From staunch little Holland came the first response. After having achieved its bravely won victory for civil and religious liberty, guided by the tolerant William of Orange, this country was among the earliest in Europe to recognize the intellectual and financial expediency of possessing Jewish inhabitants. At first barely endured, through his integrity and courage, the Hebrew, by slow degrees, gained for himself a higher position in his new home.

In the seventeenth and eighteenth centuries, to be called a Holland Jew was a title of much distinction, and the Amsterdam colony, composed for the most part of Spanish and Portuguese brethren, was famed throughout the continent as a model of cultured elegance.

The Academy of Poetry, originating in this city in 1676, was directed by Manuel de Belmonte, a Jew, whose pride of race must assuredly have been gratified by Isabella Correa, one of the most prominent members attending the meetings of the association. Her fine translation from Italian into Spanish of Guarini's "Pastor Fido" achieved for her a European reputation.

From days immemorial, Holland and England have possessed many traits in common. Hand in hand, with steadfast faces ever turned toward the aurora of progress, these two countries have given the world many beautiful lessons. As if emulous of the humane policy espoused by its neighbor, after the lapse of centuries, England again demonstrated an inclination to admit the Jew.

In Elizabeth's time, we read of a shipwrecked Jewess, Maria Nunes by name, whose beauty excited the curiosity of the Virgin Queen. At the instigation of the captain of the rescuing ship, an English nobleman, who had fallen a victim to his passenger's charms, Maria Nunes was summoned to court, where, as an especial tribute to her loveliness, she was invited to ride, side by side with good Queen Bess, through the streets of London. It is further related by chronicle that the enamored captain pleaded in vain with the maiden to abjure her religion, that he might make her his bride.

In view of this pretty story, is it presumptuous to suppose, that the favorable impression made on the English nobility by this worthy daughter of her race, did much to help to dispel the prejudice existing there against the Jews?

A strange anomaly in history is the fact that the Jews who lived at Venice in Shakespeare's day were among the noblest specimens of their kind. As fickle in its government as the sunsets that gilded its coasts, the Venetian Republic by turns tolerated and humiliated its

Jewish inhabitants. At the present moment, the Hebrew colony, consisting of some six thousand souls, was permitted unmolested social intercourse with the Christians.

Amidst the heterogeneous elements comprising so large a community, there may have been a Jessica, there may have been a Shylock, but authentic records give us no trace of such characters. They tell us, however, of a new Hebrew-Italian school of poetry, among whose protagonists were two women, Deborah Ascarelli and Sara Copia Sullam.

Of especial interest is the life of the latter. Beautiful and highly gifted, the possessor of an extraordinary mind, in which the genius of poetry and of philosophy were blended, the writer of a treatise on the immortality of the soul, which even Graetz extols for its masculine vigor, and the main figure in an episode, in which a lovelorn and proselyting priest is the hero, and she, the steadfast and faithful Jewess, the heroine, the story of Sara Copia Sullam is imbued with all the interest of a romantic tale of fiction.

As the eighteenth century neared its meridian, dim heraldings of better days began to penetrate the stifled atmosphere of the Ghetto. Here and there, amidst the sorely pressed multitude, a few faint glimmers of the speedily approaching Renaissance made themselves perceptible. After so many years of abject self-suppression, the Jews were beginning again to appreciate the glory of the individual and the glory of the race. In the words of the prophet: "The breath came into them, and they lived, and stood up upon their feet, an exceeding great army."

Guided by the pillar of fire, emblematic of progress, like his ancient namesake, the first law-giver of Israel, Moses Mendelssohn led the Jews out of the land of bondage, which is ignorance, into the land of promise, which is civilization. His resuscitating influence pervaded every department of human existence, and such was the living force of his example, that never once, even in his own home, did Moses Mendelssohn descend from the pure ideals which, he considered, should constitute the character of every normal child of God.

His attitude toward women was ineffably beautiful. Who does not know the exquisitely pathetic tale of his wooing? His views on the education of the sex, notwithstanding a somewhat incongruous assent to old-time marriage customs, were far in advance of those of his contemporaries.

Side by side and on a perfect equality with their brothers, the Mendelssohn girls received the best education that was then procurable. By the celebrated men and women who congregated at the philosopher's home, Dorothea, Recha and Henrietta Mendelssohn were deemed no small attraction. The eldest daughter, particularly, was noted for her logical and vigorous mind. Of all the children of Moses Mendelssohn, Dorothea appears to have been the one who most largely inherited her father's gifts.

In spite of an exceedingly uncomely presence, her remarkable conversational powers and uncommon amiability made this woman a centre around which the younger members of her father's circle loved to assemble, and after Moses Mendelssohn's death, when this *rendezvous* was no longer in existence, Dorothea, as the wife of Simon Veit, presided over a salon which took equal rank with that of Henrietta Herz and Rahel Varnhagen.

In Frederick the Great's time, Berlin was a very primitive place. With the exception of the inner court circle, where an unpatriotic adulation of everything French, to the exclusion of everything German, was the mode, little or no cultured society existed. The king, who counted such men as Lessing, Mendelssohn, the von Humboldts and the von Schlegels among his subjects, was utterly apathetic to the possibilities of an indigenous German literature.

Would these intellectual pioneers obtain recognition, they were forced to appeal to a higher and broader tribunal. The middle classes of the Prussian capital were a stolid, frivolous set, completely immersed in material, vain pleasure. There were no literary clubs among the men, no salons among the women. With the exception of a few Jewish houses, where Moses Mendelssohn's example was still being followed, there was no place where men and women could exchange intellectual confidences.

Speaking of this period, Henrietta Herz says: "I do not consider it an exaggeration to maintain that there was no person who then resided at Berlin, who afterward distinguished himself, who did not for a shorter or greater length of time frequent our circle."

The writer of the above assertion is elected by many authorities the Madame Récamier of Germany. Beautiful as a siren, the wife of a noted physician and *littérateur*, mistress of half a dozen languages, and the hostess of one of the most popular eighteenth century salons, the name of Henrietta Herz is an imperishable memory in the social annals of her country. Once Schleiermacher likened her to Ceres, in token of the ability she possessed to develop, among her acquaintances, the best and noblest blossoms of human nature. "Inspire, but do not write!" said Le Brun to Madame de Rambouillet. It is not known whether Henrietta Herz modeled her career upon that of her French predecessor, but it would seem so, for notwithstanding her eminent talents, she never achieved an independent literary reputation. A few pages of personal recollections, published shortly after her death in 1847, and a translation of Mungo Park's "Travels in Africa," are the only works proceeding from her pen.

Rahel Levin Varnhagen, "the dear, good, little woman with the great soul," as Heinrich Heine fondly calls her, was the third member of the Berlin Salon Triumvirate. Her husband was Varnhagen von Ense, a German nobleman of literary eminence, whose chief distinction in the eyes of posterity is his friendship with Göthe, Schiller and others of his celebrated contemporaries, perpetuated through many volumes of correspondence between himself and his wife.

The Göthe cult, which has waxed to such great proportions during the latter half of this century, was first started in Germany through the exertions of Frau Varnhagen. Love for the author of Faust was a sure passport to her heart and home, where even such men as Heinrich Heine and Ludwig Börne first had to take the oath of allegiance to its patron saint, the "open sesame" that admitted them through its portals. In perspicacity of mind, earnestness of purpose and uprightness of character, Rahel Varnhagen perhaps exceeded her two friends; but they were all children of one era, their virtues and their foibles were but a part of the storm and stress period of thought, out of which everything that is best in this world must grow.

Each human soul is an exaggerated or lessened quotation of the spirit of its age. Dorothea Mendelssohn, Henrietta Herz and Rahel Varnhagen were no exceptions to this rule. Their vagaries, some of which, to a more sober day, seem almost to savor of license, are only the natural overflow of intellectual and animal spirits enfranchised from centuries of Ghetto-suppression. When a dyke is destroyed, it is the head-waters that are always the most tempestuous.

In 1790, the French Republic, true to its principles, tendered unrestricted privilege of citizenship to the Jews under its dominion. Following close in its wake, Napoleon Bonaparte, in his triumphal marches through Europe, did much to soften the condition of the Hebrews residing within the conquered territory. The convocation, by his order, of the great Sanhedrim at Paris in 1806 once again renewed the memories of ancient Palestine.

The spirit of "live and let live," the imperishable distinction of the nineteenth century, has been of most benefit to the House of Israel, whose marvelous adaptability to every changing condition, marks it as one of the superior races of mankind. His very intensity of character, a cause for commendation as well as criticism, makes it possible, with favorable surroundings, for the Hebrew, in the short space of one generation, to transform himself from a creeping, cringing peddler into an upright, polished gentleman.

If this be apposite to the Jewish man, how much truer must it be of the Jewish woman, whose temperament of sex naturally constitutes her the quicker of the two in responding to the best variations of her environment. Everywhere, in answer to the broader possibilities of the present era, have the women of Israel kept equal pace with the men.

Fanny, the sister of Felix Mendelssohn, is the composer of many of the "Songs Without Words" attributed to her brother. A too faithful adherence to her father's narrow conception of what was best for her sex alone prevented her from producing works, which would have given her a like reputation with the composer of "Elijah."

Caroline Stern, the inspirer of one of Heinrich Heine's first published poems, and Caroline Gomperz Bettelheim, the famous Austrian court contralto, are among the modern Miriams of their race.

The actresses, Rachel Félix and Sara Bernhardt, both at one period members of the *Comédie Française*, are too well known to require more than passing mention.

Many of the members of the German, French and English branches of the Rothschild family have distinguished themselves by their musical and literary achievements. Betty, the widow of James Rothschild, is noted all over the world as a patroness of learning. As far back as 1849, she demonstrated her interest in the advancement of women, by offering a prize of five thousand francs to the young girl who should show the highest proficiency in Hebrew-French translation. Solomon Munk's celebrated edition of Maimonides' "Guide for the Perplexed" owes its origin to her munificent liberality.

The name of Grace Aguilar, author of the "Women of Israel," "The Vale of Cedars," and other famous works, is a household word. Lady Magnus' "Jewish Portraits" and "Outlines of Jewish History" are familiar to English readers on both sides of the Atlantic.

A remarkable character, whose endeavors in behalf of the higher education of women and the dissemination of the Free Kindergarten System through Germany, have placed her among the prominent benefactors of her sex, is Lina Morgenstern. When Froebel's doctrine was still viewed as the scheme of a wool-gathering reformer, this far-seeing woman took up cudgels in its defense. For her disinterested devotion to her sick and wounded countrymen during the Franco-Prussian War, she has been the recipient of many orders of decoration. In spite of such multiform practical activity, Frau Morgenstern is the author and translator of numerous well-known books. Her "Children's Paradise" has gone through four editions. As charter member and president of the "German Housekeepers' Union," an association with ramifications all through the Fatherland, and editor of "The Journal for German Housekeepers," she still continues, undeterred by advancing age, to maintain an active interest in all matters homogeneous with her chosen subjects.

The blessings of the oppressed and afflicted, arising from all sides to honor the most humane of the centuries' benefactors, are indissolubly interwoven with the memory of Judith, the wife of Sir Moses Montefiore.

At the head of the Jewish writers of this country is Emma Lazarus. She and Heinrich Heine are the two greatest poets produced by the Hebrews in the present century. Between herself and her German co-religionist there was much in common. Both were burdened by the irrepressible *Weltschmerz* of their nation, and both were Greeks as well as Hebrews. Incontestably, it is this propinquity of spirit that elects Emma Lazarus the best of Heinrich Heine's English translators. An imperishable monument erected by her to the memory of the Passion of Israel is the collection of prose poems entitled "By the Waters of Babylon."

Henrietta Szold, Annie Nathan Meyer, Josephine Lazarus, Mary M. Cohen, Minnie D. Louis, Nina Morais Cohen and Martha Morton, are only a few among the many of our countrywomen, whose achievements serve to perpetuate the undiminished glory of hoary-headed Israel.

If the measure of a nation's fame be the standard maintained by its women, then this Congress of Jewish Women, the first in its history, is a renewed pledge of the immortal possibilities of the Hebrew race.

A potent factor toward the production of one of the finest accomplishments of the age—the *fin de siècle* woman—is the club.

All over the United States, in city and in hamlet, are ethical, philosophical, historical and political organizations, whose one great aim is the betterment of humanity, through the elevation of the sex. The majority of the members of these clubs are Christians, but few of them are Jews; the history of the position of the club, in the chronicle pertaining to the advancement of Jewish women, is, therefore, yet an unwritten page. The fact that the honored president and projector of this present congress is an enthusiastic club woman, should be eloquent testimony in favor of the further extension of organization among the women of Israel.

This is called the "Woman's Age," and America is called the "Woman's Paradise." The intellectual and civic liberties more and more accorded to our sex, are open to Jew as well as Christian.

In the college, at the polls, in the home, in the church, woman is assuming an equal place with man. Shoulder to shoulder with her Christian sister, is the Jewish woman yoked to the eternal chariot of universal progress, underneath whose star-driven wheels all social barriers, products of a past, effete age, are forever ground into oblivion. Higher and higher into the "Heaven of Borderless Futurity" does this chariot ascend. See! out from the clouds the man of the past extends his hand to crown the woman of the present, for—

>"All that doth perish
>Is but a symbol,
>All that is futile
>Here becomes deed,
>The indescribable
>Here it is done;
>The Woman-Eternal
>Leadeth us on!"

JEWISH WOMEN OF MODERN DAYS.

(Discussion of the foregoing paper.)

Henrietta G. Frank, Chicago, Ill.

The woman of our day, like Eve, the All-Mother, stretches out her hand for the fruit of the tree of knowledge that she may know good from evil; though she lose the paradise of ignorance, she may gain the field of honest endeavor. The serpent appears to her not as Satan, the tempter, but rather as the companion of Minerva, the symbol of wisdom and of eternity. If Adam had eaten more freely of the fruit tendered him by Eve, his descendants might have become too wise to deny to women capabilities equal to men's. Would Adam have given Eve of the fruit, had he been the first to taste of it? Adam now permits Eve to enjoy the fruit, while he digs about the roots of the tree, until he lands at the antipodes in his effort to reach final causes.

What is woman's sphere? Whatever she can do, and can do well. No amount of cultivation will enable her to perform duties for which nature has not fitted her; like her brother, she may become warped, or remain undeveloped, but she cannot be trained contrary to the laws of her own being. The exhibits in the department of ethnology at the World's Columbian Exposition, entitled "Woman's Work in Savagery," demonstrate that woman has been chiefly responsible for the origin and development of the arts of peace.

Did the Germans copy from the Orientals, or did the German Jews copy from the Germans, their dislike of learned women, and their approval of Paul's injunction, that women keep silence in the churches? The Jewish masculine mind is apt to share with the German, a certain frowning down upon intellectual endeavor in women, outside of the accomplishments that are considered pleasing. We attribute it to the love of thoroughness and of originality, which they share with the Germans, and to their contempt of half-knowledge, of a smattering, of a dallying with the arts and sciences. Yet a slight acquaintance with the best is better than complete ignorance. Amateurs make the most appreciative audiences, for, in the spiritual sense, it is true that to him who hath, shall be given. Men are short-sighted to ignore the power of women as co-workers; the dangers which beset us need women as well as men to counteract them.

In Israel's history, even in the most primitive stages, a high position, both by affection and custom, was accorded to the wife and mother; her dignity and independence were always guarded, as with no other nation of antiquity. Some of the most beautiful stories of the Bible and the Talmud deal with the relations between mothers and children; the wife is the help-meet, the equal of man, in all affairs, great and small, pertaining to the welfare of the family. The ancient idea of marriage was to increase the family of the bridegroom, not to found a new one. "Thy God shall be my God" had a different and more restricted significance to the ancient Hebrews than it has for us. The wife of olden times did not enter into the full privileges of her position until she had become a mother, the mother of a son; the line of descent was through the male heir, the daughter did not inherit. Later, in talmudic days, the daughter might inherit when there was no male heir. The Jewish model wife in Proverbs is shown versed in all the arts and industries necessary to the production of objects of use and ornament in the household, and possessing sufficient authority to buy a field, if she deemed it advisable.

Wives and maidens in Israel had far more liberty than the Oriental woman of to-day, nor were they kept in seclusion as were the Greek women of their time.

There was no woman question among the Jews; every woman was cared for by her family; there were very few unmarried women; bachelorhood was unpopular. As all industries clustered around the home, all were profitably employed.

The ethical and social side of the woman question, which inquires how to make of woman a factor with equal rights and equal duties, according to her powers, for the good of society, was solved by them, but conditions have so changed, that the problem must be solved anew. It was true then, as it is now, that if woman gains, the nation gains through her; as mothers, women mold the character of the nation, they influence their children in the most plastic years of their lives.

Some of the learned rabbis of talmudic fame were in favor of instructing the girls as well as the boys in the Law, but the opposite view, that to initiate one's daughters in the Law was baneful, finally triumphed, and the daughters were relegated to the home; at a later period, we hear of women who were thoroughly versed in the studies pursued by their husbands and fathers, and fully shared their intellectual life.

When their opportunities are taken into consideration, it must be said that the Jewish women of our day have allowed themselves too often to become mere lookers-on at the rich banquets of study and of broad, practical work. It was not always so. Our history teaches us, above all things, that the arguments now used for the advancement of women were practically illustrated by the hundreds of Jewish women, whose names are recorded in the annals of time, who distinguished themselves by their work outside of the confines of home, besides wearing the crown of perfect wifehood and motherhood. We hear of them in mediæval times as poets and writers, as philosophers and physicians, as women of affairs, aiding their husbands in great undertakings or, when widowed, engaging in them alone. Naturally those who were distinguished were exceptions. There never can be a dead level of excellence, else there would be no need of history, nor any possibility of development. Jewish women were zealous in promoting the spread of knowledge; in the days when printing was first introduced, we read of Jewish women who established printing-houses, who were practical type-setters before our Manual Training School was dreamed of; who not only helped to print the great works of the past, but also wrote books of instruction, of history, of songs and popular tales, who expressed themselves, as well as gave wings to the thoughts of others. Some of these women were German and Bohemian, most of them were Italian and Spanish Jewesses. In all manner of occupation, in trades, industries and professions, they contributed their share to the progress of culture. Spanish-Jewish women helped to bring about a revival of Hebrew poetry, to which they gave back grace and beauty and lyrical warmth. From the time they had no longer to tremble for their own lives, they made their lives of use to others, less fortunate than themselves, and many are the philanthropic missions in which they engaged.

The effects of the Thirty Years' War, which plunged Germany into barbarism, and of the Cossack invasion of

Poland, which brought endless suffering, were disastrous to the culture and development of the Jews. The Ghetto reared its walls about them, and they withdrew from the common life, into an atmosphere of extreme ceremonialism in religion, and of separation in the ordering of their lives. Had it not been for the elevating influences of their home life, and for the fostering of their intellect through biblical and talmudic studies, their keen interest in the philosophy and the casuistry of talmudic problems, the Jews must have succumbed to the systematic vilification and oppression, their allotted portion during the ages when they were virtually slaves in most European countries.

One cause of the adaptability of the Jew was his knowledge of languages; he always could think and express himself in one language besides the Hebrew; and if to know a language is to enter into the soul-life of the people that speaks it, he must have developed his powers of adaptability through this knowledge. Spanish and Italian Jews spoke and wrote the language of their respective countries perfectly, and even *Juedisch-Deutsch* is a language and not a jargon, we are told.

Owing to the restrictions and disabilities under which the Jews labored in the years succeeding their bitterest persecutions, the Jews learned to consider themselves, in their prayers at least, as living in exile; their thoughts were turned to a restoration to Palestine; they wished to remain strangers in a strange land, in customs and ideals. Even in language, they became separated. The importance of Moses Mendelssohn for the Jews lay in the fact, that he re-opened the gates of the Ghetto of language and of thought, in translating the Pentateuch into pure German, and that, as a writer, he entered into the literary life and general culture of his day, and stood abreast of the great thinkers of his time. Yet he remained an Oriental in the strict observance of all the forms and ceremonies which had come to be identified with true Judaism. After the revival of the spirit of culture brought about by his writings and efforts, a re-action set in; many turned away from Judaism after a hard struggle, because they could not reconcile themselves to the external observances that were demanded; dogma and tradition brought religion to a stand-still, it became a routine, in which the form was observed, but the spirit neglected. The new birth, in which life was freed from its encumbrances, had not yet come, and those who turned away were not sufficiently in advance of their time to find their way out of the labyrinth. Some merely strained at a gnat; they turned from ceremonies, which had ceased to have a meaning for them, and threw themselves into the current of mysticism and romanticism which then prevailed. Rousseau's early ideas, which he himself repudiated in his later years, had been perverted into a negation of the laws of society governing man; a loosing of bonds in every direction, a confounding of liberty with license was deemed a return to nature. It was deemed less heroic to suffer than to change conditions.

Mendelssohn's daughters belonged to those who deserted the old faith. Dorothea was attracted by the æsthetic side of Catholicism; she loved the music, and the dim religious light, falling through stained-glass window-panes; the externalism of the church attracted her, the externalism of the synagogue repelled her.

Many of the women who formed a social and intellectual power in Berlin, and whose salons were oases in the desert of Berlin society, felt a great chasm between their own lives and thoughts, and those of their co-religionists, who still adhered to the letter of the law. That which their ancestors had loved, had no attraction for them; Judaism meant only legalism to them. They believed they were creating a new world of thought, and they broke with their own past and the slow process of development in Jewish circles. Women prize social life more than men; these women prized the social equality that was denied them as Jews, and thus became renegades, trading their birthright for a mess of pottage. The heroines that courted death, and inspired their children to defy torture rather than renounce the faith of their fathers, were no more. Among the men, some forsook the ranks in order to worthily employ their talents in careers that were closed to the Jew, and some thought they would make life more easy for their children.

In our day, here in America, the Jew suffers under no political disabilities, and his educational advantages are growing each year, the portals of schools and universities are open to him.

What are the tendencies of the modern Jewish woman? In how far does she partake of the broad life of her non-Jewish sister? What should she assimilate, what must she avoid, what has she to give?

The Jewish woman needs to be more noble, more self-sacrificing, more alive to the ideal, if she would be worthy of those who have preceded her. Let her study the history of the past, if she would comprehend the present. Let her counteract all narrowness, by cultivating the great force of intelligence, the subduer of evil. The mother is still the most potent factor in the world; let her live up to the high standard set her by the Jewish women of the past, whose lives were devoted to great interests. We need more thoroughness in our work, whatever it be.

Judaism means progress, America means opportunity. Judaism has within itself the power to assimilate the best thought of the time. The world to-day recognizes in woman a help in the progress of the world toward a higher civilization, and if Judaism would be true to itself, Jewish women must break the shackles that bind them, and again take a deep interest in the great concerns of life.

If the World's Congresses have proved anything, they have proved that the essential qualities of womanliness, of grace and charm, are heightened rather than diminished by the best mental equipment and the greatest cultivation, and that women are working faithfully and earnestly in research and scientific pursuits, as well as in education and philanthropy.

There is a positive need for women to keep in touch with the political history of our own country and of all the contemporary movements; the politics of to-day forms the history of to-morrow. While we have only an indirect interest in politics at present, we need, for our own intelligence, to follow the great movements of to-day. It is a matter of moment to us how Zeus parcels out the land, the marts, the rivers, and how the earth is being appropriated to man's need and greed. It broadens the mind, as travel does, to send it out over the universe; it prevents us from dwelling too much upon trivial things. The woman who takes an intelligent interest in the great questions that are agitating the world, will not, therefore, become indifferent to the duties of her own individual sphere; the habit of study begets system, and a systematic ordering of one's time helps wonderfully in the performance of duties near at hand.

It is not an absolute necessity to have a society with president and officers in order to accomplish something. We can improve ourselves without coming to a certain place at a certain time to discuss a plan of work, a philosophy, a literature. But how many of us are quite independent of the inspiration and sympathy of minds in touch with our own? Genius needs no club for development, but unfortunately genius is rare, and ordinary gifts need a stimulus. Some there be, who need to come only to teach, but most of us need to learn. Clubs and classes have been of vast benefit to women, they have taught the value of co-operation for noble ends. Man must work, and so must woman. Nature avenges herself for the neglect of faculties, and powers that lie too long dormant become atrophied. Woman as homemaker, as purveyor of happiness, as possessor of the fine art of housewifery is needed as much as ever, and her life in the club can but be helpful in all these directions, because she learns to understand herself, and to rise above pettiness. The education received within the club will fit her to take up duties outside of it.

Many Jewish women of America and of Western Europe are taking active part in intellectual labors, in art and music, in philanthropy and education, and are working as journalists and writers. While all cannot distinguish themselves in these paths, all can cultivate the best within themselves. Life, too, is an art, the art of living is one that we must foster for ourselves and for others. In our social life, we must cultivate the amenities and all that is refining, all that tends to make it beautiful and perfect, and to lend it a lovelier setting. Whether as wife, the counselor and help-meet, as mother, the guardian and inspiration, as intellectual and practical worker, the Jewish woman of to-day can be guided by the lives of the Jewish women of the past.

At the close of the session, by request of the Chairman, the Rev. Dr. K. Kohler, of New York, and the Rev. Dr. E. G. Hirsch, of Chicago, addressed the meeting.

TUESDAY, SEPTEMBER 5, 1893, 9.30 A. M.

Mrs. I. S. Moses was introduced by the Chairman as the honorary presiding officer of the session.

WOMAN IN THE SYNAGOGUE.

RAY FRANK, OAKLAND, CAL.

Duality manifests itself in all things, but in nothing is this two-foldness more plainly seen than in woman's nature.

The weaker sex physically, it is the stronger spiritually, it having been said that religion were impossible without woman. And yet the freedom of the human soul has been apparently effected by man. I say apparently effected, for experience has demonstrated, and history records, that one element possessed by woman has made her the great moral, the great motif force of the world, though she be, as all great forces are, a silent force.

It may be true that sin came into the world because of the disobedience of the first woman, but woman has long since atoned for it by her loving faith, her blind trust in the Unknown. Down through the ages, traditional and historical, she has come to us the symbol of faith and freedom, of loyalty and love.

From the beginning, she sought knowledge; perceive, it does not say wisdom, but knowledge; and this was at the expense of an Eden. She lost Eden, but she gained that wisdom which has made sure of man's immortality.

She walked upon thorns, she bled; but so sincerely repentant was she, so firmly rooted had become her faith in the Almighty, that no amount of suffering, no change of time and circumstance, could destroy it. With repentance something had sprung up, and blossomed in her being, an imperishable flower, beautiful, fragrant, making the world bright and sweet.

This flower twined itself round man, its odors refreshed and strengthened him; its essence healed him when wounded, and nerved him on to gallant and noble deeds. It is the breath of life in him, and he must needs be careful of its clinging stems, its tender leaves, for they are rooted in a woman's heart.

In mother, wife, sister, sweetheart, lies the most precious part of man. In them he sees perpetual reminders of the death-sin, guarantees of immortality. Think, woman, what your existence means to man; dwell well on your responsibility; and now let us turn to that part of time called the past, more particularly biblical days. The religious life of the early Israelites is so closely interwoven with their domestic and political life, that it cannot be separated and treated alone. Amidst all kind of tribal and national strife, the search for knowledge of Javeh went on in so even a way, so indifferent to men and things, as no other investigation has done. The soul of mankind could not be quieted concerning this matter, and religion from its very nature evolved itself. That this was, in its entirety, due to no one people is just as true as that it was due to no one sex.

To the Israelite, because of his sensitive, superior nature, was revealed that first great truth of "I am the Lord thy God," and to them, throughout the generations, was given the command to spread His truth. But when the Lord said to Moses, "And ye shall be unto Me a nation of priests and a holy nation," the message was not to one sex; and that the Israelites did not so consider it, is proved by the number of women who were acknowledged prophets, and who exercised great influence on their time and on posterity.

The Talmud speaks of seven prophetesses: Sarah, Miriam, Deborah, Hannah, Abigail, Huldah and Esther. Ruth not being mentioned in this list, we infer that she was regarded simply as a religious teacher. Except in the Talmud, Sarah is not mentioned as possessing the inspirational power, which made the prophets of old; yet, there is that chronicled of her which gives rise to the assumption that, for a time at least, she was the greatest of them all. For in Genesis xxi. 12 is recorded the only instance of the Lord's especially commanding one of His favorites to listen carefully to a woman: "In all that Sarah may say unto thee, hearken unto her voice."

Evidently, the Almighty deemed a woman capable both of understanding and advising.

That Miriam, the sister of Moses, was a woman of extraordinary mind is evidenced by the words of Moses to herself and Aaron when he journeyed to the mount; and from the prominence given the word *prophetess* prior to recording the words of her triumphant song, it is evident that she must have been one of the leaders in Israel before the journey across the sea was made.

The one compliment paid Moses for his faithful service is that which speaks of him as a man of exceeding modesty; and it is pleasant to reflect that in the words of Israel's greatest woman, Deborah, can be found that same beautiful characteristic. When reminding Barak that, if he goes not alone to smite the foe, to a woman will be accredited the glory, she speaks as though loth that it should be thus; and when, in the name of Javeh, she leads the army, she says not, "I will do this or that," but, "Barak, up! for this is the day on which God will deliver Sisera into my hands." Of great modesty was this wife of Lapidoth, whether as ruler, warrior, poet or prophet; a woman whose influence in her time was mighty, and whose glorious, inspiring words still live.

The life of Hannah inculcates more deeply a lesson which we women must learn than that of any of our sex mentioned in the Bible. Greatest and best among women is she who is a wise mother; for the children are the Lord's, the heirs of Heaven. Blessed beyond all is she who dedicates her offspring to the Eternal. Who need wonder at the song which rose so joyously from the heart of Hannah, for she was truly an inspired prophetess, she was a wise mother!

Abigail, Huldah and Esther are the others mentioned in the Talmud. The story of the latter is so well known, her courage and piety are so justly celebrated on our Feast of Purim that I will not dwell longer upon them. From the scarcity of names mentioned, we are not to conclude that only a few women were teachers in Israel at this time; but rather that to woman was entrusted all that appertained to the domestic life; and in the performance of these duties her personality was merged in that of her husband. That she was capable of performing heroic deeds is evidenced by the legends of Jael and Judith. The intense excitement of the periods in which these women lived is supposed to have permitted them for a time to forget strict morality and loving mercy. Crude and almost repulsive in their invention, the narratives serve to show that weak woman was regarded as capable of performing for God and country heroic deeds, deeds from which strong men might have shrunk. Her faith under the most trying circumstances was sublime; and nothing more effective is recorded of piety embracing death than the martyrdom of the Maccabean Hannah or Miriam, who unhesitatingly gave to immortality herself and her seven sons. Other illustrations pale beside this magnificent heroism of a woman in whom rested the Almighty.

From any point of view, enough has been recorded to show that when she led, she led successfully. However, the ancient Jewish woman was, above all, wife and mother, and as such she was a religious teacher, and closely associated with what might be called the temple-worship of those days. The life of the woman of patriarchal times was clean and elevating, there was nothing slavish about it; and when one considers that the Jewish Law permitted polygamy, and that even with the debasing influences of harem life instituted by Solomon, the Jews became a monogamous people, one can understand the extraordinary influence of the Jewish woman to whom this important fact is due.

"One woman, a good one, is the light of a man's existence," sang an inspired sage.

Women of other nations soon learned to contrast the life of the Jewish woman with their own, and the first converts to Judaism were women from the neighboring idolatrous tribes. The emotional nature of Jewish women made them fit instruments to celebrate the joys of heaven and earth, and the finest things in our sacred literature are believed by many critics to have come spontaneously from our women's hearts and tongues.

If the woman of apocryphal times does not always appear sharply outlined in her work, it is, as we have said, owing to the deep workings of the wife and mother principle, which was striving to manifest itself as the axis of woman's world. Slowly, unevenly, events moved round, and in the Græco-Roman period we find the capricious jolts and jars lessening, until in mediæval times the Jewish wife represents all that is pure and noble in womanhood.

During the Græco-Roman period, two queens stand out as prominently influencing religious matters. Queen Salome, who was born in Jerusalem about the year 143 B. C., was of great wisdom and remarkable energy. Filled with the spirit of the Chasidim, with ideals pure and lofty, she early resolved to aid the faith in which she believed. The times were among the fiercest recorded by Israel, and great diplomacy was necessary to avoid dissensions. But through disasters of every nature, she remained constant to her principles, and at all times level-headed. Her tact and her power to remain impassive under the most awful circumstances are almost unparalleled in history. Her sole ambition was to preserve to the people their Pharisaic worship, and this she did by the most heroic teachings.

Among proselytes, Helena, Queen of Adiabene, born 152 years B. C., is mentioned in the Talmud as having done much for Judaism. She and her son were both converted to this faith, and in turn became teachers of religion, remaining true to the Jewish nation to the end.

The position of the mediæval woman differed from that of her ancient sister. Forced by circumstances at times to become a leader, her personality no longer merged itself in that of her husband, but ran parallel with his. Tribal wars for political supremacy did not now agitate the people, for existence had, in most cases, become an individual struggle. The princes of Judah were dethroned, their lands, the possession of strangers; yet the law lived, better understood and more sacredly guarded than ever. That this was owing, in the greatest degree, to the women is shown by the numbers mentioned in the Talmud as learned mothers and teachers. The Jews were stripped of many precious things by their oppressors, ofttimes their relentless persecutors, yet the Torah held such consolations that the family-home became to the Jew the most beautiful, the most sacred thing in the world. Of the love of a pure wife and reverent, obedient children, nothing could rob him, and he was, indeed, blessed beyond all that sought to harm him. The prophecy of Lemuel's mother had been faithfully realized; and as we look through the mist of centuries, the sunlight clears grayness, and we read: "Many daughters have done virtuously; but thou excellest them all."

True help-mate was the mediæval woman, combining with greatest intelligence, stern purpose and the softest maternal qualities.

During the period of happiness permitted them by Moorish and Spanish rule, our women rose to eminence intellectually and socially. But note how the learning always leaned toward the elevation of the home. That part of the Bible which concerned the home life became their especial study, and as practical preachers of religion, they have never been excelled, for they practiced what they preached.

Among the women of early mediæval times, Ima Shalom, Rachel and Beruria are representative. The father of Ima was president of the Sanhedrim, and a descendant of Hillel. Her husband, the most noted rabbi of his day, found in her an intellectual equal, and many were the knotty questions submitted to her judgment. Had it not been for the self-sacrificing and deeply religious nature of Rachel Sabua, history would scarcely have had an Akiba, while Beruria, wife of Rabbi Meïr, who lived about 100 A. D., was of such powerful intellect that she became noted throughout the land. All that she said concerning disputed points of the Halacha received the attention of her contemporaries. Poetry and prose testify to her worth.

Graetz mentions Bellet, the daughter of Menachem, who lived in Orleans in the year 1050 A. D., as one who was talmudically learned, and who taught the women of her town their religious duties. Hannah, sister of Rabbi Jacob Tam, of Orleans, and a whole circle of learned women in the family of Rashi, of whom may be mentioned Rachel, his daughter, and Anna and Miriam, his granddaughters, were highly educated, and acted as teachers of religion. They paid particular attention to instructing women regarding culinary matters, on which Mosaism laid the greatest stress.

Zunz calls the mother of the chief rabbi of France, Mattathias Ben Joseph Provenci, and wife of Rabbi Joseph Ben Jochanan, "well nigh a lady rabbi," and accords her great praise for her original and sensible interpretation of the dietary laws.

Rabbi Samuel ben Hallevi, who flourished in Bagdad in the year 1200, had a daughter, Bath Hallevi, who delivered in public biblical lectures to men. She was screened from her audience by sitting in a kind of box whose windows had in them panes of opaque glass.

A rabbinical college had for its principal Miriam Shapira, and her lectures to the students are said to have compared favorably with those of her contemporaries. Dolce, wife of Rabbi Eleazer ben Jehudah Rokeach, of Worms, a remarkably learned woman, lived a saintly life, preaching to the women their duties. She with her two children died the death of a martyr, being slain by the Knights of Malta, at Erfurt, in 1214.

In the Hebrew encyclopædia compiled by Dr. Goldman and his associates, and edited in Warsaw in 1818, is found an account of a remarkable woman, Donna Benvenida Abarbanel. Her husband was treasurer of the king of Naples, and into her charge the prime minister of Naples gave the education of his daughter, the princess Leonora. The intelligence and righteousness of Donna Benvenida were known throughout the land, and her association with the princess continued long after the latter's marriage. It is said that her royal charge esteemed her as a mother, and that in all her work this good Jewess never forgot her creed and her people.

Inasmuch as all appertaining to Judaism belongs to the temple, so the connection of this great woman with the synagogue is not to be doubted.

In about 1532, the priests who presided over the Inquisition petitioned the king to drive out the remnant of Jews from southern Italy. The petition was granted. But Donna Benvenida, with great diplomacy, succeeded through the princess in having the edict revoked. From various writings by the clever men of that day, one learns that the highest praise was given this woman.

From the book of the memorial of the dead of the Jewish congregation at Worms, I have taken the following names, they serving to show what the women of Israel at this time did for religion. Here is an epitaph: "Eva, daughter of Isaac Leipnitz, wife of Abraham Samuel, Rabbi of Worms. Her name shall be remembered because she was profoundly learned, and because she was conversant in the Bible and all its commentaries and the Midrash. There was no woman before her so deeply learned." " Remembered, the aged Rebecca, daughter of Jeremiah Neustadt, because she regularly attended synagogue, morning and evening, devoting all her life to benevolence. She spun without charge *Tzitzith* for all who needed them, and gave of her own money to the synagogue." "Remembered, the pious and esteemed Miriam Sinzheim, daughter of Joseph Sinzheim of Vienna, who went regularly to the synagogue, morning and evening, praying with devotion and giving all her life to benevolence. She supported students of the Bible in various congregations, especially in ours of Worms. She builded the synagogue of the great Rabbi Rashi (Solomon ben Isaac), establishing free seminaries and stipending students." Women of the nineteenth century! These are but a few names from among the many on the old grave stones, testifying to the splendid work done for the synagogue by women, at a time when obstacles made up their lives. In the early part of the eighteenth century, Krendel Steinhardt, a member of a gifted family of rabbis, obtained distinction for her knowledge of the festival prayers, the Machsor, and for cleverly interpreting the Midrash. She was known as the "Rebbezin." Sarah Oppenheimer, daughter of the chief rabbi of Prague, wrote a Meghilla, a scroll of the book of Esther, while Sprenza Kempler, blessed with beauty, knowledge and piety, could quote the Mishna from memory. Bienvineda, wife of Rabbi Mordecai, of Padua, was of such rare intelligence that she held disputations on the Talmud and the Mishna with some of the greatest scholars of her day.

The list is a long one, and each name reflects intelligence and piety. But enough has been given to disprove all doubts as to the Jewish woman's capability in religious matters, both as pupil and instructor. If to the men of these times be accorded credit for having performed their duties well, if as scholars, as expounders of the Law, they live in fame, what shall we say of the women who, under the most adverse circumstances, rose to eminence in this same field of labor? With one or two exceptions, they were all wives and mothers, most of them wives of rabbis, and in the discharge of their duties no one thing was done at the expense of another.

Intellectually they were the compeers of their husbands; practically, they excelled them. They built synagogues, controlled colleges, and stipended students. All in all, they have in the past earned the right to the pulpit, even as nature created their sensitive beings to act as its finest interpreter.

Jewish woman had earned the right to the pulpit, though she never formally asked it of the people, but that they would not have wholly opposed it, may be inferred from a romance of Bernstein's, "Voegele, der Maggid," probably founded on facts.

Voegele was an itinerant preacher, and that she combined the lovable qualities of the woman with her chosen work is shown by the fervent words of the hero who says to her, "Your hand makes the *Bethhamedrash* light." To our times and to our country in particular, the Jewish woman is indebted for many changes in her relation to the synagogue, and this progress is mainly due to one man, whose decided stand as a liberalist, in all matters concerning woman and her work, earns our hearty thanks. I refer to our revered rabbi, Dr. Wise, of Cincinnati.

With added privileges and numberless innovations, let us see what is the religious status of the Jewish woman of to-day. Compare her with the woman of the Apocrypha we will not, for it would be unjust to both. The one was the result of a great spiritual revelation and chaotic material circumstances pressing against and whirling round each other, leaving as a resultant the keen-visioned, practical woman of the Middle Ages, one whose knowledge was of men, and whose wisdom was of God. Calamitous as were the days, our mothers rose to meet them, each time victorious. Their children received, as a heritage, patience, courage, fidelity, reverence, honest, God-fearing souls, the richest treasures of men. What matter how the winds of fortune blew, the Jew was secure from total shipwreck. He carried as a talisman the instructions of his mother. When persecution drove him from shore to shore, he journeyed across unknown seas, and finding a new Canaan cried, "Hear, O Israel, the Lord our God, the Lord is one!" and so dedicated a new home.

Centuries have passed; the wilderness is the pride of the world, for it is all a land of freedom, of homes; and the Jew, we find him so grateful that he has well-nigh forgotten to what he owes his salvation. He has forgotten, else how explain the empty temples, the lack of religious enthusiasm, lack of reverence of children for parents, lack of that sacred home life which has made us an honored place in history? That our women have not made of themselves Dinah Morrises and "Voegele der Maggids" we can forgive, but that we have removed so many of the ancient landmarks which our fathers established, can we forgive ourselves for that?

That we have not possessed ourselves of the wisdom of her who builded her own house can hardly be pardoned us, for what can replace the priceless love which has bound the members of the Jewish family to each other and to their God? Learning is not wisdom. Innovation is not progress, and to be identical with man is not the ideal of womanhood. Some things and privileges belong to him by nature; to these, true woman does not aspire; but every woman should aspire to make of her home a temple, of herself a high priestess, of her children disciples, then will she best occupy the pulpit, and her work run parallel with man's. She may be ordained rabbi or be the president of a congregation—she is entirely able to fill both offices—but her noblest work will be at home, her highest ideal, a home. Our women, living in a century and in a country which gives them every opportunity to improve, are not making the most of themselves, and to the stranger, the non-Jew, who views us critically, we are not entirely an improvement upon our mothers of old. We may dress with better taste, we may know more *ologies*, we may discuss high art, but we no longer offer up such reverent homage to the Almighty, as that which was given in times of direst distress and persecution, and which yielded so rich a harvest as an America, in which to enjoy life and liberty to the utmost. How is this liberty enjoyed? Go to the synagogue on Friday night; where are the people? Our men cannot attend, keen business competition will not permit them. Where are our women? Keener indulgence in pleasures will not permit them. Where are the children? Keenest parental examples of grasping gain and material desires will not permit them, and so the synagogue is deserted. Go there on a Saturday, the day of rest, of holy convocation. Where are the people? Our men are at their shops, our women doing the shopping, calling, or at the theatre; *every one and everything can be attended to but God. For Him they have no time.* With whom lies the blame? Where are the wise mothers of Israel to-day? As we sow, so we must reap. Costly temples with excuses for congregations will not do, friends. Better the old tent for a dwelling, the trees and skies for synagogues, and reverent, God-fearing men and women, than our present poor apology for religious worship.

The world calls the nineteenth century Jew materialistic, the Jew denies it, but denial is not refutation.

It is time we stopped calling ourselves chosen, it is time we stopped living upon our past, time we prove we have been chosen a nation of priests by fulfilling His law. Many an one has been chosen for some noble mission who never attempted its completion, and it would be illogical to credit such an one with any great merit. That we are now in the position of backsliders is owing to us women.

Where are the Hannahs who cry as she of old, "For this lad did I pray; and the Lord hath granted me my petition which I asked of Him. Therefore also have I lent Him for my part to the Lord; all the days that have been assigned to him shall he be lent to the Lord."

Sisters, our work in and for the synagogue lies in bringing to the Temple the Samuels to fulfil the Law. As mothers in Israel I appeal to you to first make of our homes temples, to rear each child a priest by teaching him to be true to himself.

If the synagogues are then deserted, let it be because the homes are filled, then we will be a nation of priests; edifices of worship will be everywhere. What matter whether we women are ordained rabbis or not? We are capable of fulfilling the office, and the best way to prove it is to convert ourselves and our families into reverent beings. To simply be ordained priest is not enough, and the awful punishment which befell Eli is the best illustration of this. Nothing can replace the duty of the mother in the home. *Nothing can replace the reverence of children, and the children are yours to do as ye will with them.*

Mothers, ye can restore Israel's glory, can fulfil the prophecy by bringing the man-child, strong love of the Eternal, to his Maker.

The Rev. Dr. I. S. Moses, of Chicago, was called upon to discuss the paper, "Woman in the Synagogue." Miss Rebecca Lesem, of Quincy, Ill., then read a portion of a paper on "Advance Sabbath School Work," prepared for the Sabbath Visitor Association.

INFLUENCE OF THE DISCOVERY OF AMERICA ON THE JEWS.

Pauline Hanauer Rosenberg, Allegheny, Pa.

Events follow each other in natural sequence; and as by the law of universal gravitation, every particle of matter in the universe exerts an influence on every other particle, and is in turn influenced by it, so the events in history exert their influence upon those which follow, and the last epoch sheds its light on those which have preceded.

To fully understand the influence of any special event upon a particular people, a knowledge of previous conditions is necessary. Turn back the pages of centuries, and behold a small section of the Hebrew group leaving Palestine to occupy the more fertile pasture lands in Egypt. The subsequent slavery of the Jews in that country, their deliverance thence, their sojourn in the wilderness until the conquest of Canaan, are familiar. In an age when conquerors either annihilated, or made slaves of, the conquered, the Israelites amalgamated with the Canaanites, absorbing their culture, and in turn imparting the Mosaic doctrine to them. This was the beginning of their history as a nation, which, like all others, had its rise and fall. Beginning by subjugating its enemies and afterward in quest of territory and plunder, the period of war was followed by prosperity under the judges and the kings. The prophets flourished, literature, philosophy, science and arts were cultivated. Other ancient nations existed on a purely political basis with a religion as their outgrowth, but Israel was composed of a union of tribes with religion as its basis, the political union being an outgrowth and a secondary condition. The worship of one true God, Jehovah, was its supreme business and pleasure, and all the glorious and splendid achievements may be attributed to this doctrine. Judah flourished as a nation until the dispersion, about 586 B.C., when in a war with Nebuchadnezzar, Jerusalem was taken by storm, its Temple reduced to ruin, and the larger portion of its inhabitants deported to Babylon. Thus exiled in Chaldæa, some lapsed into heathenism, but many continued faithful to Jehovah, and although they could keep no religious feasts as in the Holy Land, the habit of meeting, and reading from the prophetic writings as an observance of the Sabbath, which developed the synagogue, came into use at this time. Later, Cyrus gave the exiles permission to return to their fatherland, but only a small number availed themselves of this permission. In 445 B. C. a Jew, Nehemiah ben Hakelejah, was appointed as Persian governor of Judæa. The subsequent history of the Jews in the East is identified with the revolutions frequent in that section: from a Chaldæan province Palestine became a Persian, a Greek, and an Egyptian possession, until Pompey's conquest subjected it to Roman rule.

With each change of power, the dispersing of the Jews becomes more complete; their settlement was encouraged everywhere, and under the Ptolemies in Egypt, they received preference over, and in consequence earned the hatred of, the indigenous population. At the beginning of the Christian era, the Jews were more populous and powerful in every civilized country than in their original stronghold, Jerusalem, colonies having been formed in and around Asia Minor and in Europe. The mission of the apostles having attached itself to the synagogues, this diaspora, or dispersion, of the Jews became the means of the diffusion of Christianity.

From this period, their fate and that of the early Christians were the same. They were alternately tolerated, given equal civil rights, and again persecuted and banished. Strange that Christianity, which itself struggled so bravely for existence, should become, with prosperity, intolerant of other creeds, and especially of its parent, Judaism! But no, in those dark ages nothing was strange. Given no place in the political arrangements of the world of those days, being neither nobles nor serfs, the Jews dwelt apart, performing their mission; they formed the link between the glorious past and the Renaissance, carrying a remnant of Egyptian, Greek and Roman civilization to the dawning of that brighter day, when the world awakened from its night of gloom to witness the crusades, the aurora of its day. But the splendor of its dawn became shadowed by the clouds of a gloomy morn, for at this period, nurtured by religious zeal and fanatic enthusiasm, began the deep-seated prejudice against the Jews as having been dwellers in Jerusalem at the time of the Crucifixion.

They emerge from a dark night to find civil, social, political disabilities everywhere; a deep abyss of persecution before them, a stone wall of restrictions behind them. This brings us to the fourteenth century, when Spain, at the zenith of her glory, is in the van of civilization. What was the condition of her Jews at that time?

Following the trend of migration and civilization from East to West, we find a large proportion of Jews settled in Spain, where they were tolerated, enjoying equal rights of citizenship, passing through a glorious period of literary and social activity, and during the fifteenth century holding government positions of great responsibility and emolument, thereby incurring the enmity of the Catholic citizens. The same religious zeal which prompted Isabella, under Torquemada's influence, to aid Columbus, led her to issue her famous edict against the Jews of her country, to take effect on the very day that Columbus started on his eventful voyage. Many believe his discovery to have been divine fore-ordination; but the new country was only about to be discovered, and meanwhile the Spanish, and later the Portuguese Inquisition commanded baptism or death, and many were baptized. These Marranos, as they were called, spurned by the Jews, and despised by the Christians, publicly professed Christianity, and secretly maintained Judaism; they intermarried with Christians, and rose to heights of power and dignity. Despite restrictions, many celebrated Jewish names belong to the general history of culture in the countries where Jews were resident. The Jews of Spain stand out pre-eminently as persons of extraordinary culture and intelligence, who, banished from their country with every refinement of cruelty and hardship of which the Inquisition was capable, dispersed to many lands, in all of which they were barely tolerated, carrying their culture with them. Cut off from their fellow citizens, excluded by oppressive laws from all legitimate trades, specially taxed, consigned to the narrow confines of ghettos, strictly prohibited from entering certain towns, limited in numbers in others, disabled from being members of trade guilds, such was the condition of the Jews of the world at the time of the discovery of America. There was no known country to which they might turn, and call it *home*. What wonder, then, that the new world was hailed as a divine gift to humanity, a haven of peace and good-will at last. Ah! but even here the problem of freedom must first be worked out, and the life-long traditional prejudices against the Jews were not set aside as readily as European expulsion cast the Jews themselves out of their native lands. Religious intolerance was prevalent among all peoples at that time. Education in the broad, liberal sense of to-day was unknown, and the dangerous experiment of forcing convictions was tried.

America, settled by all sects of people fleeing from religious intolerance and in search of a place where religious liberty and freedom of conscience might be enjoyed, could not long harbor bitter antagonisms on the ground of religion. "America is another name for opportunity. Her whole history appears like a last effort of divine providence in behalf of the human race." From within her boundaries emanated the grand idea of freedom, such as the world had never heard of before. Here was the dreamed-of Utopia, the New Atlantis, the land of promise that opened up the ghettos of the old world.—Liberty, I worship at thy shrine!

The spiritual re-awakening of the Jews was given its greatest impetus by Moses Mendelssohn, in Germany, who by translating the Pentateuch into the scholarly German language of the day removed the barrier reared by the use of an alien language; and the most powerful impulse to political liberation came from France under Napoleon. This period in Europe, the arms of America at the same time stretched out to receive the willing colonists, may truly be termed the Jewish Renaissance.

The early colonists in America were engaged in the arduous undertaking of settling and reducing to the requirements of civilization, a wilderness peopled by savages, who were not always friendly to the white settlers. We therefore find the settlers of all sects united in protection against their common enemy, the Indian, banded together in their common interests of protection, government and self-help. And although many Jewish names were on the lists of the rank and file, and others stand forth in glorious prominence during the early wars and the wars of the Revolution and Rebellion, the tie of a common cause makes one lose sight of this one or that one as a Jew, a Catholic, or a Protestant; we know of them only as *men* doing battle together for a great cause.

Since the western hemisphere has been opened up, a stream of immigration has flowed in steadily, people leaving the 'over-crowded countries of the old world to better their condition; some come to enjoy greater freedom, others, disappointed with their achievements, make a new beginning, whilst others still, working and slaving where toil is over-crowded and poorly paid, are anxious for their children to have better opportunities than they themselves enjoyed. The sad, disappointed and dissatisfied with the state of affairs in the old world, come to the new to build up under more favorable conditions; looking toward America to solve the problems and allay the fears menacing the nations of the earth to-day. And nowhere can one find so happy a working class or a middle class in a better, happier or more cultured condition. And that which is true of this nation in general is true also of her Jews. How truly has it been said that "Each country has the Jews it deserves."

The American Jews of to-day (and by these are not meant the oppressed Russian exiles who find a home here, but the descendants of the earlier settlers throughout the country) hold positions of influence and culture, commingle with the other citizens of the United States in all vital questions, and are in reality lost sight of as Jews, excepting in religious belief. They exert a healthful influence over immigrants from other countries, in which oppression has been the lot of their brethren, and although we occasionally hear of a wave of anti-semitism in civilized countries, nevertheless persecutions cannot become general in our enlightened age, nor endure for any length of time.

Each age has had its celebrated Jewish philanthropists, and with the favorable conditions enjoyed under the glorious "stars and stripes," Jewish hospitals, orphan asylums, free schools and benevolent institutions flourish in proportion to the Jewish population. The Union of American Congregations has for its object the dissemination of religious knowledge through the medium of its Hebrew Union College, of Cincinnati, and the congregational Sunday-schools, and is in this Congress reaping one of the best fruits of its sowing. To co-operate with similar associations throughout the world, to relieve and elevate oppressed Jews has been its noblest task, and through its agency the immigrants coming to the United States are taught self-reliance and self-help. No matter how ignorant through oppression these people are, their immediate progeny show marked signs of improvement and Americanism, and removed from the yoke of the oppressor, the third generation of this remarkable people on American soil, with their inherited powers of adaptability, will retain only their religion as an indication of Judaism.

We have followed Israel from its bondage in Egypt, through its national period, in its dispersion, during times of persecution, until we see Judaism, not as a nation or a tribe or a race, but as a religious sect; and now the Jew's nationality is like that of his Christian brother in his adopted or in his native land. The great colleges of the world are open to him, and in the short period of his liberation, his achievements have been greater in proportion to the population than those of any other people.

The influence of the discovery of America on the world at large was to revolutionize the accepted mode of reasoning; it set the philosophers to work, and assisted Bacon and later Franklin in striking the death blow to scholasticism. Thought pinioned for centuries was set free; freedom was no longer a dream, but a reality within the grasp of the daring; the bold new world with its unexplored extent invited daring adventurers, and offered an asylum for countless numbers of hitherto oppressed people. Could it help having a wholesome effect upon the treatment of the Jews?

Among the workers of all classes in America we find Jews: artisans, tradesmen, merchants, scientists, *littérateurs*, professors, doctors, advocates, diplomats and philosophers, and those who have not attained extraordinary renown are happy in being integral parts of the best nation on earth, exerting a restrictive influence upon foreign oppressors of their creed, aiding to better the condition of mankind, and working out one of the problems of civilization—to live in friendship and peace, not antagonism; in love, and not in hate; and, in all questions absorbing the nation, working hand in hand with the Christian, making a brotherhood of man, radiating an influence to all quarters of the globe, inviting citizenship. America's Jews, the descendants of foreign born citizens, enjoying liberty, enlightenment and culture for a few generations, judging by past noble achievements, hold out a bright promise of future possibilities.

"When the centuries behind me like a fruitful land reposed,
When I clung to all the present for the promise that it closed,
When I dipt into the future far as human eye can see,
Saw the vision of the world and all the wonder that would be."

INFLUENCE OF THE DISCOVERY OF AMERICA ON THE JEWS.

(Discussion of the foregoing paper.)

ESTHER WITKOWSKY, CHICAGO, ILL.

Forget for one moment that you are attending a Jewish Women's Congress in America at the close of the nineteenth century, and turn back with me to Spain, on the first and second of August, 1492. Look along the highroads leading from the cities; you will see throngs of human beings, in all 300,000 souls, journeying they know not whither, realizing only that, for no fault of their own, they are expelled from a land which has been the home of their fathers for about eight hundred years. They, the best of the Spanish kingdom, writers and scientists, physicians and jurists, artisans and farmers, were cast, impoverished and plague-ridden, upon the mercy of foreign nations. Let us follow them a little way; Portugal, for a high tax, gave them temporary shelter; the cities of Italy granted them a grudging welcome to the ghettos; Germany admitted them to a share in the persecution of their brethren; England and France spurned them utterly. In all Europe they were welcomed in but one place, in Turkey, the home of the infidel.

When Queen Isabella refused the generous offer of the Jews to share the expenses of the Moorish war, if Isaac Arbarbanel, with the tongue of a prophet, had turned upon the bigoted woman, and told her that the hand which had signed the decree of expulsion would, by its bounty, provide a resting place for the descendants of his people, he would have been called a madman.

We have the eyes of history, and once more looking back, this time to the third of August, at the port of Palos, we see three tiny vessels setting out for a journey across an unknown sea, seeking the spices and precious metals of India, but finding the New World, needed by none so much as by the children of the poor wanderers we have just been following.

When Torquemada, Inquisitor-General of Spain, holding aloft the crucifix, with fiery eloquence, reproached his sovereigns for considering the offer of the Jews, if then Isaac Arbarbanel had turned upon him, and again with the tongue of a prophet, had foretold that the Inquisition would pave the way for the first pilgrimage of the Jews to this new home, he would have been called a madman. Our scene now changes to Holland; time, about seventy-five years later. We see the sturdy Dutch people, who, by a series of fateful royal marriages, had come under the sway of Philip the Second, great-grandson and worthy descendant of Isabella, engaged in a bitter struggle to secure their ancient privileges, and to prevent the establishment of the Inquisition in their land.

When this freedom-loving Batavian people had succeeded in gaining the political and religious liberty for which they had so valiantly fought, with the logic that might have been expected of them, they offered a home and immunity from persecution to those whose faith was different from their own. As they carried this policy into their colonies, we are not surprised to find, as early as 1654, the record of the first Jews in North America in the city of New York, then, of course, New Amsterdam. It took the English Puritans a little longer to reach the logical conclusion of their religious premises, and it was nearly three centuries from the time Columbus sailed to the unknown lands, when the descendants of the early settlers agreed, in the Constitution of the new nation they were forming, that "Congress shall make no law respecting an establishment of religion, or prohibiting the free exercise thereof," thereby making a home for the persecuted of all lands and all times.

It behooves us Jews, as partakers of the bounty of this new nation, to remember the history of our people, to recall the struggle that our fathers have had to hold fast to the faith, and to understand that it is our duty to extend a helping hand to any of our brethren still bearing the yoke of oppression. No matter how ignorant, how degraded, the modern exiles may be; no matter whether we believe they are of one race with us or not, they are suffering for our religion, and for the sake of our own past, we must help them.

By educating the younger generation, not only of these newcomers, but of American Jews, by instructing it in the essential principles of culture, by surrounding it with refining influences, we must seek to stifle the breath of prejudice. There was no land of promise for the persecuted Jew of the sixteenth century; we have found one here in America; the Holy City may not lie within its boundaries, but the route thither certainly does. "Next year in Jerusalem" prays the orthodox Jew; let us hope that *here*, in the future, he may forget this prayer, believing that he has found what he has sought.

THE INFLUENCE OF THE DISCOVERY OF AMERICA ON THE JEWS.

(*Discussion of the foregoing paper.*)

MARY NEWBURY ADAMS, DUBUQUE, IOWA.

The influence of the discovery of America on the Jews was to bring them into prominence, because they had the qualities needed by the new conditions it gave to nations and religions.

When Protestantism began to disintegrate Christianity, and reason and learning were to be brought to bear on religion, and new sects formed from the study of the Bible, as human reason should find necessary to suit the modern world, then we find learned Jews were needed to translate and interpret the Bible.

Reuchlin, the humanist and Hebraist, has a statue as a promoter of the Reformation. He began true Protestantism with the demand that we use our reason in religion and in the study of Scripture.

The Christian history given to western Europe was of Rome, Constantinople and Jerusalem. When people began to reason on religion, and establish sects best suited to their needs for coming time from the Bible, the Hebrew race and Asia came in as a part of the religious history of humanity, and when the great monument was erected to Luther, statues of Jews were among those that surrounded his.

The newly discovered continents had given hope, courage and influence to Hebrews, and the public recognized their position in human progress. The revival of the study of literature and the Bible, brought about by the Renaissance and the Reformation, and the need of these in the formation of new religious sects, were beneficial to the recognition of their worth, for the value of Scripture, of literature, as above the authority of any one person or one institution, has risen with the increased power of Hebrews in society and religion. Then people, fleeing from persecution to new countries that they might worship God as seemed right in their judgment, increased interest in the Old Testament, and this had a reflex influence on Hebraism throughout the world, as Moses had said, "For it is not a vain thing for you, because it is your life, and through this thing ye shall prolong your days in the land," as "these words of the law" have done.

Venice, Holland and Spain were the enterprising, commercial governments at the time of the discovery of America, and they owed to the Jews much of their financial power, and that is the basis of influence in the world. They were travelers, and they brought knowledge that could be relied on of other countries, and could compare governments and religions. It was the Hebrew and Moslem learning that Prince Henry II. collected at his scientific college at Sagres on Cape St. Vincent that gave the navigators Perestrello and Pedro Correa knowledge for navigation. Columbus received their charts, maps, and collected astronomical and geographical learning. Christians, for a thousand years, had taught people to despise this world and the real facts of earth, but to look to Rome, the Christian Atlas, on whose shoulders government, religion and all civilization should rest.

At the time Columbus started for Portugal, Venice had Jews who for convenience established banks. London had learned the need of a Lombard Street. At

Antwerp and at Amsterdam, they were powers recognized in society and business. With new trade opening with the East Indies and America, the need of men who could speak several languages, and who had ability to make exchange of money, to be responsible for large amounts of cash, taught the business men of Europe to respect and honor Jews. For never since the overturning of the money-changers at Jerusalem, so many centuries before, in the Temple, where wealth had been safe, where the religious Temple was the court-house, under the care of priests and lawyers, who were bound by religious oath to honesty, had there been a secure place for money, or a set of people to care and be responsible for money confided to them, until this time, 1500, when in Venice and Holland there were banks kept by Jews.

With the discovery of new lands, the Jews were ready with knowledge gained by travel, with the sciences, and with money for the enterprises of discovery. These new countries not only gave opportunities for Jews, but stimulated exertions with the hope of obtaining security from the cruel thefts and persecutions of organized Christianity throughout Europe. For a thousand years, persecutions, which we never find equaled among savages, the Christian church inflicted in Spain upon these learned people, and upon the artistic and cultivated Saracens, who, by farms, gardens, architecture and the fine arts, had made that peninsula the Eden of Europe, and it was due to the learning of these Hebrew and Arab scientists that they gained knowledge to enable Columbus to sail across the ocean. Constantinople had been taken by Mohammedans in 1453. As late as 1556, the English church was burning books on geometry and astronomy, as works of heathen magic. Arabs and Hebrews had had schools for the learning of history and science for many centuries. The discovery of America making a demand for knowledge and learning brought them into prominence. They were sought for in universities.

Isabella, granddaughter of the great Philippa of Flanders, true to her woman nature, had *curiosity*, she *wanted knowledge*. She sent a Moorish botanist and a learned Hebrew astronomer with Columbus that she might have accurate knowledge of the new lands he was to find. She wanted the Arab to find new spices and herbs such as Holland women had, fruits for her plum-cake. She had to seek a Hebrew and an Arab, for Christians were not trained or learned, save in church legends and Roman history. They could not report on facts of *this* world or on the heavenly bodies accurately. They had been taught, "Come ye out of the world," and that knowledge of earth was folly, but the Hebrews were taught to enter the world, learn of it, and to enter into possession of it. "The Lord of Hosts is our God, *Maker* of *heaven and earth*, and we are His people." The Hebrews were prepared by instinct, habits and religion, by the arts that are easily transported, literature and music that could be carried in a small package, to enjoy new colonies in a new land.

For fifteen hundred years these persecuting European powers had demanded *uniformity* in religious belief, had falsified history to excuse their murders, and made opportunities to steal from the Jews to build palaces and cathedrals. They had tried to ostracize and exterminate them, but in the providence of God, the Scriptures and the knowledge of the Hebrews were the warp of the mantle raised that parted the waters of ignorance, and allowed the modern world to pass through into new scenes, new conditions, by the Reformation caused by reasoning on religion, and the discovery of a new hemisphere. Now, after four hundred years, with the impetus given trade by the opening of colonies, not a European power can go to war, or enter upon great financial operations without consent of Jew bankers in all nations. Napoleon wanted friends, he wanted money, wanted France to be cosmopolitan, so he befriended them.

As the French Revolution had given vitality and organization to the reason of humanity and the rights of mankind, and in America a republic had been formed by "We the people" for "equal rights," with methods based on the Hebrew ideal, a unity with variety in harmony, an ideal consonant with the newly discovered law of the heavens too, prayer had been answered. "Thy will" had come on earth as it is in the heavens. The method among the stars was worked out politically in government, and by variety, not uniformity, in religion. The States, like the twelve tribes of Israel, did not follow the example or commands of any person as authority, or rest on one belief, but the republic was spherical, revolving about the axis of principles deduced from the people's own best reason. The motion of the atoms causes the motion of the whole like the cosmos. So the reason of individuals organized in state government and religious sects, then again into a Union, and the science of the world expressed in political formation and religious toleration, leading to the future cosmos in religion, were the New World's adaptations of the Hebrew ideal.

The republic founded on unity in variety was an opportunity for the Hebrews to rejoice in. A government under which the president takes his oath as chief magistrate by putting his hand on the collected literature of the Jews, sanctions the collected wisdom of that people as authority. Here is the opposite of the ideal in Europe that persecuted the Jews. Here the president is but the executive hand to put into effective force the will of the people, and these laws are put into permanent form as the people's best ideals. No supernatural

Atlas holds the government on his shoulders, no individual can say, "It hath been written, but I say," and do as I, the individual, shall think right. The *written law*, as with the Hebrews, is the method of the republic, and not the command of one leader, or the example of one person. The "elders" of the people must rule, not by sentiment, but by written law. The Prophets had given promise of the coming republic, variety in harmony, not imperial uniformity.

Three hundred years of study of Hebrew literature and history shaped this government. Moses, Aaron and Miriam seemed a part of our history. The Bible was read not only at church, but in the family, daily kneeling, night and morning, at home-worship, singing the psalms, and repeating the Hebrew poetry and proverbs. When children's minds have had woven into their highest, sacred moments memories of these Scriptures, the imagination makes them not only the pillar of fire to lead, but the forming, creating power for life, their daily manna. The reading of the history of the Jews, as the ancient history of religion, shaped the imagination of the people. They read in their colonial homes, "When I consider the heavens, the work of Thy fingers, the moon and the stars which Thou hast ordained, what is man that Thou art mindful of him, and the son of man that Thou visitest him? For Thou hast made him a little lower than the angels, and hast crowned him with glory and honor. Thou madest him to have dominion over the works of Thy hands; Thou hast put all things under his feet." "I delight to do Thy will, O my God. Yea, Thy law is within my heart." "He shall cut off the spirit of princes." "He is terrible to the kings of the earth," as the republic was. "I have said ye are gods, and all of you are children of the Most High." "God standeth in the congregation of the mighty. He judgeth among the gods" (people). Here was a present, living Creator and God in America, not the history of one in Asia. "Let the beauty of the Lord our God be upon us, and establish Thou the work of our hands, yea, the work of our hands establish Thou it." These Scripture words echoed through the minds of the children in their early days, and formed the ideal for statesmen. Jefferson, in his inaugural, saw that it was a *constellation* that guided this republic, as an ideal in method.

The English church did not persecute Jews, because the kings were always needing their financial aid; they wanted the strength which Spain persecuted, and many of her people were from Holland. The Presbyterian as well as the Independent element were Hebraic rather than Roman, because of the dependence of their knowledge and forms of worship on the Bible, rather than the Christian system as established by Paul and Peter. The whole system of Rome's religion that dominated Europe, and held the people helpless during the Dark Ages was the triumph over many races of the system of *unity with uniformity*—the attempt to rest power, as they thought the earth rested, on one person. The cross has always stood for imperial power over individual life; thousands of years before, Rome had adopted it after conquering Alexandria. When Constantine, as it is said, saw the Cross in the sky, he saw the opportunity to select one religion, and make all others submit to it, all saved through one blood-sacrifice in heaven, all saved on earth by the Emperor, head of the church, and Constantinople, the imperial city, to hold Asia and Europe in subjection. Rome had conquered Africa, and she based her empire of religion on Constantine's political system, readjusted to include her diverse European races. They, too, were praying, and trying to have "Thy kingdom come on earth as in heaven," but they killed the prophets and the learned men, and, without the scientific knowledge of the law of the heavens, based their methods on Ptolemaic astronomy and Chaldæan Tarsus philosophy. There could be no peace for Hebrews with those who despised the laws of astronomy and earth, for they sang, "My help cometh from the Lord who made heaven and earth."

The Hebrews returned good for evil to the persecuting Christians, who stole their property, and scattered them by banishment. They had incited no wars nor rebellions. Again they had hung their harps on the willows, believing that their "God of Hosts, the Creator of yesterday, to-day and forever, to whom a thousand years are as one day, would turn, and overthrow, until His will was done," and humanity, born of God, again had a right to life, liberty and the pursuit of happiness.

When the ideal of an empire, unity with uniformity, rules, there can be no peace for those who differ from the head. The influence, then, of the discovery of America on the Jews was to bring them forward victorious with their banner inscribed, "Ye are gods, and all of you are children of the Most High." They could not submit to Christian belief, for it was based on depravity of mankind and the need of exterior salvation by a human blood-sacrifice. The history of a representative of God could not be an authority over the "children of God." As the power of priests with ceremonies, repeating history, declined, prophets multiplied, and thus it came about that those whose religion rested on the authority of prophets furnished the light for the day.

The art of music began at this time, and in this they won signal success. With the discovery of printing, their literature became the "high towers," the "Hill of Zion," to give law in many lands and across oceans to colonies, and thus they became the forming influence in society as well as church and state after the discovery, and important factors in all civil life.

Two thousand years ago, over the door of Hillel's school for youth in Jerusalem, till Rome's Titus destroyed it, was the motto, "The world is saved by the breath of the school children." Here the learned teacher, "a strong personality characterized by unusual sweetness and light," taught them to come into the sanctuary, and repeat the golden rule, to learn of laws, and to obey the written word. They were forbidden to follow persons until approved by the elected authority. No one individual could be an authority, only the one God through the people. "The Lord is in His holy temple"—the human mind—"let all the earth keep silence before Him." The collected wisdom of human mind of prophets and prophetesses were in Scripture as authority, not in a building, nor in one person, but in *law, literature, Scripture.* "For with Thee is the fountain of life. In Thy light shall we see light; and worship Him that made heaven and earth and the sea and the fountains of waters." A race that bringeth "good tidings, that publisheth peace," that believeth in a God that requires "but to do justly, to love mercy, and to walk humbly with God."

One influence on the Jews of the discovery of America was to make them realize, in their wide travels, that the Mediterranean Sea was not the world, and that not in walled Jerusalem or Rome was or could be the realization of God's kingdom on earth. God was not historical or geographical, but present in the human mind. With the discovery of continents, of the other half of the globe, and that the sphere was held in place by its own motion, came cosmopolitan ideals that nations, too, are held in equilibrium by vitality in all their various activities, that it is the people with freedom in various lines of activity that turns a nation on its axis with safety. So the Jews with world-wisdom have entered into modern, social life as a potent force. At the ballot-box, they have confronted, in a solid body, enemies of the republic from Europe. They are the friends of the public schools, patrons of fine arts, and sustain, quietly and as law-abiding citizens, the power of government; for the discovery of America loosened them from their bonds to Jerusalem as their home, and fastened them to people who accepted their Scripture as law and leader. They have become the cosmopolitan element, and are at home where law and commerce go. From 300 to 1500, Jews were treated in Europe worse than beasts or savages. What a dawn was the discovery of a new hemisphere that the old hemisphere could not rule over, and the establishment of a republic with a heterogeneous people that must become one by forming and following law! A full history of the influence on America of the Jewish financial ability, the ethical teachings and religious methods needed in this new land, is a volume yet to be written. This race obeys law that is accepted by law-makers. They denounce individual assertion of democracy that would say, "It hath been written, but I say." They hold to obedience of written law as authority, till another written law is accepted by those in authority. Anarchists do not come from this race or this religion. Modern history has awakened to the ethical value of their long experience with high aims for human benefit, and has renewed "faith in the one God who turneth and overturneth till His will is done," and His way is won. "The fountain of their patient faith was thought, and faith in God." Europe's rejected stone has become the cornerstone of the United States.

In this Parliament of Religions, this Congress of Hebrew women can turn to their Scripture, and read

Micah iv. 2, "Many nations shall come, and say, let us go up into the mountain of the Lord. And He shall judge among many people, and rebuke strong nations afar off, and they shall beat their swords into plowshares, and their spears into pruning hooks; nations shall not lift up sword against nations, neither shall they learn war any more. But they shall sit every man under his vine and fig tree, and none shall make them afraid, for the mouth of the Lord of Hosts hath spoken it." *For all people will walk in the name of his god, and we will walk in the name of the Lord our God forever and ever* (Micah vi. 4). For, saith He, "I brought thee out of the land of Egypt, and redeemed thee out of the house of servants, and I *sent before thee Moses, Aaron and Miriam.*" If by the memory of Moses "they are to remember and show themselves men," let us remember Miriam, and *exalt womanhood*. The serving qualities in this helpful sister of old that foresaw coming good to a people, and protected its life, are repeated down through the centuries to this day. As the time has come when, as Joel ii. 28 said, "your daughters shall prophesy" and "upon the handmaids in those days will I pour out My spirit," then it is time that not only Jewish women, but all women who would have liked to have the great Miriam give her prophecy, now work out into action what she would have told us to do. She could say, "I girded thee, though thou hast not known me."

Miriam does not belong alone to Jewish women. She is leader of the womanhood of the world. All Bible-reading nations honor her memory. "The battle is not to the swift, nor the victory to the strong," but to the organized forces. This has always been women's way, to unite their forces by sympathy, and let superior numbers with intuitive tact take the place of individual might and force; so thought and reason were first generated, and the desire to pass these on to their children began history. Proverbs xv. 22 says, "Without counsel, purposes are disappointed, but in the multitude of counsels they are established." Then let us now in this multitude of counsels, with the help of the International Council of Women, encircle the enlightened women of the world in a Miriam sisterhood, and work out into womanly deed what centuries ago she would have bidden us do. We, too, must use our foresight to protect, on the stream of time, our deliverers. Moses and Aaron as commanders and institutions have for centuries held sway, but the prophet bears witness that God said Miriam came with equal authority. Delay not, then, to form special denominational organizations to do the work the time demands. Miriam is leader for all women. Her prophecy was silenced, but shall not be lost, but be resurrected, and revered by us all.

For centuries we have learned of the great Jewish women, but for you to be in union with us you need to know of all Gentile women, whose lives have been "light and instruction in the way of life." The great Abbess Hilda, of Whitby, who was to England her Miriam, sent to Rome in 650 for the Empress Eudocia's (Athenais) transcript of the Bible story of creation, and thus introduced Hebrew literature into the abbey, where she was educator and the venerable Bede. She presided over a double monastery of monks and nuns. Over her high seat was the motto, "True life of man if life within." She taught too, "In Thy law is light. I delight to do Thy will, yea, Thy law is within my heart." She inspired, and gave opportunity and encouragement, so that Caedmon could write the first English poem on *Creation*, a suitable subject for his work, the germinating of a new language that now circles the earth. He was led by Hebrew thought, translated by a woman, and taught by a woman; but Abbess Hilda was the protecting sister watching an opportunity for him. She is the true founder of the English church. She first protested against Rome's control of Britain's religion. This was the rising of that spirit from western waters, which felt the tides of world's oceans; it protested against Rome's Mediterranean Sea dictation. Hebrew women must include her with many others among their star-women to light them on their way.

There are the great women of Holland and Germany, and France has a host of them, Catholics, Protestants and Rationalists. They are a part of the galaxy of womanhood. There is St. Catherine, of Siena, who did so much to introduce diplomacy to replace war, who developed the Italian language for common people to learn high truths hid in Latin, and was "peacemaker between cities," the stateswoman of her time. She belongs to the class with Miriam. They have all been helpful sisters, guarding an ark in the stream of time, containing a good force which they foresaw would deliver them from the enslaving authority of some Pharaoh.

We want a history of civilization written showing the work of women for the benefit of common life, of civil peace, and religious aspiration. There is cumulative evidence that these women of the past, who are found in all nations and faiths, are one with us in ideal. They, being women blessed by the Holy Ghost, had faith in the divinity of the human soul, and were mothers of more than animal life. They gave vitality to souls by faith and thought.

"Awake, awake, put on strength," as in the ancient days, in the generations of old. "Rise up, ye women that are at ease, hear my voice; ye careless daughters, give ear unto my speech."

As in the beginning, so now, every day has oppressing Pharaoh leaders that would enslave to build. Let your Jewish women's council, when organized, be a basket to protect those principles that are helpful, and you will give law to the future. To protect your spirit, your ideal, organize, unite your forces, weave them, and pitch them both within and without, and in time the learning of the world will recognize, and add wisdom to, your spirit, for the "Lord of Hosts is your strength," and the Sabeans of stature shall say, "Surely God is with thee."

Tuesday, September 5, 1893, 2.30 p. m.

Mrs. Minnie D. Louis, of New York, was presented by the Chairman as the honorary presiding officer of the session.

WOMEN WAGE-WORKERS: WITH REFERENCE TO DIRECTING IMMIGRANTS.

Julia Richman, New York.

This is an age of progress; and, surrounded as we are to-day by every evidence of the astounding advance that the nineteenth century has carried in its train, I feel that I am flinging down a challenge that will, perhaps, bring me face to face with a volley of rhetorical bullets, when I assert that in no other country and in no other direction is this progress more noticeable than in the relative position to man and the affairs of the world that woman occupies to-day. This advance has been made in almost every grade in society, in almost every walk in life; but so far as my own personal observations have permitted me to go, so far as my own experiences have enabled me to judge, it is my belief that this change, this revolution, yes, this progress is more noticeable in the position held by the Jewish women of America (notably the descendants of European emigrants driven from their homes forty or fifty years ago), than in that of any other class in our cosmopolitan community.

Many conditions have conspired to bring about this change: the general advance in the education of women;

the desire to give children greater educational advantages than the parents enjoyed; the financial value of woman's work; the frequent necessity for women to contribute to the support of families; the growing conviction that there is not a sufficient number of marrying men to supply all the marriageable girls with good husbands—these are but a few, with only one of which it is my privilege to deal, viz., the financial value of woman's work.

Perhaps it was due to custom and tradition, perhaps due to our oriental origin, but notwithstanding the fact that there may have always been among us a certain number of Deborahs, Ruths and Esthers, in general, the wives and daughters of Jews were, and in many parts of the world unfortunately still are, regarded as man's inferiors, their chief mission in life being to marry, or rather to be given in marriage, to rear children, to perform household duties, and to serve their lords and masters.

This is an age of progress; and thousands of women, many of them good, true, pure, womanly women, have discovered for themselves, or have been led to discover, that there is, at best, only an uncertain chance of real happiness facing the woman who calmly settles down in her parents' home, to perform, in an inane, desultory way, certain little household or social duties, who lives on from day to day, from year to year, without any special object in life, and who sees no prospect of change, unless a husband should appear to rescue her from so aimless an existence. Having made this discovery they try to join, and frequently, in the face of opposition, succeed in joining the ever-increasing army of women wageworkers, striving to lead useful, if sometimes lonely lives, with the hope of making the world, or that little corner thereof into which their lines have fallen, a little better and a little brighter than they found it.

I speak of such as women wage-workers, although many of them labor for no more substantial pay than the approval of conscience, and the satisfaction of feeling that it is God's work, however imperfectly done, that they are doing. With this class others must deal; for me it is enough to thank those whom I have met, for the inspiration their work has so often been to me, and to point out, humbly and modestly, how their future efforts may make life sweeter for the class whose work and condition must form the main topic of this paper—the immigrant wage-workers in America.

Who are our women wage-workers? From the writer or artist who receives thousands for a single work, to the poor overworked girl in some pest-hole, called a factory, killing herself by inches for a couple of dollars a week, there is so wide a range, divided into strata, sub-strata and veins leading to or from these sub-strata, that it is practically impossible to mark off, with well-defined lines, the different classes of woman's work. Perhaps the simplest classification on practical lines would be in general terms:

Women engaged in professional work.
Women engaged in domestic service.
Women engaged in store or factory work.

The professional workers, excluding writers, artists and all other classes requiring special talent in addition to long training, let us, for convenience, divide again into two classes; the one class, including teachers, governesses, companions, kindergartners, typewriters, stenographers, bookkeepers, trained nurses, etc., demands, first, a general education, in a greater or less degree, with a thorough knowledge of the English language; and, second, some special course of instruction, to which, in most cases, months, sometimes years must be devoted. The other class, a type best represented by dressmakers, milliners, manicures, masseuses and hair-dressers, demands little general education, in which a thorough knowledge of the English language is not an essential, a marketable value of which can usually be acquired by a special course of instruction, which can be completed in a few weeks.

This first class of professional work is, with very few exceptions, not open to immigrants, particularly not to the class with which American Jewish philanthropists have to deal, Russians, Poles, Hungarians and uneducated Germans. The exceptions would include those young women, who, by unusual educational advantages in Europe, may possibly have been fitted to give instruction in music, German, perhaps French, or in kindergarten methods; but the well-educated female immigrant is not plentiful, and the competition for positions of this nature is great, and I am afraid that discouragements drive such applicants too frequently into the factories and shops, where their surroundings are neither educating nor refining.

Into this second class of professional workers, I should direct as many capable immigrants as the demand for such work would justify. To be sure, some preparatory instruction must be furnished. Upon what lines this is to be done, I shall try to suggest later on.

The workers, whom, in general terms, I have placed under the head, "Women engaged in domestic service," are the cooks, laundresses, waitresses and chambermaids, children's nurses, seamstresses, ladies' maids and general houseworkers. And when we have found a sound, practical, reasonable plan for directing the tide of immigration into this channel, we shall have solved the most perplexing woman's problem of the day.

Good servants are in greater demand in all parts of the United States than any other class of labor, and yet, while thousands of homes, many of them good homes, are open to these homeless, friendless girls, we find them living in miserable tenements, slaving in dismal factories, forming corrupt associations, losing their health morally as well as physically, turning their faces away from a life incomparably better than the one they follow,—and why?

It is hardly proper that, in a paper prepared to advance the interests of immigrant working girls, I should put in a plea for the housekeeper of to-day. But the sight of the hundreds of homes which are annually broken up, because incompetent servants make housekeeping, if not marriage, a failure, the knowledge of how these housekeepers drift into the evils that the idleness of hotel or boarding-house life engenders, and the certainty that many a matrimonial craft has met shipwreck, the indirect if not the direct cause of which has been the servant question, force me to emphasize the fact, that it is not alone the poor and the ignorant that have need of our philanthropy. If, from the plan I shall attempt to outline later on, any good may come, it is not the immigrants alone, it is a whole generation of housekeepers who will be benefited.

And now we come to the third class, "Women engaged in store or factory work." Perhaps this class comprises more grades of work than could be classed under any other general head.

The manager of one large dry-goods house reports to me that he employs women as buyers, forewomen, dressmakers, milliners, saleswomen, cashiers, stock-girls, office-assistants, bundlers, operators, addressers and scrub-women; while a manufacturer of tin toys uses female help exclusively for painting on tin, cutting tin, packing toys, making paper boxes, and working foot presses. There are almost as many grades of woman's work as there are branches in every style of factory work. A word, now and again, is all that I can say in reference to these.

Saleswomen in large establishments are, on the whole, fairly well paid; but this avenue is closed to the immigrant, until she shall have mastered the English language to such an extent that there is no room for misunderstanding between herself and her customer.

"Figures" in wholesale cloak and suit houses are well paid; their hours are short, their work never onerous, and "between seasons" they have little or no work to do. But, perhaps, no other class of working women in large cities is so directly placed in the way of temptation, and the mother who lets her daughter, particularly if she be attractive and vain, take a position as a "figure," has need of all our prayers added to her own to protect her girl. You, who are doing such zealous work among working girls, try to reach this class. God help them! They have need of you.

Until I commenced to systematically collect data for this paper, which data have been furnished me by the owners of large manufacturing industries in New York City, and by working girls with whom I am intimately acquainted, I am afraid I shared the only too general opinion, that factory girls are an overworked, underpaid, much persecuted class of wage-earners. Now, I am hardly prepared to say that girls are never overworked or never underpaid, but I am prepared to assert and to prove that in New York City, at least, there are hundreds of shops and factories, well lighted, well ventilated, controlled by humane forewomen, where girls can be contented if not happy, and where the pay for satisfactory work is good, in many cases excellent. I do not, for one moment, claim that there are no factories, life in which must be torture to the poor girls therein employed; but these are in the minority, I think vastly in the minority in those industries largely controlled by Jews.

I take keen pride in re-quoting an extract taken from the government report on "Working Women in Large Cities," quoted by Mrs. Campbell, in her article on "Women Wage-Earners," published in the July *Arena:*

"Actual ill-treatment by employers seems to be infrequent. Foreigners are often found to be more considerate of their help than native-born men, and the kindest proprietor in the world is a Jew of the better class."

Such being the case, it becomes an obligation on the part of those whose aim it is to benefit the immigrant and the working woman, to organize a factory committee, whose special work it must be to act as an intelligence bureau, to direct the proper class of workers toward those factories whose proprietors can appreciate and properly remunerate good work.

Probably, the manufacture of clothing and cloaks gives employment to a larger number of immigrant Jewish girls and women than does any other single industry in New York City, and, unfortunately, many, perhaps even most, of these women are compelled to run heavy machines, in badly lighted, worse ventilated dens. The manufacturer is only indirectly to blame for this, owing to the pernicious "middleman" system; and let me say right here that if "*the kindest proprietor in the world is a Jew of the better class,*" there is no employer of our Jewish working girls who shows less kind-heartedness to his employees than these Jews of the other class, call them middlemen, or sweaters, or what you please. They are, with few exceptions, so hard, so harsh, so grasping, so unreasoning, and so unreasonable, that on several occasions, in my capacity as president of a Working Girls' Club, I tried to find better paying positions for some of these girls, in order to take them away from shops owned or controlled by their own fathers. I recall one case distinctly—a girl, not over fifteen, whose father runs a shop for the manufacture of ladies' wrappers—over twenty machines in two small rooms lighted by kerosene lamps, the air vile, the language not less so, the employees paid by piece-work, laboring from seven in the morning until after ten at night, and for this, the girl I refer to received three dollars a week, of which she paid her father two dollars and a half for board. I saw her growing hollow-eyed, round-shouldered, narrow-chested, with a never-ceasing pain in the back. It was not until I found a place for her in which she earned six dollars a week, working daily from 8 to 6, that her father would let her leave his shop, and then only upon her promise to pay him four dollars a week for board.

It is this class which requires our attention. It is in these sweaters' shops that the immigrants congregate, and it is away from these dens that we must turn the tide of women-workers. But how? I regret that I had not the time to obtain statistics from all the great manufacturing industries in the country, but from six of them, manufacturers of cloaks, ladies' underwear, men's shirts, tin toys, cigars and ribbons, I have obtained much valuable information, valuable not only because it shows existing conditions, but because it furnishes the facts which should indicate the means for arranging and systematizing a well-defined plan for directing immigrants toward those industries wherein their capabilities will command the best price, and sending the incapables in those directions where their incapability will do the least harm to themselves, their fellow-workers and their employers. In certain industries, only a partial knowledge of the English language is required; in others, girls who do not speak any English can find employment, in some classes of work, the foremen prefer German and Bohemian hands; in others, Poles or Russians are preferred.

All who have supplied me with information are unanimous in their statement that, for the same grade of work, there is no difference in the pay given to immigrants and to native-born, and in most cases, women receive the same pay as men for the same kind of work. The same manufacturers assert that the foreigners and the native-born women in their employ affiliate readily with each other, that only in the rarest instances does any ill-feeling prevail, and when such is the case, the foreigner is responsible, usually because her personal habits are such that she becomes objectionable. It is a customary thing for the native-born to show a desire to help the immigrant where the latter appears worthy of such help.

To note down in greater detail the general conditions of our factory girls would take time and space that ought better to be devoted to suggestions for the future, and so I must pass on to that point, stopping just a moment to quote from a letter written to me by a manufacturer who personally superintends a large factory: "I have been employing help, principally the class you are interested in, for thirteen years, and my experience has taught me to discriminate very sharply against certain classes of immigrants. I will cite two:

"First, Italians of South Italy. They are uncleanly, and in painfully many instances, seem to lack the germs, so that development has no basis to start on.

"Second, Russian-Polish Jews. They are suspicious, dissatisfied, and always want pay and preferment ahead of the knowledge and dexterity acquired. They are servile, almost cringing, when they start; they soon become arrogant and impertinent, and have almost a craze to get away from actual work themselves, but want to get at the commercial side, to start for themselves, and employ others to do the work. They also marry young, and come under another general class I discriminate against, viz., those nationalities that marry young. It is a great deal of trouble and expense teaching girls a trade, and if they abandon the trade for domestic duties soon after learning it, we are 'out' on the transaction."

How to improve the condition of the present army of working women is a problem which our working girls' clubs and our sisterhoods are slowly but bravely solving, and will you pardon me if I forget my theme for a moment, in order to pay tribute and to offer my thanks to the founder of the working girls' club movement, to Miss Dodge, the truest, grandest, noblest woman I ever met, a woman whose smallest act serves as an inspiration to those who try to humbly follow in her footsteps? If we but stop to contemplate the breadth and magnitude of the magnificent philanthropy which is the outgrowth of her personal influence upon a handful of working girls, we have no right to pause or hesitate in organizing a kindred movement, for fear of failure. Nothing fails that is properly conceived, carefully carried out and zealously promulgated, and to those pessimists who may declare that the following plan or some modification thereof is Utopian or impossible, I can only say, "Look at the Association of Working Girls' Clubs, examine into its history, see what it has accomplished, and then withdraw your prophecies of failure."

It has been truly said that the first aim of every effort intended for the benefit of the mass of workers is to disentangle the individual from the mass. In work such as I hope to outline, this disentangling of the individual is essential, as the entire success of the scheme depends upon the judgment displayed in selecting the proper work for each individual to do. Why make a poor dressmaker of one who with a little help might have become a competent nurse? Or why make an inferior typewriter of a girl who might have become a skilful milliner? In general, the plan is this:

In every large city establish a working women's bureau or agency on strictly business principles. This is not to be a charity. Working women as a class ask no charity; as Mrs. Lowell states the case, "Charity is the insult added to the injury done to the mass of the people by insufficient payment for work."

This bureau should be operated on the same general basis as teachers' or dramatic agencies, or even intelligence offices. Every candidate for a position of any nature under the head of woman's work must be properly registered, and must pay a small fee as soon as the bureau shall have furnished her with employment of the kind required. The bureau, through its agents, which, outside of the necessary clerical force, should be composed of an unlimited number of volunteers, must place itself in communication with shops, factories, mills, stores, families and every other field wherein women are employed, and must agree to furnish competent help of every kind upon demand. The volunteer corps of agents to supply factory hands should be selected from many and varied sources. Wives and daughters of manufacturers, fore-women in shops and capable working girls, who could gain a knowledge of conditions within factories and stores that might be withheld from the casual observer, should be largely represented. There should be a separate corps of agents to supply help to families, from governesses down to scullery maids, if necessary. Still another corps must take charge of special help: the dressmaker, the masseuse, the skilled nurse, etc.

The first outlay for an enterprise like this would necessarily be large, but, after a time, the bureau might become self-supporting. That this is not too optimistic a view becomes evident when you calculate the enormous amount of money that manufacturers, heads of families and others who employ female help expend solely in advertising in the columns of the daily papers. Why should not such money be turned to the practical use of some intelligent movement like this? Could we not train the employer to see that well-selected help, which a reputable organization could at all times furnish, is worth the payment of a fee equal to the price of an advertisement? Could we not, at the same time, show the immigrant that furnishing her with employment of a suitable nature, in an establishment that the same reputable organization feels no hesitancy in recommending, is also worth a fee?

Do you realize how many thousands of dollars are annually expended in a city like this or New York in fees at intelligence offices, to secure, in most cases, thoroughly incapable domestic help? If we could establish, in connection with this bureau, a training school for servants, from which we could supply competent cooks, laundresses, nursemaids, waitresses, etc., tell me, you housekeepers who hear me, would there be any lack of dollars flowing from your pockets into ours? And this brings me to the most important point in my paper. Strange that a spinster, above all, a school teacher, one who is supposed to have escaped the cares and worries of housekeeping, should feel so deeply upon a matter which has no bearing upon her profession; but realizing how many young housekeepers lose health and happiness, observing how many lovely homes are annually broken up, and seeing how many husbands seek comfort at the clubs only because the housekeeping wheels run off the track, how can any woman feel unconcerned as to the result? And then look at the other side. How can any woman with feeling look upon the hundreds of young girls living in squalid tenements, (did I say living? it is barely existing) bending over machines in crowded factories, surrounded in the evening by coarse, if not evil influences; how can she, I say, seeing this, and feeling that in hundreds of families these same girls could find easier work, comfortable beds, good food and refined surroundings, how can she help passing judgment on some one that this condition prevails? What right has she to keep quiet, when raising her voice in protest may make at least a few women pause to think?

And why is it that girls are so loth to enter domestic service? The poor girls and their mothers are in part to blame, because they have not been trained to do housework; but is there nothing on the conscience of the housekeepers? Do you think if tradition (or is it perhaps only report?) had not led these girls to feel that in entering domestic service, they were losing all their independence, and were often placing themselves in the way of petty meannesses which tyrannical mistresses practice in their little kingdoms, that they would so resist every effort to make them enter into private homes?

May I quote once more from Mrs. Campbell?

"In the matter of domestic service, even after every admission has been made as to the incompetence and insubordination that the employer must often face, the Commissioner for Minnesota, after stating the advantages of the domestic servant over the general worker, adds that only about a fifth of those who employ them are fit to deal with any worker, injustice and oppression characterizing their methods."

What a startling accusation! Only one housekeeper out of every five fit to be the mistress of servants! I spoke of a training school for servants in connection with this bureau—but who will organize the training school for mistresses?

Now, how could a training school for servants be arranged? My idea is somewhat like this:

Lease or buy (when the money shall have been advanced) a large house; furnish it with offices, reception room, bed-rooms or dormitories, bath-rooms, kitchen, dining-room, laundry and nursery. Rent out the bed-rooms to respectable immigrant girls, who have no homes, and who otherwise must drift into tenement boarding places, already overcrowded; furnish them with good, plain board at a moderate price; furnish, perhaps, table-board for those who prefer to sleep elsewhere; do their laundry work and sewing at the lowest figure possible. Also arrange to take in, at low figures, laundry work, plain sewing, mending, perhaps even dressmaking for such other immigrants as are not boarders or lodgers at the bureau. Here we have a regular source of income in addition to practically improving the lives of these boarders. Utilize the house by forming classes of resident girls who are unemployed, to do the general work, bed-making, washing, ironing, cooking, house-cleaning, mending, etc. This gives the opportunity for training girls as general house-workers, chambermaids, plain cooks, laundresses, seamstresses and waitresses.

A capable girl who is willing can learn very quickly how to adapt herself to one particular class of work, and there need be no lack of applicants, if the bureau furnishes good places as soon as pupils are sufficiently proficient. A strict register should be kept, not only of the qualifications of girls, but of the shortcomings of mistresses. Women who do not treat help well must be taught better, or must be "boycotted." In the same way, classes should be formed in dressmaking, millinery, manicuring, hairdressing, etc.

All this instruction should be given primarily to train the pupils to make a living, but a second advantage appears in this: in practicing work of this kind, the girls are gradually acquiring habits of greater refinement and culture. Table manners and personal habits will improve, and with their improvement a long stride will have been taken away from the old landmarks of ignorance and vulgarity.

An arrangement might be made whereby poor women, for a small fee, could be permitted to leave babies or small children in the care of the bureau for several hours each day, and these little ones would form the practice material by means of which a class of children's nurses could be trained. And so the work could grow in every direction.

I feel that I have but crudely expressed what I have in mind, but no plan, however cleverly designed, is ever worked out just as it was planned. As work of this kind grows, the experience of the workers, and the needs of the work will, from time to time, suggest ways and means for its development, which none but the inspired could have foreseen.

The Jews of America, particularly the Jews of New York City, are, perhaps, the most charitable class of people in the whole world. Time, labor and money are given freely in some directions. But charity is not always philanthropy; and we have reached a point in the development of various sociological problems which makes it imperative that philanthropy be placed above charity. The need of charity must disappear as we teach the rising generation how to improve its condition.

Almost all the female immigrants who come to this shore, through lack of knowledge as to the means by which they can swing themselves above the discouraging conditions which face them, sink down into the moral and intellectual maelstrom of the American ghettos, becoming first household or factory drudges, and then drifting into one of three channels: that of the careless slattern, of the giddy and all-too-frequently sinful gad-about, or of the weary, discontented wife.

We must disentangle the individual from the mass. We must find a way or several ways of leading these girls, one by one, away from the shadows which envelop them, if not into the sunshine of happiness and prosperity, at least, into the softening light of content, born of pleasant surroundings, congenial occupations, and the inward satisfaction of a life well spent.

Working girls' clubs are doing a grand work, but these clubs never reach the lower strata. There must be something before and beyond the working girls' clubs, something that shall lay hold of the immigrant before she has been sucked down into the stratum of physical misery or moral oblivion, from which depths it becomes almost impossible to raise her.

In this age of materialism, in these days of close inquiry as to the "Why?" of every condition, it has been claimed that the ever-increasing proportion of unmarried women among the Jews of America is largely due to the independent position women make for themselves, first, by becoming wage-earners, and second, through the development of self-reliance brought about by societies, working girls' clubs and kindred movements. If marriage always meant happiness, and if celibacy always meant unhappiness, to make women independent and self-reliant would be a calamity. But, in the face of so much married unhappiness and so much unmarried contentment, it is hardly pessimistic to wish that there might be fewer marriages consummated, until the contracting parties show more discrimination in their selection of mates.

The saddest of many sad conditions that face our poor Jewish girls is the class of husbands that is being selected for them by relatives. It is the rule, not the exception, for the father, elder brother, or some other near relative of a Jewish working girl, to save a few hundred dollars, by which means he purchases some gross, repulsive Pole or Russian as a husband for the girl. That her whole soul revolts against such a marriage, that the man betrays, even before marriage, the brutality of his nature, that he may, perhaps, have left a wife and family in Russia, all this counts for nothing. Marry him she must, and another generation of worthless Jews is the lamentable result.

I wish it distinctly understood that there is no desire on my part to disparage matrimony; indeed, happy wifehood and motherhood are to my mind the highest missions any woman can fulfill; but in leading these girls to see the horror of ill-assorted marriages, I intend to teach them to recognize the fact that many of them may never find suitable husbands; and recognizing this fact, they must fill up their lives with useful, perhaps even noble work. Should the possible husband fail to appear, their lives will not have been barren; should he come, will a girl make a less faithful wife and mother because she has been taught to be faithful in other things?

And so I could go on showing how, in every direction, the harm and the evil grow, until the day will come when charity, even with millions at her disposal, will not be able to do good. It is easier to save from drowning than to resuscitate the drowned. Disentangle the individual from the mass; create a new mass of disentangled individuals, who shall become the leading spirits in helping their benighted sisters, and with God's help, the future will redeem the present and the past.

WOMEN WAGE-WORKERS: WITH REFERENCE TO DIRECTING IMMIGRANTS.

(*Discussion of the foregoing paper.*)

SADIE G. LEOPOLD, CHICAGO, ILL.

It is with pleasure that I add a few words to the excellent and instructive paper just read, and in expressing my appreciation thereof, state those points that most appeal to me, in this question of women as wage-workers, with special reference to directing immigrants. The story of the working woman, in one large city, is, with trifling differences in conditions, the story of the working woman in all, and everywhere the fact obtains, that while in the better order of trades, woman may prosper, in the greater proportion, wearing and unceasing labor serves simply to ward off actual starvation, the "life-limit" in wages having been established long before the term became current in political economy. That woman is a permanent and conspicuous factor in the labor market of her country, the three million now earning their livelihood in the United States, at an average weekly income of five dollars and twenty-four cents, will bear witness to. The better paying trades are filled with women who have had some form of training, or have, by passing from one handicraft to another, found that for which they have most aptitude. It is to sewing, however, the most overcrowded, most underpaid, of all vocations, that all the more helpless of the vast army turn at once. It is here that the immigrant, bewildered, penniless, ignorant even of the language of the land she has entered, seeks her precarious subsistence, her sole method of obtaining work often being through the medium of the middleman, or so-called sweater. According to the seventh biennial report of the Illinois bureau of labor statistics, there are, in Chicago alone, 666 sweat shops, and 10,933 persons connected with them, working either in the shops or at home; as this inquiry was not made during the busiest season, it is the judgment of the agents that there are probably 800 such shops and 13,000 people deriving work and wages therefrom. The new factory and workshop inspection law of the State of Illinois, passed by the thirty-eighth General Assembly, the most rigid State law ever enacted on the subject, provides that each workshop shall be kept in a cleanly condition, and in forbidding that any female be employed in any factory or workshop more than eight hours in any one day or forty-eight hours in any one week, and by prohibiting the employment of children under fourteen years of age, it strikes at the very worst evils of the sweating system, which means the maximum of profit for the employer, the minimum of wages for the employed. We should all welcome the public sentiment that aims at the betterment of the hard conditions the poor groan under, and, by giving our hearty co-operation to the inspectors in their work, make the enforcement of this just law possible. Mrs. Florence J. Kelly, the Chief Inspector of Labor for this State, said to me in a recent conversation on the subject, that it "is to the credit of the Jewish manufacturers that they were the first to respond to the new order, and cheerfully posted the revised rules upon the walls of their factories."

The terrible struggle for existence at the bottom of the social ladder grows ever fiercer, and no pen can picture the want and the privation that prevail among the proletariat. Helen Campbell, whose investigations, published under the title of "Prisoners of Poverty," created a wave of indignation against existing circumstances, says, in one instance, in regard to the workers in the wretched tenements of New York: "As one woman selects, well pleased, garment after garment, daintily tucked and trimmed and finished beyond any capacity of ordinary home-sewing, marveling a little that a few dollars can give such lavish return, there arises, from narrow attic and dark, foul basement and crowded factory, the cry of the women whose life-blood is on these garments. Through burning, scorching days of summer, through marrow-piercing cold of winter, in hunger and rags, with white-faced children at their knees, crying for more bread, or silent from long weakness, looking with blank eyes at the flying needle, these women toil on, twelve, fourteen, sixteen hours, even, before the fixed task is done."

How can we save our immigrant from the horrors of such an existence? Held down by her own incompetence, powerless to help herself, and if she be a mother, unable even to protect her little ones from the impurity of their surroundings! The women's protective agencies, with all their nobility of purpose, can hardly reach her; the trades' unions of the working women themselves, and there are six of them in Chicago, with all their power for improvement and capability of broadening the character of their members, by teaching them to think rather of the good of the all than of the part, are still beyond her. A trip through the densely populated quarters of our city will discover to us whole settlements of foreign nationalities, affiliating neither with each other nor with the people of the country they seek a living in. Packed together in hovels, or worse still, in teeming tenements, they acquire not the virtues, but the vices, of their neighbors, the children naturally not escaping contamination. Philanthropic aid on the part of the many has thus far not availed, nor has the individual himself succeeded in ameliorating his own condition. To me it seems, as Mary K. Young says, that in centering our energies on work among the older people, we are beginning at the wrong end of the question.

Whatever we may attempt, this generation must still toil and suffer and weep; it is the old story of the children of Israel wandering in the desert; they may look into the promised land—it is for their children to possess it. With the mother we can do nothing. Marrying young, as Russian Jews will, she is old at thirty; the outgrowth of a civilization that looks upon woman as an inferior being; beset with all the superstitions that centuries of religion's darkness have put upon her, unenlightened, and in some instances ignorant of the simplest laws of household cleanliness, her one strong passion is her love for her children, through them alone can she be reached. Her daughter rushes to the factory, working with intelligence and precision, oftentimes for no compensation, to learn a trade; proud of her work, she is the brightest element in immigrant labor. Not over modest, she owns one beautiful characteristic, the giving freely her scant wages for the support of the family; but domestic service, as a means of gaining a livelihood, is to the Russian girl the very badge of slavery. Could we but teach her that this department of woman's work is not the very depth of degradation, one side of the question might be solved. Were such service placed upon a strictly business basis, and its social disabilities removed, with justice for a foundation, and a strict fulfilment of duty as an understanding on the part of both mistress and maid, this task might be more easily accomplished.

As early as 1868, women like Gail Hamilton advocated the establishment of industrial schools, so that more practical shape might be given to the higher education of women. Such schools, established now and modeled after the Cooper Institute of New York, might have, as their work, the studies of dressmaking, telegraphy, stenography, bookkeeping and typewriting.

Ask the teachers of the night classes held in connection with our Jewish training school on Judd street, what they are doing for the young women of the Russian quarter. As an example, in three months, a course of dressmaking is there completed, and the skillful graduate is enabled to earn from one dollar a day and upwards by serving in private families. English is taught there, and history and geography, valuable not only from an educational standpoint, but in offering something better than these young girls can ever know in the narrow, untidy confines of their homes, and keeping them from the demoralizing associations otherwise sought and found on the streets. These night schools, with their capable, self-sacrificing teachers, and social settlements, like Hull House, with noble women like Miss Jane Addams at their head, are powers that work only incalculable good. Reforms require patience; one can not have seed and flower and fruit at once, and the very child is the seed, the industrial school, in its largest sense, the agent, which brings the best within it to a glorious fruition. We must begin with the little ones, for it is more possible to train the habits of the young than to change those of the old, and it is easy to remove prejudice and distrust and even the taint of evil surroundings from the heart of a little child. The right to be joyous and pure is born in every little one, and to teach it "neatness and cleanliness and a love of nature and its fellow man" is the very foundation of the kindergarten system. It is from the kindergarten that "the poorest child takes home to the tenement house something strong enough when growth has come, to abolish the tenement house forever." To develop, not only the mind, but the heart and the hand, makes pauperism impossible, and builds up within it the power of becoming the future self-supporting citizen. A training from the beginning, that beauty and order and law are the ideals that must govern our daily striving, that work is honorable and a love of it a power to sweeten life, is the groundwork of a better order of society. Were each member of the human family to receive an education sufficiently wide to give him the necessary skill to earn a fair livelihood, the sweat shop might be abandoned, and the grinding out of life with the slow toil of the needle be known no more. Well were it for the general population, if industrial schools were established in every ward of every city. Until that is done, however, the duty devolves upon us to build them in the heart of the districts where the Russian Jews abound, for we must take care of our own, first, because their own prejudices preclude their going to others for aid, and second, because it is to our own interest to do so, they being looked upon by those, not familiar with the true conditions, as typical of our own culture and civilization and religion.

If we can successfully combat the tendency, so apparent amongst our immigrants, to herd together in certain sections of our cities, which, in consequence, have virtually become a new Ghetto, we shall have taken a mighty step toward the solution of this vexatious problem. These Ghettos are not an advantage either to the Jewish communities at large or to the Jewish refugees themselves. None will dispute the desirability of detaching the individual from the mass, but whoever will attempt this will be met at once by the natural instinct of people in such circumstances, to crowd together, impelled by the instinctive belief, that in greater numbers there is safety for them and the assurance of sympathy; while again, and this is a factor of no small moment, their religious ideas and habits and customs make for herd life, and are fatal to individual location or independent regeneration. The evil is so great, the question so wide in its ramifications, that more reforms than one must be accomplished. There is merit in every method, and whatever be done, the best we can hope for practically, for the time being, and until our whole social order is reorganized on a basis of greater justice and fuller love, and cemented by stronger sense of responsibility, is to work a palliative, not a cure. Life, however, demands certain work of each one of us, and each has a part to play in the sad drama of his unfortunate neighbor's existence. The main thing for the women whom fortune has placed in positions of advantage is, of their own accord, to cross the chasm that separates them from their sisters in what is falsely called the lower order of life. They will find, beyond a doubt, that while they themselves may have the capacity of giving much, these immigrants that are in such dire need, may compensate them most amply by showing them a phase of life, which, under an unattractive exterior, may cover in many cases, a crystal spring of possibilities, the best and the noblest.

Mrs. Henry D. Lloyd spoke on the same subject, treating more particularly of the phase presented by domestic service. In the general discussion that ensued, Miss American, of Chicago, and Mrs. Helen Kahn Weil, of Kansas City, took part.

THE INFLUENCE OF THE JEWISH RELIGION IN THE HOME.

MARY M. COHEN, PHILADELPHIA, PA.

This subject has been selected, first, because of its vital importance, and second, because it is one that seems incapable of being controverted. I feel well assured that no student of sacred and profane history will doubt the premises which I shall endeavor to present.

I believe sincerely that the influence of the Jewish religion upon the home is a truth so deeply established that all liberal thinkers have but one opinion about it. But there are, in this world, many thinkers not yet able to think liberally, that is, they have been trained in a certain groove of thought, and there their minds remain, according to their education, their environments, their beliefs. It sometimes happens, even among Christians of the kindliest nature and the warmest sympathies, that they have never come in direct contact with families of so different a creed as that upheld by the Hebrews. It has been the experience of the writer, over and over again, that members of the popular religion have observed, "We have never known any Hebrews. What are their views? What are their observances? How does their religion affect the home life? Tell us all that you can."

It is largely with reference to this absence of knowledge of the way in which the Jewish religion enters into the home life that I am urged to deal with the theme before this religious congress of the Columbian Exposition.

There is very little doubt that the idea with which the Jewish religion was planned was to so engraft it upon the home life that the two should be inseparably joined. The observances of the faith are so entwined with the every-day atmosphere of the home as to make the Jewish religion and the family life one, a bond in sanctity. In this sense the synagogue is the home, and the home the synagogue. I mean that the intelligent and devout Hebrew parent is the priest or priestess of the family altar. There is no need, if there is a desire to worship the God of Israel, to visit the sanctuary; it is always right and appropriate to enter the House of God, but it is never indispensable for the performance of religious service. The prayers for the Sabbath eve, the prayers for the Sabbath day, for the fasts and festivals, can be as feelingly and efficiently rendered in the home as in the synagogue. The service on the first night of the Passover can undoubtedly be far better observed in the home than even in the sanctuary itself. It is true that certain ceremonies were given with the condition that they were only to be performed in the place where the Temple stood, but these were comparatively very few. Among them was the very positive command, " Thou mayest not slay the Passover within any of thy gates which the Lord thy God giveth thee, but at the place which the Lord thy God will choose to let His name dwell in, there shalt thou slay the Passover at evening."

Many visitors to synagogues at the time of the Passover Festival are surprised not to see there the sacrifice of the paschal lamb, but this rite was to be performed only in the Temple, so that since the dispersion a lambbone has been substituted as a reminder of the ancient ceremony.

The greatest benefit derived from this close connection between the religion and life is the fact that the religion thus became an intensely practical one, and yet lost nothing of its inspired ideality. It was not possible for the Jew to forget his allegiance to Judaism. In the morning when he arose, the binding of the phylacteries turned his thoughts heavenward; before partaking of food, the immersion of the hands in cold water truly reminded him that "cleanliness is next to godliness." At the close of the meal, the Hebrew grace expressed his gratitude to the eternal Father for His bounties. In the daily events, in the transaction of business, either within or without the home, the influence of the religion was very seldom absent.

It was especially noticeable in the times when the Jews were restricted to life in the Ghettos, that it was very difficult to see just where the religion ended and the home life began. Many of the people, deprived of opportunities of worship outside of the Ghetto, concentrated all the fervor of their nature upon the home observances; sometimes this was carried to an injurious extreme, resulting in an exaggerated superstition, which drew down the contempt of many a more enlightened and more favored outsider. In this regard it is impossible to refrain from alluding to one of the most striking Jewish books which has been issued this year. Mr. Zangwill's story, "The Children of the Ghetto," is a work which, when taken up by Christians, often impresses them most unfavorably as a picture of the Jews; but when carefully studied by critical, and yet sympathizing, Hebrews, it is not in the least misunderstood. We have in that, to be sure, a very depressing presentation of Hebrews in the east end of London, with their tawdry clothing, their wretched dwellings, their pinched means, their indescribable privations. Yet with it all, deep down in the soul of the Hebrew in the Ghetto, man, woman, or child, is the wondrous loyalty to the

God of the people. We see this in Esther Ansell, who, although transplanted when a girl from the Ghetto into the luxurious home of her patroness, Mrs. Goldsmith, finds, without exactly understanding why, no satisfaction in the wealth surrounding her. It is seen, too, in the half quaint, half pathetic scene, when Moses Ansell is summoned to his son's deathbed, and although the jargon which the father speaks has to be translated to the son, there is a clear understanding between the two that it is the glorious declaration of the Unity, the "Hear, O Israel, the Lord our God, the Lord is One," the Hebrew's dying confession, which is to be uttered at that awful moment.

On the other hand, turning to the Jewish home life of this country, we find that the religion has a powerful effect upon the pursuits cherished in the home. This will be seen particularly in the cultivation of the art of poetry. I will venture to quote a verse from a poem entitled "*Rosh-Hashana*," the Jewish New Year.

> "One word—ere once again we turn a page
> In this great volume of the countless years
> To mark another epoch of our age,—
> One word, and we resume life's hopes and fears."

This production evinces something of the power of the religion in the home life; the gifted writer has no doubt traced these words at the close of one of the most solemn Hebrew festivals. Not in the synagogue, not in the office, not in the school, not in the place of amusement, do these high, poetic inspirations arise, as a rule, but in the home. The creator of these poetic lines just quoted, is a young Philadelphia Hebrew, whose work will be seen to have ethical significance as well as rhetorical grace; after the day which stimulates all the religious fervor that a Jew possesses, he sits in his library, and traces on paper what we may hold in our hearts forever. We all know how closely associated were the sudden religious awakening and the literary home life of Emma Lazarus: her splendid poems, such as "The Crowing of the Red Cock," "The Banner of the Jew," and "The Feast of Lights," might have sprung from a soldier in battle, or a fiery, wandering exile; yet they were written in the quiet study of a New York Jewess; these examples are but two out of a large number that will, I think, testify to the truth of my assertion.

The influence of the religion in regard to dietary laws is perhaps one of the most marked in close connection with the home routine. In addition to the various observances commanded in the Bible, tradition and the Rabbis have made it customary for Hebrews to partake of special kinds of food on certain festivals; we see this in the use of white stewed fish for the Passover, in the additional decoration of the table during Pentecost, in the serving of apples and new honey on the New Year. The praises of fried fish as prepared by Hebrews have been eloquently set forth, but where is the writer who has done justice to the glories of the white stewed fish as it appears on the Passover table? Golden balls, of delicate flavor, surmounting slices of the whitest halibut; cayenne peppers, with circles of lemon, adding brilliant color and spicy taste to the compound; over all the yellow sauce, almost jelly-like in consistence. Those who have spoken of Judaism as a "kitchen religion" lose sight of the fact that spirit and body are equally in need of nourishment, and that to closely associate the material and the religious is to dignify the one without injuring the other.

There are many other special dishes transmitted to us by tradition for minor festivals. These little customs serve to bind the religious and the domestic life very closely together, and who can doubt it that sees the blessing given by parents to children on the Sabbath eve, or witnesses the solemnity of the *Kiddush*, the wine which celebrates the approach of the bride, the Jewish Sabbath. I can never see, in the sometimes punctilious care with which some Hebrew women prepare their homes for the religious festivals, the ground for annoyance or ridicule which it seems to furnish to many critics; to me it presents a beautiful union between the religion and the home. The Jewish faith is not to be worn as a cloak on the Sabbath or the festival in the synagogue, and then to be cast aside before entering the portals of every-day existence; it may be carried as a veil, but through it should be seen, still showing brightly, the purity of the domestic altar.

The Jewish wife and mother, as a rule, is faithful to her husband and children. Her religion teaches her to fulfil every duty to these near and dear ones, and in addition, to exercise as generous a hospitality as her means will permit. From the time when Sarah entertained the angels until to-day, the chain of kindly feeling toward the traveler or the visitor has never been broken; in fact, the well-to-do Hebrew woman holds it a privilege to share the fruits of the earth with any one less favored, and knows that in so doing she is only obeying a divine behest: "And thou shalt rejoice with every good thing which the Lord thy God hath given unto thee, and unto thy house, thou, with the Levite, and the stranger that is in the midst of thee."

The influence of the Jewish religion upon the home is of great importance in determining exactly the niche which the inmates are to occupy in the history of moral forces affecting other peoples. For instance, inasmuch as a Hebrew woman *is* a Hebrew woman, just so powerful are her character and her example. There are plenty of merely cosmopolitan women, open to the guidance of every creed or no creed, as shifting fancy may dictate; such women may be lovely and excellent in many ways, but they will scarcely command the admiring respect, the deep sympathy, the earnest fellowship, which a loyal Hebrew woman receives in overflowing measure from the world at large. Her chief value to the people of other beliefs is that she is a worthy daughter of Israel, in the home first, and then everywhere. Husband and children in the Jewish home show to the wife and mother a profound affection, and hold her in the greatest honor. Jewish men are almost invariably domestic, valuing their homes as the union of material and spiritual good.

The influence of the Jewish religion in the home may well be treasured as the keystone to the lasting happiness and usefulness of all the nations of the earth.

THE INFLUENCE OF THE JEWISH RELIGION IN THE HOME.

(*Discussion of the foregoing paper.*)

JULIA I. FELSENTHAL, CHICAGO, ILL.

The code of ethics held to be correct and practicable by right thinking men is the same, unaltered, that was taught in the Book of books thousands of years ago. The commandments of the decalogue and the other moral laws, congruous with the same, are of as vital importance now as when first proclaimed to the emancipated Israelites. To the obedience to the Ten Commandments is due, primarily, the survival of the Jews. Since two thousand years they have been a national nonentity, playing the part of scapegoat in the drama of the nations, and scattered throughout all lands. The wonder and the question arise, to what is due the Jews' perpetuation? The strongest bond to unite them one to another was religion. How potent a factor this is, in the life not only of individuals, but of races, is observed, when we remember that Greece and Rome, with their splendid civilizations and their vast achievements in art and legislation, have vanished. They, too, had a beautiful belief in higher powers, full of poetry and ideality, but differing in the fundamental idea of monotheism and stern morality. Judæa, inferior in the arts both of war and of peace, exists, a witness to the truth of the idea, that there is but one God, the Father of all, who holds the fates of His children in His hands, and who does all for the best. He loves what is good and hates the bad. This is and was the keynote of the Jew's religion. But, as in other religions, the cardinal idea alone did not form the substance of Judaism. Around this central idea clustered, during the lapse of centuries, a mass of additional doctrines, laws, traditions and customs, which formed the network of the religious practices of the Jews. This accumulated mass of ceremonials was like embroidery so intricately worked that one could scarcely discover the original texture beneath. The various observances, finding equal importance in the eyes of the devotees, were not restricted to holidays and Sabbaths and to fulfilment in the synagogue alone, but almost every daily action of man or woman, in the household and out of it, was accompanied by the performance of some religious rite, which none was too ignorant or too enlightened to omit.

Therefore, when one considers the influence of the Jewish religion on the home, it must not be forgotten that every department of life was permeated with religion, and the home principally, was the centre for the fostering of these religious and moral truths. A people which believes that religion is not for any distinct time or place, but that it must enter all phases of life, is virile.

Many of the most powerful moral forces were continually brought into action through this constant association of religion with life, through the agency of prayer and countless religious practices. The deeds and duties which are essential in high-minded, moral living were religiously practiced in Jewish homes, because prompted by religion. By indicating a few of the daily observances, this may be made apparent. No one, from the babbling child to the feeble grandfather, rose in the morning without uttering prayers of thanks to God, and invoking His divine grace for the coming day. At night, before retiring, the last conscious act was the saying of a prayer. Before every meal grace was said, and afterward a prayer of thanks was again recited. It was a religious duty to visit the mourner and the afflicted, and the poor received the graceful charity prompted by the beautiful Jewish laws. Scarcely a Jew was so poor as not to entertain some one of his poorer traveling coreligionists on the Friday evening, not as a troublesome beggar, but as an honored and welcome guest at the table. So, by the aid of these few illustrations, can be traced gratefulness, sympathy, charity and hospitality. Such paramount duties as the obedience of children to parents, strong mutual attachment between the members of a family, etc., were faithfully fulfilled. Be it remembered that these customs just alluded to were not merely social usages, but religious duties, which entered the very sinews of life, and if many of them were mechanically performed, their significance nevertheless impressed itself on the minds of the participants. Thus the home became a bulwark of moral and social strength, impregnable by reason of the religious atmosphere that pervaded it.

In this connection, it may be remarked, as a noticeable fact, that wine, which played an important part in all holiday and Sabbath celebrations, never became a baneful influence in their lives. It was looked upon, like any other food product of the earth, as a gift from God, and the blessing or thanksgiving was always pronounced before partaking of it. Intemperance and dissoluteness, those two cardinal vices which have wrecked so many homes, are sins which have not, as a rule, allured the Jew. The praise is scarcely due to the man, but to the Jewish laws, so wisely framed, and to the customs, so beneficially impressive. Simple fidelity to these laws and customs was enough to guard him from temptations, and keep the peace and purity of his home intact.

During the centuries of persecution and migration, the home and the synagogue were the only places where the Jew could find relief from trouble and care. The broader arena of life, where men might enlist, and find intellectual exercise and pleasure, was closed to him. Inasmuch as unfriendly and tyrannical governments refused their Jewish subjects any participation in the pursuits dear to patriotic and high-minded men, there remained for them only the narrow channel of bread-winning. They were only too thankful if their endeavors to earn a livelihood were unmolested. What would have soon dwindled into the most narrow materialism was redeemed by the purity of their home life, permeated with poetical and homely illustrations of their faith. The synagogue and the home were sanctuaries, on whose altars the burdens of life might be cast, and love and peace be found. In this respect, persecution proved a blessing to the dispersed. With the sword of an innocently incurred hate ever hanging over them, home-ties were firmly knit, and the small communities living behind Ghetto walls were bound together as one family. So does misfortune often carry a blessing in its train. Fearing evil from without, they found peace within the Ghetto walls.

The Jew, distinctly Oriental in some respects, has avoided, as if by instinct, some of the Eastern vices and failings, notably the institution of harem life and the notion of the inferiority of woman. Though woman's sphere was limited, within it she received the loyal love due her, as wife and mother and queen of the household. The father, on the other hand, was vested with a sort of patriarchal dignity. He was the protector and guardian of his loved ones, and his authority was final. Filial and conjugal duties were zealously performed, but particularly did old age meet with veneration and regard.

Owing to necessary brevity, many elements of domestic Jewish life, possessing beautifying and elevating tendencies, must be omitted, but I cannot refrain from mentioning the Passover, Sukkoth, Chanukkah and Purim, which gave great opportunity for the play of joyful, religious emotions in the home, whose influence was felt long after the occasions themselves were over. But most valuable was the Friday evening celebration. How impressive, when the father, returning from divine service, folds his hands upon the bowed heads of his children, giving them his blessing, thus imbuing the child with filial love and veneration, and himself with the moral responsibility toward his offspring. To see the members of the household assembled around the brightly lit and festive table, welcoming the bride of the Sabbath with hymns and praise, presents a picture of true religious fervor and piety. A number of writers, mostly German, have caught this undercurrent of beauty in the lives of a hampered people, who quietly passed their days in the shadow of Ghetto walls, and have portrayed them in works of fiction. Kompert, Bernstein, Franzos and Sacher Masoch, have been among the most successful of these writers. Prof. Oppenheim, an able artist, has preserved these features of the past for the profit and pleasure of later generations, by painting a series of pictures, representing typical scenes, such as the interior of the synagogue on various occasions, holiday celebrations, observance of the Sabbath eve, etc.

Since Mendelssohn's time, many of the barriers which separated Jew and Gentile have been gradually removed. Simultaneously with the granting of civil and religious rights, the Jews were given intellectual freedom, and minds trained for centuries almost exclusively in the study of the Bible, the Talmud, and their numerous commentaries, eagerly sought the avenues open to them. Politics, journalism, law, letters, medicine, etc., had many a Jewish follower. The horizon widened, and religion no longer played so important a part in their lives. How did this react on their home life? The dietary laws, formerly a prominent feature in the daily routine, fell among many into disuse, until now they are "honored more in the breach than in the observance." Many of the customs, which had accompanied the wanderers from land to land, were forgotten or ignored. In Russia, Eastern Austria and adjacent provinces, the old customs still prevail to a great extent, but in Western Europe and in our own country, circumstances have almost compelled a change, and we have had to adjust ourselves to a new order of things; a simple task for the Jew, who, although preserving some distinctive traits throughout all the ages, has nevertheless always affiliated himself with the country of his adoption.

Many of the moderns have cut loose from ceremonialism. Whoever has considered the rise of races or religions knows the importance of ceremonies and symbols as social factors. As civilization advances, these forms lose their power and significance, so that if they are still to have a value, it is as historical reminders and relics.

This value is denied by many, but even were its importance to be granted, the complications of our busy life are such that many rites, beautiful and significant, are difficult of performance. Doctrinal belief, many maintain, would suffice for any religion, but granted that this were so, we would still have to admit that mere adherence to a number of articles of belief would be only the skeleton, which must be clothed with the flesh of imagery and form to make it a living reality. This was a necessity in the childhood of the race, and in a great measure it will always be necessary. Now, when many assume that we are arriving at the vigor of maturity, it is deemed useless to surround ourselves with any forms. It remains to be seen whether religion, shorn of all symbolic rites, can still exert as potent an influence on the home as of yore. Formerly the Jewish religion was treasured and preserved in synagogue and the home alike. Now our temples are mostly lecture-halls, and in our homes many rites are omitted.

Under any and all conditions, it is of the utmost importance that the home life, as the basis for true national prosperity, should be elevated and elevating. This, united with the fact that there are many tendencies in modern life apt to lower the standard of social purity, should make us consider well before discarding entirely an element that has been so vast a power for good during so many centuries.

WEDNESDAY, SEPTEMBER 6, 1893, 9.30 A. M.

Mrs. Pauline H. Rosenberg, of Allegheny, Pa., was introduced by the Chairman as the honorary presiding officer of the session.

ISRAEL TO THE WORLD IN GREETING.

Cora Wilburn, Marshfield, Mass.

Unto the world, with Time's Peace-offering,
What treasure gifts does Ancient Israel bring?

Heart-stirring melodies, the aspiration
Of martyred souls, that death of torture braved;
The breath Divine of answering inspiration,
While fierce the fires of Persecution raged.

The boundless Trust, uplifting captive sorrow,
From Israel's stricken heart, enkindled hope;
That evermore the dark, uncertain morrow,
Flushed with the glory of the Future's scope.

Faith in the Name Ineffable—Unspoken!
Leading throughout the centuries' darkened maze;
Glad benedictions wrung from hearts long broken,
Of heroes, slain on unmarked battle-ways!

Grandeur of Womanhood's exalted duty;
Self-abnegation that Life's all bestowed;
Sunshine and storm of Love's illumined beauty,—
Crowned Purity, with light of heaven that glowed!

High, reverent awe, the soul's reflecting mirror,
That guards within illimitable Truth;
Kept 'mid the stress of Superstition's terror,
In the religious soul of Age and Youth!

The Patriot's iron will, all hardships daring,
For native land, and Freedom's light within;
With Lion shield of David onward bearing
The soul's abhorrence of the Traitor's sin!

Vibrating unto heart and brain responsive,
The ancient record, and the by-gone song,
Attest in triumph-strain and hymning plaintive,
The sweet forgiveness of a Nation's wrong!

More than by reach of word of earthly meaning,
Unto the world does Ancient Israel bring;
Time's righteous victory of ascendance gleaning,
While low accordant chimes of Freedom ring!

Unto this gathering of the World assembled,
What treasure-gems does Modern Israel bring?
In the far silence freighted souls have trembled,
Nor heavenly message dared the minstrel sing.

Now, broadening Light sheds radiance of the Morning,
Great souls hold vigils 'neath the glow divine;
Despite of threatening Russia's bitter scorning,
What gift brings Israel to *Our Country's Shrine?*

The olden reverence, graced with dear remembrance,
Its holiest fervor, heritage of days;
That with the New Life's vast, diviner semblance,
To God's high purpose heart and spirit sways!

The joy of Manhood's soul-emancipation;
Glory of Woman's heart-ascendancy;
Blent with the home-life's threefold consecration
To noblest aims of human destiny.

Rose-flowers of Feeling; sun-rayed Gems of Thought,
Into one hallowed wreath of Memory wrought.

Love for the Stars and Stripes! all power transcending
Imagination weaves of soaring dreams;
Truth's vowed allegiance with all heart-hopes blending,
As affluent Life with high endeavor teems.

In daily service of humanity,
Shared sweet and irksome tasks of Liberty!

The Mind's advance, in Israel's modern story,
Keeps evermore abreast of Truth and Time;
As Godward tending, Science wields the glory,
That guiding leads to long-veiled heights sublime.

On loftiest summit, as from lowliest place,
The garnered favors of Celestial grace,
Shed benedictions o'er the human race.

TO THE WORLD IN GREETING—WILBURN.   131

Only, as children love *the Mother* best,
We cling unto the dear, ancestral breast.
Not loving less the differing souls we meet,
In mart, or home, or on the busy street,
But as our kindred all. 'Mid din of strife,
We know the mandate, with old wisdom rife:
"The righteous of *all* nations shall Eternal Life
Inherit." Long-kept, cherished Truth!
Newly engraved on heart of Age and Youth,
Attests Our Father's universal care,
While Faith uplifts the adoring search of prayer!

And *tears* we bring! for helpless thousands call
On human help, as deepening shadows fall;
Portents of storm, and strife of bigotry,—
E'en o'er Columbia's stronghold of the Free!
Grief-thrilled, true souls To-day, as ere the light
Pierced the deep gloom of Egypt's rayless night,
Wait prayerful for the blest Deliverance gleam,
Beyond the Prophet's hope and Poet's dream!

Peace! with thy gracious splendors manifold
The sway of Truth let captive eyes behold!
The boundless trust of ancient days renew!
E'en though he reached thy sacred havens through
Red seas of carnage! For the menaced life
Of Freedom calls for ending of the strife,
That holds the world in bondage to its fears;
With grief of longing fills the waiting years;
Marring the grace of Justice in the land,
At lawless bidding of the blood-stained hand
Of Tyranny. Though not "for me and mine,"
The fell intent of secret hordes combine;
Though safe beneath the Starry Flag *we* dwell,
Dare we assert that with us all is well?
While homeless brothers may not seek their bread,
On native soil; but cringe 'mid phantoms dread
Of Famine, Murder, Pillage, women slain!
Are *we* so deadened to another's pain,
In arms of luxury lulled, that willingly,
We shackle *here* the soul of Liberty?

America! thy grateful Israel gave
Her life-blood, equal with thy "free and brave;"
For the safe-keeping of thy holy stars,
Thy Hebrew soldiers wear the battle-scars.

They share the country's glory; and its shame,
When Force and Fraud their dastard deeds proclaim;
Shall Russia's shadow dim *our* record's fame?

Forbid it, God ! enthroned in earth and heaven!
Forbid it, hearts of His Compassion filled!
By all the Light of Inspiration given
To souls that would Thy Freedom Temples build!
Let not the Cossack hand's brutality
The bulwarks of the People's Sovereignty
Assail, while dawns the Twentieth Century!

Greeting to Israel still in captive chains!
Greeting to all in Freedom's wide domains!
Not Toleration, but Fraternal Love,
Be the New Era's olive-bearing dove!
Only a foeman he who bars the way
To holy Freedom's universal sway.
Where the Great Name Ineffable is spoken,
Life's tributary prayer is heavenly token,
And frankincense of praise; brothers and sisters we,
Clasp hands of service for humanity,
Heart-linked for earth and Immortality!

CHARITY AS TAUGHT BY THE MOSAIC LAW.

Eva L. Stern, New York.

> "Sing heav'nly Muse that on the secret top
> Of Oreb, or of Sinai, didst inspire
> That Shepherd, who first taught the chosen seed
> In the beginning, how the heav'ns and earth
> Rose out of chaos. . . . .
> And chiefly Thou, O spirit, that dost prefer
> Before all temples the upright heart and pure,
> Instruct me, for Thou know'st; Thou from the first
> Wast present, and with mighty wings outspread
> Dove-like sat'st brooding on the vast abyss
> And madest it pregnant: What in me is dark,
> Illumine; what is low, raise and support;
> That to the height of this great argument,
> I may assert eternal Providence,
> And justify the ways of God to men."

This shepherd of Milton's song was Moses, the lawgiver, the simple man of meekness, who alone of all mortals breathed into by the breath of God, stood face to face with Him; who alone of earth's men held converse with Him, and was the elect of righteousness and holiness to receive from the divine spirit the decalogue, so simple in its comprehensiveness that we teach the babe to lisp it, and yet so deep, grand, severe, that it awes the savage in his lawlessness. It is the mighty pile upon which the Christian world rises, and upon which is built the destiny of the whole human race. From these Thou-shalt-nots have risen the nations' glory —morality and lawfulness, and from that solitary Thou-shalt issues the crowning aureole of life, which sits like a star on the mother's brow, and wraps the father in a cloth of purple.

The decalogue attests the sovereignty of God, a teaching which goes like an æolian sigh through the code of Moses: "I am the Lord your God which brought you forth out of the land of Egypt." As a prelude to his grand system of laws, he reminds the Israelites of their deliverance from the taskmasters of Egypt, to render them merciful to the oppressed, and to make them protectors and friends of the downtrodden and all those who sue for mercy from man. "And thou shalt remember that thou wast a bondman in the land of Egypt." This enslaved condition of the Jews for four hundred years has tempered the spiritual teachings of the world by having developed a Moses. It has put into touch with each other men of widest lives, of extremest education, of conflicting faiths, and this link between men is *Charity as taught by the Mosaic Law;* "it humanizes religion, and religionizes humanity;" it is the ethical basis of Judaism, as Judaism is the bedrock of all religions; whatever may have come after it, there was nothing before. What is the essence of charity as taught by the Mosaic law? It is merciful conduct to man, beast, birds in the air, fruit-bearing trees, to everything animate and inanimate under the wide expanse of heaven. There is a reason for every precept in the Law, and every reason teaches equity, mercy, justice, courage. The Mosaic code has, for its *direct* object, the cultivation of a spiritual and holy life, the inculcation of patience, modesty, humanity, sympathy for the poor and the sick, of help for the weak, of release for the slave, of compassion for the hired man and the debtor, and above all of the necessity of *education*, which is the fountain whence well-springs of good impulses gush. Though the Law impresses the precept of charity on the people—in fact, rabbinical writ says: "He who practices love and charity fulfils the whole law of Moses,"—it does not commiserate the poor man to the extent of commanding self-abnegation. It says: "Every man shall give as he is able, according to the blessing of the Lord thy God, which He hath given thee," and the Talmud comments on this: "Whoever wants to enrich the poor must not give more than the fifth part away, otherwise the giver may some day impoverish himself, so that he will be thrown upon society."

This humane and judicious law was carefully observed by the Jews of the Middle Ages, and even to-day, here in our midst, we have Jewish philanthropists who give a tenth of their earnings to the poor and the needy, and though this unselfish charity is unstintingly dispensed, it is given with a wise heart, lest the poor should organize themselves into bands of idle parasites, and paralyze society. When the great philanthropist-banker Itzig, of Berlin, gave wine to the sick and the poor, he persistently asked the return of the empty bottles, to show these helpless creatures that everything was of use, that his wealth did not blind him, that though they had consumed the wine, the vessel which had held it for them could be of further use in serving others.

How beautifully this contrasts with the godless emperors of Rome who lavished wealth indiscriminately, striving to win fame by ill-considered liberality; "they fed the rabble with corn, wine and oil," and thus encouraged idleness and dissipation, countenancing the rich who encroached upon the rights of the poor. This, too, is in opposition to the Mosaic teachings, which insist upon the rich man's calling in the poor to his table, and forbid hurting his feelings by even staring at him while he eats, lest it be taken for the arrogance of riches or the pride of ownership of the food he gave. Says the Law, "If the man be poor, thou shalt not sleep with his pledge, in any case, thou shalt deliver him the pledge again, when the sun goeth down, that he may sleep in his own raiment." This would keep the lender to the poor from asking his garments as a pledge; or at least it would secure the garment as a covering for his limbs, when the poor man lay down to sleep. And in addition, it ordains, "When thou dost lend thy brother anything, thou shalt not go into his house to fetch his pledge, thou shalt stand abroad, and the man to whom thou dost lend shall bring out the pledge unto thee." This would prevent the lender from acting in an arrogant manner, or from domineering over the less fortunate man.

The Greeks of antiquity were likewise munificent in their gifts, but with the ulterior object of displaying their wealth to the populace; it was a sort of advertisement for the rich man; but the Jews of this time were practicing the *letter* of the Law. Almost in every town there were synagogues, where not alone the one, true God was worshiped, but where instruction was given, and charity practiced in all its branches.

The Jews have a sympathetic, responsive nature, and on account of the hardships undergone by their race, they are so knitted in soul to one another, that they nurse their sick, help their poor, soothe the widow and the orphan, and entertain the stranger, from instinct as much as from education. Consequently, all this civilizing humaneness was found in towns where Israelites dwelt, and up to the destruction of the Second Temple, they lived in the spirit of the Law.

Then came Christianity, a modification of these practices under better organization, learned from the Romans, for the latter have excelled, in history, as leaders and organizers. In addition to Christianity's having this incalculable advantage, it had converts from every quarter, who willed large sums to its institutions, and consequently put it in possession of a large territory. This left the Israelites in fewer numbers, and made them fall back into a solidarity of purpose, which intensified their brotherhood and their sympathies for one another.

However, though Christianity grew abroad, and was enriched by Roman converts, who enabled it to do much fine charity, its ethics were nourished at the bosom of Mosaic teachings; virtues were adopted from the Mosaic code, and the merciful words, "When thou cuttest down thy harvest in thy field, thou shalt not go again to fetch it; it shall be for the stranger, for the fatherless, and for the widow;"—this merciful precept had lain in the heart of Jesus along with the love of the man, Moses, who bequeathed it to his people.

The widow and the orphan claimed the especial love of the legislator, and everywhere he speaks of them, and enjoins man to be concerned about them, and provide for their wants.

"When thou beatest thine olive tree, thou shalt not go over the bough again; it shall be for the stranger, for the fatherless and for the widow."

"When thou gatherest the grapes of thy vineyard, thou shalt not glean it afterward, it shall be for the stranger, the fatherless and the widow," for out of the mighty depths of his heart, he foresaw that woman, clinging in her nature, would be doubly weak when the stronger arm was snatched away, and with her children would be among strangers. While the letter of the Law commands commiseration for the widow and the fatherless, it is in the *spirit* of the Law that the Israelite best serves the Master, a spirit that can best be understood by God, for the Jewish heart goes out to these unfortunates, expands for them, and contracts again with them enclosed. The strong man takes charge of the widow's affairs, advises her, comforts her, and in every provision includes her before himself. If the fatherless lose this last, loving parent, the orphan is adopted, taught in the Law, given a trade together with the more fortunate child, and when ready for matrimony, if a girl, a good husband is secured for her, nor is she left portionless; if a man, a good wife is sought for him, and in most instances he is provided with the means for establishing a household. Jewish Orphan Aid Societies have existed in large and small communities from the early centuries. We have them in almost every town and city in the United States; and they give sums of money and outfits of necessary clothing to the orphan. In Europe, among many, is the society founded in Berlin by Daniel Itzig, providing liberal dowries for poor brides. This is a duty of the Jew to an orphan.

Together with the widow and the orphan is mentioned the stranger. The stranger, supposed to have left his country, his kinspeople and familiar scenes, so dear to the heart, his body worn with travel and emotion, sometimes with hunger and thirst, must be allowed to gather the fruits of the field, left for him by the gleaners, that he may sustain life, as the story of Boaz and Ruth well illustrates. The stranger is invited to the homes of his brethren in faith, and is compensated there for what he has left in his own land. The stranger is coupled with the brother, "And if thy brother has waxed poor, and fallen in decay with thee, thou shalt relieve him, *yea, though he be a stranger* or a sojourner; that he may live with thee." This is one of the beautiful qualities of the family life of the Jews; their concern for one another, their respect for father and mother, and their cheerful hospitality. In Jewish communities there also exist brotherhoods, which have for their purpose benevolence to the stranger, who may chance among them, and one historian tells us that, in many instances, a poor Jew has traveled through the greater part of

Europe without much more than a penny in his pocket, his brethren feeding and clothing him, and then giving him a letter of recommendation to his co-religionists in the next town to which he wanted to go.

Mosaic charity inculcates fellowship, a responsiveness to the joy or the sorrow of others, be they kinsmen or strangers. "Thou shalt not oppress a stranger, for ye know the heart of a stranger, seeing ye were strangers in the land of Egypt."

There is a very fine, humanizing law on usury, which says, "Thou shalt not lend upon usury to thy brother; usury of money, usury of victuals, usury of anything that is lent upon usury," and this law was observed until the early Middle Ages, when the Jews were forced into disregarding it by being deprived by the rulers of countries of other channels of livelihood. The precept taught the lesson to lend to the poor without exacting pay for what was lent, so as not to make the poor poorer, and as Philo interprets it, "Considering that *gratitude* may in some degree be looked upon as interest repaid at a more favorable season for what was lent in an hour of necessity."

Mercy, twin sister of charity, is extended also to the hired man, "The wages of him that is hired shall not abide with thee all night until the morning." This is a consideration the heart can readily understand, for the laborer fortifies his strength with thoughts of his pay and of the comfort it will afford those dependent upon him, and if, when the sun sets upon him, his heart is cheerful, he brings better strength to his labor the following day, while if he is tricked out of his wages, in addition to his waste of energy, he suffers disappointment, which eats away his manhood, a quality of suffering which we are forbidden to inflict upon beasts, for "thou shalt not muzzle the ox when he treadeth out the corn." With the same divine conception of mercy, instruments of labor are forbidden to be taken away or taxed, if their owner needs them to gain a livelihood: "No man shall take the nether or the upper millstone to pledge; for he taketh a man's life to pledge." Would not this mean, besides, preparing poverty for a man who would otherwise be happy, because industrious? Thus, when the unfortunates are committed to the charity of man, the wisdom of the Law streams forth like the word *God*, written on the mitre of the high priest. Everything has a claim on man's mercy, and the Mosaic code would have the creature made "in the image of God," resemble his Creator by cultivating in him the divine attributes of *virtue, justice* and *mercy;* many splendid blossoms have bloomed on the tree of life, and showered down leaves to make a soft bed for the poor, and have shed fragrance, and lent strength to those who needed comforting.

In every century Mosaic charity has communicated its spiritual essence to society at large, and has given to the needy a friend and support. Antiquity records the charity of Helena, Queen of Adiabene, and her son Monabazus, both proselytes to the Jewish faith, who labored to relieve the people during the great famine in Judæa by distributing food and money among them, and down through the roll of ages we come to our modern times! Moses Montefiore and his gentle wife Judith exemplified, in the highest degree, what charity was, taught by the Mosaic law. Fancy these two inspired beings moving calmly side by side to relieve stricken families of whatever faith, wherever found, crossing seas to pour gold and comforting words upon suffering fellow-creatures in the Holy Land. Then, when this sympathizing wife is laid in the bosom of the earth, look once more at this angelic old man, ninety-seven years old, braving the dangers of a long journey again, his seventh trip to Damascus, to let fall his charity like the soft dew from heaven.

Regard the multiplicity of charities of Judah Touro. Besides endowing orphan asylums in many cities of the United States, he left fifty thousand dollars for the poor in Jerusalem. And who can estimate the charities of the Rothschilds! they support whole towns in the Holy Land, and in European cities, schools, colleges and synagogues are drawing their maintenance from their coffers, while, but a short while ago, one of their chateaux with its beautiful grounds was converted into a home for the poor and the sick.

Baron Hirsch may be called the noblest exponent of Mosaic charity, and if the stones preached sermons, and if the stars above were tongues, they could not tell of the many hearts he soothes, the many agonies he palliates, the many lives he saves for usefulness.

Mohammed said, "Solomon was sent by God to illustrate His attribute of wisdom, Jesus, His righteousness, and Moses, His providence." Would it not appear that such men are sent always to confirm a providence which never lessens? For "Mercy, first and last, shall brightest shine." Almsgiving is a cardinal requirement of the Law. The first fruits of corn and wine and oil and flocks were to be given to the priests, because in their holy office they could not till the ground, or tend the herd, and supplementing this there is the finest of human laws:

"Six years let the inhabitants of the land enjoy the fruits as a reward for the acquisitions which they have made and for the labors which they have undergone in cultivating the land; but for one year, namely, the seventh, let the poor and needy enjoy it."

Can we overestimate the quality of these precepts? One of the Greek philosophers has said about them,

"Who would deny that these go to the very furthest extent of humanity, unless he had tasted of this sacred code of laws only with the edges of his lips, or unless he had not reveled in its sweetest and most beautiful doctrines?"

These doctrines are like strands of assorted pearls, and lie deep in Jewish hearts; they are the strength of their strength, and appeal to the reason and the tenderness of Jews. Like a cry come up these words to them, "For the poor shall never cease out of the land, therefore I command thee, saying, thou shalt open thine hand wide unto thy brother, to thy poor and to thy needy in thy land."

This age is made glorious by its development of woman; little by little she has pulled herself up from depths, in which she was but little above or better than the brute animal.

Who in the whole history of the world was the first to elevate woman? to teach delicacy to woman? to command honor of woman, and to insist upon her rights? It was this same law-giver, Moses, who has purged and cleansed the morals of the world from the inner circle to the greatest. He purified thoughts about woman, and created for her a place in life, next in dignity to man. And as dews from heaven bring forth the sweetness from the rose to exhale upon the air, so have these tender laws about woman, this care and love developed her heart, and the world is happier for having had noble women who are sainted in the minds of men because of their charity and soft comfortings.

We have spoken of Judith Montefiore as her husband's inspiration, how she helped him in his humanitarian work, but she did much charity of her own accord. She gave from her own means in a queenly and gracious manner regardless of the creed of the beneficiary; it was the needy human being she sought to befriend, not the adherent of a church or the believer in a dogma.

In Berlin and Vienna there lived benevolent daughters of Daniel Itzig, nine sisters, cultured, beautiful and gracious, each possessing many accomplishments, and trained to be merciful to the needy, and good to the poor and the sick.

Here, in America, there issues a light from the grave enshrining Rebecca Gratz, a Philadelphian. She attended the synagogue on every Sabbath, and during her whole beautiful life "never went astray in the slightest instance" from ancestral teachings, and her charities, many and far-reaching, were conceived in a liberal spirit. She included suffering humanity in her plans of mercy, and refused to draw the line at creed; her heart was a mine of compassion for those who most needed it, and she bestowed it lavishly upon them. She founded the first Hebrew Sunday School in America, and was its superintendent for thirty-two years, and helped to found the Foster Home, the Fuel Society, the Sewing Society and the Hebrew Benevolent Society. Her friend was Washington Irving, who was a great admirer of her mind and heart, and history has it that once, when visiting at the home of Walter Scott, he learned of "Ivanhoe," then in process of writing, and that Scott was casting about to introduce a Jewish heroine into the novel. Irving described Miss Gratz, and grew so enthusiastic over her that Scott drew a character from his description. When his book was completed, he asked Irving how the "Rebecca" of "Ivanhoe" corresponded with his original; it is, indeed, a fit monument unto so sweet a life as Rebecca Gratz lived.

And now while we write of noble women who lived with their palms turned outward, and illustrated Mosaic charity, let us not forget a great woman whom the

Talmud honors with the name of "daughter of God," that woman whose maternal affections beatified her life, and who clasped to her womanly heart the crying child from out of his green cradle, wherein he rocked upon the water, the Egyptian princess, Pharaoh's daughter—who adopted the babe, and cared for it, and loved it with a mother's love, and called him Moses.

Thus God chose a woman to execute His design to preserve to the world the greatest good it has ever known, through this man Moses, whose laws will last until heaven comes down to earth, and God walks abroad on the face of the deep.

For, to quote Moses' own words, "My doctrine shall drop as the rain, my speech shall distil as the dew, as the small rain upon the tender herb and as the showers upon the grass."

WOMAN'S PLACE IN CHARITABLE WORK—WHAT IT IS AND WHAT IT SHOULD BE.

CARRIE SHEVELSON BENJAMIN, DENVER, COL.

In a far-off country, where the snow rests eternal on the mountain tops, there towers a grand mountain peak covered with shining snow as with a bridal robe. Its crest is raised in high majesty against the blue sky, a vast, white, towering mass of resplendent crystal, whose dazzling beauty fills the trembling air. Royal dignity shines from the gracious forehead; delicate grace permeates every outline of rock and snow—a sweet and glorious presence. The simple people of the mountains hundreds of years ago paid their tribute to womanhood by naming this peak "Die Jungfrau." The appellation implies that beauty and grace are woman's heritage from all generations; homage and adoration, her rightful dower. She is the wind of the evening and the spice of the forests transformed into a presence, the glory of sunshine become material, the white foam of the ocean moulded into exquisite form, and the gleaming snow turned into lovely flesh. The radiance of the enduring stars is her soul, the *charity* of God is her heart. And this that scattereth abroad help like light among the children of men is—*woman*.

With such a heritage as her special dower, with such a mission as her special duty, with such a banner as her special sceptre, why need woman seek other rights and other spheres? At the recent Women's Congress held here, one of the apostles of the new creed of women—the right to be men—in speaking of woman's sphere, said, "Why, she hasn't even a hemi-sphere." We think she has not only a hemisphere, but the whole world, with which to play shuttle-cock, if she will but use the proper battledore. A rabbinical story relates that twelve baskets of gifts fell from heaven, and that Eve secured *nine* while Adam was picking up the three. And we are inclined to believe that since then she has obtained the use of all.

At any rate, in the field of charity, which is almost co-extensive with the field of human action, there is no one to dispute woman's rights, no male angel Gabriel standing with flaming sword at the gate, saying, "Thus far and no farther." Here she can be a priestess to herself and to others. Had this field of woman's usefulness and special fitness been cultivated with half the zeal that has been devoted to the so-called woman's cause in other directions, the fig-tree had sprung up instead of the thistle. Did woman understand that this is her strength, of which, unlike Samson of old, she cannot be shorn, she would not be at the mercy of every Philistine who mocks at woman's rights and woman's sphere.

Woman's fitness for the work of charity is emphasized throughout the old Hebrew writings. According to their idea the perfect woman must possess energy, strength of purpose and active zeal in ministering to the poor at her door, giving them her time, her trouble, her loving sympathy. She *may* open her mouth to wisdom, but her tongue *must* know the law of kindness. As the needle to the pole, so should a true woman's heart turn to deeds of charity. If man's proper study is man, woman's proper study is charity. This is the work that lies nearest her, and should be dearest to her. She herself was a gift of God's compassion for man, when God saw that it was not good for man to be alone. Hence she is an attribute itself of a divine charity.

Ruskin writes, "A woman has a personal work and duty relating to her own home, and a public work and duty which is the expansion of that. What the woman is to be within her gates as the centre of order, the balm of distress and the mirror of beauty; that she is to be without her gates where order is more difficult, distress more imminent and loveliness more rare."

The conclusion of the whole matter is this: Let woman's rights become woman's duties, and woman's suffrage humanity's sufferings, and let her remember that though she have the gift of prophecy, and understand all *onomies* and *ologies* and the mysteries of spheres and hemi, yea, demi-spheres, though she speak many languages with the tongues of *men* and of angels, though she be clothed in splendor, so that not even Solomon in all his glory was arrayed like one of them, if she have not charity, it profiteth her nothing.

What is this charity, this bright jewel in woman's crown of glory, which is co-eval with the ages? For, in the Mosaic institutions, there abound laws which inculcate tenderness, compassion and merciful care for human kind and the lower animals. Doubtless, the ferocity of a nomadic race was greatly restrained by these humane enactments, and the sweet amenities of life were encouraged to blossom even amid the sterility and desolation of the Arabian desert. What is this charity of which the unthinking prattle, and which earnest men and women find it an herculean task to grapple with? Everything that can *uplift* the condition of that great mass of poverty and ignorance, which forms the lowest and largest stratum of civilized societies, comes under the definition of charity. Everything which seeks to *remove* the curse of poverty from those upon whom it has come down, not only in hereditary entail, but upon whom it has held mortgages before even the deeds were put into their hands, is charity. And everyone, from the legislator who makes wise laws for the benefit of the poor, to the young girl who persuades a maidservant to lay aside some of her earnings instead of squandering them, is an agent in the cause of charity.

If it is true that charity covers a multitude of sins, it is also true that it brings to light a multitude of virtues. If use and abuse enter into this field, it is only because human nature will not change, even though benevolently disposed both to give and to receive. The uses of charity, like those of adversity, are sweet. The abuses of charity, like those of experience, are steppingstones to higher things. If charity succeeds in uniting doubters, atheists and devotees under a common creed— that of humanity—it fulfils a divine mission. If it notices one raven's fall, and uplifts it to a purer atmosphere, it asserts man's likeness to God. If charity unlocks the left hand as well as the right, it explodes a poor theory, and removes a honeyed morsel that has been chewed too long. The fear of disobeying the command that the left hand shall not know what the right hand gives has, in many cases, paralyzed the right hand altogether. It would be as well to let the left hand into the secret. There are a few persons capable of silent and unrecognized labors for the poor, but the larger number must always be stimulated by the recognition of the world. If charity gives employment to the idle rich, let alone to the idle poor, it prevents much mischief. If it asserts its claim as woman's prerogative, it gives the woman's cause an impetus devoutly to be wished. If a *true* charity teaches a *false* charity that there is no cause for a pæan of self-gratulation when reports, newspapers and pulpits announce that in one year so many cases were relieved by donations of money and food, or so many poor families were given traveling expenses from one city to another, it asserts its higher and better aims. If charity succeeds in basing its operations on a strictly *quid pro quo* principle, and thereby blots out from its vocabulary the word *relieve*, and substitutes the word *prevent*, it will then indeed " drop like the gentle rain from heaven."

Of the abuses of charity more can be said. It is abused by the individual who gives indiscriminately, and by the individual who receives with the same indiscrimination. It is impossible to stir the surface of any of our charitable institutions without discovering the wholesale imposition practiced. If a charitable door is opened, whether it lead to a benevolent individual or to a benevolent society, the throngs that enter are mainly shams and cheats. The fault often rests with a charitable system which shifts the duties of a whole community to the shoulders of a generous, but not always judicious minority. If the alms capriciously bestowed in a single month were, at the end of that time, collected and distributed with order and intelligence, the result would prevent pauperism from following in the wake of charity.

Organized or scientific charity aims to correct this evil. The time has passed for the Charles Lamb-like philosopher to sneer at scientific charity. It is as sensible to sneer at scientific physiology, or scientific anatomy, or at scientific anything else, as at scientific charity, which is merely a phrase describing an intelligent system of treating poverty, founded on the widest actual experience and the most careful thought. The amelioration of humanity under its varied phases of misfortune must become a science, the appliances of which must be carefully studied, or the obstacles to good works will be increased. The spirit of association involving unity of purpose also involves division of labor, so that individual charity in the shape of personal contact and friendly visitation is not excluded. While it offers the means of realizing the loftiest enterprise, it also gives efficacy to the humblest efforts.

Of many charitable institutions, both public and private, there is no end, and their name is legion. Millions of money are expended every year in benevolent work by countless charitable societies and countless institutions. Among these the Jewish charities assume no mean proportions. Judaism, in its broadest sense, is synonymous with humanity, and the expression, "rich as a Jew," is merely negative, implying that there are no *poor Jews* depending on any but their own charities. There is no philanthropic work where Jewish women, when permitted, do not take an active and a leading part. Yes, our cities are full of charities, some languishing for lack of funds and personal interest, others flourishing with noble endeavor and achievement. Our cities are also full of persons who give freely, and who seem ready to plunge recklessly into the formation of still more charity-societies and buildings. And yet much of this must be effort absolutely wasted, since poverty increases, ignorance runs riot, and crime keeps pace with these. It strikes us that an increase in the number of churches erected bears an inverse ratio to that of charity institutions. Besides, more churches do not always imply more church-goers. But more charity buildings seem to augment the ranks of the poverty-stricken. "The poor ye always have with you," is true, but it is equally true that much brick and mortar, many asylums and institutions are only a panacea for ills, not a cure.

Preventive and *educational* charity—this is the remedy. Some one has said that nudity and rags are only human idleness and ignorance out on exhibition. Every charity, no matter how important or how beautiful, that does not tend to prevent the evils of idleness and ignorance, defeats the very end for which it exists. Give work to the able-bodied idle, and you do much to empty refuges for the unfortunate. Establish an orphan's society that shall possess not one brick in the way of an asylum, but that shall create a thousand new homes, individual homes, for a thousand street Arabs, and you have a remedy for juvenile pauperism. It is the influence of work over idleness, of homes over institutions, that is needed. Volumes full of truth and eloquence might be written on this subject. But the pen of the writer would have to be dipped into a sunbeam to write, with sufficient eloquence, of the benefits of the education of the poor. It is a well-worn axiom that where ignorance prevails there is the greatest amount of pauperism and crime. If much cannot be done with the old and hardened pauper something can be done with his child. The prophecy of Fichte is true, "The first generation will be the only one upon whom it will be necessary to use constraint." Succeeding generations will lean toward education as the flowers toward the sun, as the dry leaves to the refreshing rain. Much has been done, but there is much more left undone. There are times when the limitations of man's power to help man's need drive one into despondency and despair. We reap our little corner, and see the wide fields stretch beyond, not only unsown, but unploughed.

Who shall take these matters in hand? Shall they be left to legislation? Yes, if legislation were ideal. Look at Europe; its very heart is being eaten out by the cancer growth of all sorts of dreadful *isms*, because of too much, or perchance too little, legislation. Look at our own country. Legislation has much to answer for, and its responses, like those of the oracle of old, are often unsatisfactory, if, coming from a silver State, I may be permitted to criticise recent legislation.

And in this connection I may be pardoned if I speak with special pride of Denver's charities at all times, but especially in these times that have tried its soul. When a legislation, without legislating, shut down Colorado's mines, and thrust thousands of men with their dependent families out into a sea of trouble, Denver's men and women came nobly to their relief. The history of its Governor's misunderstood remark of "blood to the bridle" has been written up and spread abroad in article upon article, and illustrated in cartoon upon cartoon, by newspapers that are fond of sensations, and by those whose printers' devils, were there no sensations, would cry for "copy" in vain. But what about the *unwritten* history of the deeds of charity done in Denver? When in one night like magic there sprang up, in the open field, hundreds of homes in the shape of tents for the homeless, provided with food for the hungry? What about the public works pushed for the sake of giving employment to the idle? What about heaping coals of fire on the enemy's head by sending car-loads of food from Denver to the unemployed of "gold-bug" New York? Colorado's skirts may be trailed in the dust, but with such a record, her head must rise peerless to the skies. Hence it is evident that, until a legislation becomes ideal, nothing can touch the evils of poverty so well as the work that can be done outside of State and even church by those who have the heart to feel, the hands to do, and, above all, the time to do it in. For the real growth of philanthropic work depends upon the time intelligently devoted to it.

It seems conclusive that it is to woman that we must look as the invincible agent in this work. She is divinely appointed, and innately fitted, and for the most part endowed with what is of essential value—leisure. To the unoccupied woman the plea arises loudest. When we speak of unoccupied women, we mean, not only the familiar type of the woman indifferent to all things, but also those who live in careless comfort, and who sometimes satisfy their half-awakened consciences by giving to the poor what they can readily spare from their well-filled larder and press. Often the quality of such charity of cold victuals and old clothes is much more apt to bless those who give than those who take, by relieving larder and press of burdensome effects. We also include those women who pass long mornings at society sewing-circles, full of the idea that they are discharging their duty to the poor, when the essential labor of personal contact, of judicious investigation and education is left undone. Such sewing has to be done, but let it be relegated to the pauper women who are supported in idleness, and be paid for. There is an appallingly large class of these unoccupied women, rich as well as poor, and it is vastly important to develop this wasted power into labor for the common good. Work is the appointed lot of all, and neither the lazy rich nor the lazy poor can escape this edict. Position, influence and wealth are not indispensable. The widow's mite of *time* serves here as the coin of old. "Every man hath business, such as it is," and indeed the most delicate butterfly of fashion sighs: "I am so busy," but the question should be forced upon you, pretty butterfly, "What *is* this business?" Suppose an ideal legislation should place a levy on your time in favor of the unfortunate, after the manner of the tithes of feudal times? Suppose an ideal legislation should draft you into a standing army of women of leisure to do charity service? and train you in the best tactics of social usefulness, thus teaching you that only by having the interests of the poor at heart can you become a good citizen, thereby also perpetuating the idea that you cannot live to yourself alone, but must bear others' burdens? It would tax the limits of this paper to enlarge upon the beauties of such a scheme. We can give only the merest diagnosis of the disease, and only hint at the remedy. If to do were as easy as to suggest what were good to do, chapels had been workshops, and poor men's unsafe tenements sanitary cottages. Did every spark let fall from the pyrotechnic display of eloquence offered within these walls at the myriad congresses held here, take effect, there would arise a conflagration, compared with which your fire of '71 would be as "moonlight unto sunlight, and as water unto wine."

It is an old legend of just men, *noblesse oblige*, or superior advantages bind you to larger generosities. Hence the more gifted the woman, the more goods she is endowed with, the more leisure she possesses, the greater the demands on these resources.

Bentham's principle, "the greatest good to the greatest number," is most true of charity. The benefits of the more fortunate must be bestowed on the less, or they convict themselves of unfitness to possess their advantages. Surely the graces of culture and wealth will not be thrown away if exercised among the humblest and the least cultured, for they need them and must have them, or they will remain blind forces in the world, the levers of demagogues, who preach anarchy, and misname it progress. There is no culture so high, no refinement of wealth so exquisite, that it cannot find full play in the broadest field of humanity, and there shed a light which shall illumine surrounding gloom, and without which life is like one of the old landscapes into which the artist forgot to put the sunlight. If your fruits are gathered up in storehouses and barns, they must decay and die. If your coin is put into chests and vaults, the moth and rust must corrupt and destroy it.

No matter what her walk in life may be, woman can take up arms in the cause of charity. Whether she be on the highways or in the by-ways, she can find ample scope for her energies in this work. Whether she walk in the day-nurseries, through the kindergartens, in the industrial schools, out in the trades with the wage-earners, into the tenements, into the hospitals, out in the streets, into the homes of the poor and the rich—"the ways, they are many, the end it is one." It is said that women have a mania for organizing, and that doctors encourage this as a cure for nervous prostration. This sly insinuation, with all its attendant sneers, would lose its force, did women put forth all their executive efforts in ways for which they are pre-eminently fitted, and for ends universally good. If woman must be an organizer, with all the influence which that implies, let her emphasize the fact at her meetings, clubs, and congresses, that woman's sphere may comprise, among other things, suffrage, dress reform, and charity, but that the greatest of her duties is charity. If the woman's-rights woman thinks, with Mrs. Browning, that "male chivalry has died out," let her remember that in the cause of charity "women may be knight-errants to the last. A greater Cervantes shall arise who will make his Don a Donna."

When woman shall walk (uprightly) in the many ways that charity opens for her, we shall see that a new political economy will arise that shall be to the old science what the spirit of modern religion is to the ecclesiasticism which has been its unwilling mother. Let woman, obeying her divine mission, be the modern Heracles to set free the modern Prometheus. The rocks will take up the chains that long fettered his limbs. The hungry vultures of pauperism, ignorance and crime will feed on the carcass of worn-out life, not on the throbbing heart. The fire of a divine charity, filling the earth, will flame back to the sun by day and the stars by night. "Watchful angels will not wear their faces veiled, and shadows will mimic substance no longer."

WOMAN'S PLACE IN CHARITABLE WORK—WHAT IT IS AND WHAT IT SHOULD BE.

(*Discussion of the foregoing paper.*)

GOLDIE BAMBER, BOSTON, MASS.

Woman's place in charity, to-day, is that of a self-constituted agent for the distribution of food, fuel, clothing and money. Suffering and pitiful want appeal mightily to her tender heart, and alms-giving follows. This is but a "sop to Cerberus," however, and while it relieves the sensitive susceptibilities of the giver, fosters rather than diminishes pauperism, the evil which charity aims to obliterate. In my work among the poor, I have found them, as Tolstoi says, "As other men are," difficult to assist without devoting time and care to them; their wretchedness is not to be relieved by the mere giving of a bank-note.

Since, then, material aid is obviously insufficient to do more than relieve for the day or the hour, it is in the field of æsthetic charity that we must labor to obtain permanent results. If our aim is to effect a change, to redeem the poor and uplift them from their sordid surroundings, we must devote time and thought to the character and need of the individual.

In Boston, we have commenced with the children, trusting through them to influence their elders; they are the future citizens, and in them we are not obliged to contend with confirmed habits, old-world prejudice and superstitions. Their fresh, young minds are open to every new impression, and they readily adapt themselves to changed conditions. The civilizing and educating influence of the public schools is not undervalued, but we consider it necessary to supplement this by special schools, where more attention may be paid to the individual requirements, to the assimilation and growth of American ideas.

Three years ago, through the interest and sympathy of Mrs. J. H. Hecht, an Industrial School was opened with twenty miserably unclean and melancholy little girls for pupils. The school numbers to-day one hundred and fifty tidy, self-reliant little women, and they are not half of the number of those who are clamoring for similar advantages. Our first step in character building, after we have won the confidence of the child, is to impress upon its mind the necessity of cleanliness; appreciation of the hygienic value is encouraged by the distribution of free bath tickets, but it would have been impossible to furnish a practical illustration, and enforce neatness with these unfortunate children in their soiled shreds and tatters, if the Hebrew Ladies' Sewing Society had not come to our assistance, and provided shoes, clothing, and new material. Self-respect and industry and order were then developed by teaching the child to keep its clothing in repair. For this, classes were formed, after school hours, in plain sewing, darning and mending. This intimate association with the children revealed to us the deficiency of their moral and religious training, and a Sabbath School was the outgrowth. The instruction is not dogmatic, and observance of the forms and ceremonies is not strenuously insisted on so much as an intelligent conception of and adherence to the vital principles of Judaism.

Knowing that these girls would be obliged to contribute toward the general support of the family at the earliest age that the law allows, we endeavor to render them capable of filling good positions. The time after school hours was found to be all too short for thorough and systematic training, so evening classes were inaugurated; there sewing is taught in all its branches, both hand and machine work; cutting of white clothes; dress making and fitting by chart and measure, and millinery making and trimming. We are in direct communication with the principal business firms, who send to us for help, and we hear only praise of the neatness and efficiency of our pupils.

Good manners are cultivated, and opportunities are given the children at religious festivals, concerts and entertainments to meet and mingle with those more favored children who know the charms of a refined home. Friendly relations have also been established with the parents of our pupils, and they have been urged to encourage their children to put into practice the knowledge gained at school. We soon became aware of the ignorance that prevails in these households of how to perform the commonest tasks, or prepare the simplest meal. One feature of the industrial school is the Country Week. During the first summer we attempted cooking and kitchen gardening with excellent results. The utility of such instruction was clearly demonstrated in the improved conditions of the homes. Extension of our future work will therefore be along these lines. Another much appreciated feature of the school is the lending library.

These advantages offered to the girls excited the interest and envy of their brothers, who repeatedly appealed to us for corresponding opportunities. It was finally decided to open a boys' club, and a more motley group than the fifty ragged, dirty newsboys and bootblacks who assembled on the first evening, it would be difficult to find. The consternation of the ten or twelve merchants and college men who had gathered to assist us soon gave place to profound interest in their novel occupation. The aims were the same as in the girls' school, to establish habits of honesty, industry and cleanliness, and arouse a spirit of self-reliance and self-respect. As with the girls, a practical illustration of the motto, "Cleanliness is next to godliness," was first insisted on. The depth of enthusiasm of the Harvard man, who himself washed and combed a bright-eyed little gamin, was not participated in by all; but night after night, after study and business hours, social and household demands, these earnest men and women devoted themselves to the making of worthy American citizens. Lectures, readings, debates, informal talks on social, religious and scientific topics, music, games and gymnastics filled the evenings of these boys, and withdrew them from the evil influences of the street. Among the two hundred neatly dressed, well-mannered fellows listening intelligently to a lecture on "The opportunities that America offers to the immigrant," delivered before them last June, it would have been difficult to recognize the fifty original members. Interest in our work is so widespread that we hope soon to have a well-equipped building, to be devoted solely to the education and development of Jewish youth.

This wave of interest has extended even to the parents of our pupils, and renewed fervor in the work of the Sewing Society, and increase in the ranks of the district visitor are direct results. Although more tact and discretion are required, previous attempts in the way of furnishing employment, amusement and instruction to the adults, have proved how much can be accomplished in arousing their dormant self-respect and independence. One visit to their squalid habitations will convince you, as no printed or recited story can, of the necessity of "better dwellings" societies. After such a visit you will not doubt the guarded rumors of immorality said to exist there; moral cleanliness and well-being are greatly dependent on environment, and such surroundings are degrading and debasing. There is room for more Jewish women on the roll of the society which compels the Board of Health to condemn and landlords to pull down unfit dwellings, and erect in their stead convenient, well-ventilated apartments.

No society has greater influence in this work of elevating the poor and fitting them for improved conditions than the Boston Women's Educational and Industrial Union, numbering Jewish women among its members. The Young Women's Hebrew Association, although established only two years ago, is also an important factor in the redemption of the poor; it relieves immediate want, provides physicians and nurses, and gives occasional outings to the children. A day-nursery and a diet-kitchen are among their plans for the immediate future.

Tchernystchewsky, in his book, "What's to be done?" deals with the very people, the problem of whose salvation we are trying to solve; from his statements and by our own experience, we learn that it is only through association, by actual contact, that we may hope for their regeneration. The dread of disease and contagion should not separate us from our unfortunate brothers and sisters, especially as with crowded thoroughfares, public conveyances, places of amusement, and money, the universal medium of exchange between rich and poor, teeming with germs, we cannot expect to enjoy immunity from disease, even if we keep away from the poor.

Wherever and whenever a well-directed movement is inaugurated for the betterment of downtrodden humanity, woman's wisest energies should be employed. Her place is in a field of usefulness, bounded only by her good intentions.

All Israel suffers in the degradation of its poor; woman is the Messiah come to deliver them from their second bondage of ignorance and misery. She is the educator, the reformer, and the reward of her labor will be the evolution of a nobler race of worthy citizens and respected members of society.

WOMAN'S PLACE IN CHARITABLE WORK—WHAT IT IS AND WHAT IT SHOULD BE.

(*Discussion of the foregoing paper.*)

R. W. NAVRA, NEW ORLEANS, LA.

When we turn to the consideration of a subject as far-reaching as the one now before us, it must be remembered that it is an inherent law that the actual facts of the present and the possible ones of the future are influenced by those of the past.

Therefore, we, who stand to-day with the broad light of civilization illuminating all avenues of thought, with the gleam of "right purity, right truth, right rapture" shedding rays into the misty future, must seek for the spark of this brilliant and intelligent illumination in the comparative twilight of the past. The vista thus presented is almost endless. Even in the primitive creed of the ancient Greeks, we find that the pure and beautiful woman whose form always stood as a type of the most exalted virtue, the one whose arms were entwined about the figures of Hope and Faith, *Charity*, was considered the greatest. If, then, even with such rivalry, the figure of Charity stood supreme between the other Graces, surely the crown, sceptre and mantle of that rank, which has descended through the ages on all women, must determine the supremacy of her position in the world's charitable work. As the gradual and imperceptible changes of the social scale have taken place, and the intellectual ranks given to woman have become established, she has assumed the position of almoner, as alleviator of the sufferings of others, striving to maintain her position as a true disciple of the great Queen Charity, who was so worshiped and so deified in the past.

We of to-day who see constantly the great need in our cities among all sorts and conditions of God's people, all races, all ranks, all creeds and all characters, especially since the great immigration of Russia's persecuted Jews, must feel that there is a vast field for the executive ability of woman, as well as for all her tact, diplomacy, patience and untiring effort in educating the young. It has been my personal experience, and from such data we consciously and unconsciously form our conclusions, that the mere question of money-giving or of gaining subscriptions for charitable work is, especially among the generous-hearted people of our sect, and in our Southern city, not the most difficult problem to solve. Rather the most formidable, because it entails both good and evil, is the *injudicious giving of money to the poor*. Cases occur to my mind in which some modern Crœsus, moved by a sense of pity aroused by a tale of distress, recklessly gives to the applicant enough money to entirely upset his domestic economy, and to make the privation of to-morrow the harder to bear, because of the plenty of to-day. It is for this reason, and because I always believe that in organizations and institutions the judicious expending of the funds entrusted to its officers is of paramount importance, that I often wish it were possible for me to head a crusade, which would find followers in all the world, against careless and unthinking charity.

Surely, then, the wise administration of the alms of those who give is a mission worthy of Mrs. Jellyby herself. Yet we women who have laughed at that clever caricature have sympathized sweetly with the absorbing interest of this poor enthusiast in the savages of Borrioboola Gha, while the members of her own household were even wilder and more uncivilized. This involuntarily reminds me that it might be well for us all to remember that there is a place for women in the "Charity which begins at home," and that those who have really filled the highest place in the world's work, are the women who never permit a conflict between the duty that lies within and that which is without their gate. If, then, there is one woman who has listened to me to-day who will carry home with her, among the many souvenirs of this more than marvelous exposition, one little thought, uttered from out of the fullness of my heart, may it be this: when she rejoices in the pre-eminence of woman in charitable work to-day, let her feel that she is in the position of *guide* to those who give carelessly, and let her remember always to ascertain the wants as well as the position of the applicant. Also, that absorbing as outside work may be, there is a duty that lies nearer, the one which must be fulfilled to those dear to us, whose claims are undeniable. Then, too, hidden from others, there is a sanctuary within our souls, at the shrine of which we lay our sacrifices, and it is then that we remember that there is a charity which speaketh no evil and thinketh none. This truth exemplified in noble lives has done more than anything else to keep bright the halo that surrounds the figure of Charity—for

"In Faith and Hope the world will disagree,
But all mankind's concern is Charity."

WEDNESDAY, SEPTEMBER 6, 1893, 8.30 P. M.

The interest in this evening's session was so great that it was found necessary to hold an overflow meeting in another hall, over which Mrs. H. Frank presided, and at which all the papers read in Hall 7, the usual meeting place, were repeated.

ADDRESS.

Hannah G. Solomon, Chairman.

In the first days of the week, I had decided to say a few words of welcome to the fathers and brothers who might attend this evening's session. But so generous has been their attendance during the week that words of welcome are superfluous. But one thing I will say, and that is, that if there is one lesson more beautiful than all others which Israel has taught the world, it is that of the position of woman. Love for the mother, devotion to the wife, sacrifices for the children, these stamp Israel of all times as a civilized nation. And if this week we have been spelling "Jewish Woman" with a capital "J" and a capital "W," it is not less true that we believe you all capital fellows. It is not vain-gloriously, or in a spirit of boasting that we have been rummaging the pages of history for the illustrious daughters of Judah, nor do we strive to shine by reflected light. But we have come to teach and to learn. In the pages of history, in the lives of the heroes and heroines, the destinies and possibilities of a people are written. In them, we have been trying to discover ideals for ourselves, our daughters and granddaughters.

I hope I shall not be too severely taken to task for saying that I am proud of the record made by Jewish women during the past week. I am proud of the earnestness shown, best attested by the facts that all our essayists, with one exception, were here to read their own papers, and that our delegates have come from the remotest points to be with us; proud of the unselfishness of the women; of the lack of vanity shown by the women of our city, who left every place in the programme to the women of other cities, accepting only the places left. All this, I think, argues well for the woman-soul of the future that is to lead " upward and on."

PRESENTATION OF THE HYMN BOOK.

E. FRANK.

Mrs. President, Ladies and Gentlemen:

When first the subject of a religious congress was spoken of, the idea suggested itself to a few of our ardent workers that no more fitting time or opportunity would ever present itself for the revival of our forgotten and scattered hymns than at this first Jewish Women's Congress. That it is peculiarly woman's sphere to introduce divine and sacred music into the household is self-evident; why should not we, then, deem it a duty to become familiar with the beautiful echoes of the past and the histories that surround them?

It is an admitted fact that many of our co-religionists have created the most beautiful and sublime works in the world of sound; is it possible that the music in connection with the divine service is of an inferior quality? No; and yet we have searched so little for its beauties. I believe the main reason for this lack of knowledge has been the want of some book to bring it to us in an easy and intelligent manner, and I am sure the compilers of our Memorial Book have accomplished this end. Let these songs be heard, and they will need no praise to recommend them to you.

To many, these revised melodies will bring memories of the sweet and pathetic incidents of their past lives, when, surrounded by those who have long since departed, they knew no greater pleasure than to make their Sabbaths and other holidays perfect so far as their simple mode of living allowed. A feeling of reverence and piety is with us as we gaze on these pictures of the past, and why must the sentiment of the old be thrust aside for the rush and hurly-burly of the present? We have always been called a people of sentiment, though we must refute statements that attribute to us merely sentiment without ability to act.

Music fostered and sung on all occasions can lead us to the greatest of deeds, and then, when within our heart of hearts we feel that we are doing our best, what care we whether "sentiment" is still said to be the main feature of our individuality?

In our new and easy methods of teaching in the Sabbath School, it has been found unwise and unnecessary to bother the children with the study of Hebrew, but music, the language understood by young and old the world over, must not be buried, and let us hope that our book will fulfil its mission, and every home give it a welcome.

> "Music! Oh, how faint, how weak
>   Language fades before thy spell!
> Why should *Feeling* ever speak,
>   When thou canst breathe her soul so well?
> Friendship's balmy words may feign,
>   Love's are even more false than they;
> Oh! 'tis only music's strain
>   Can sweetly soothe, and not betray."

MISSION-WORK AMONG THE UNENLIGHTENED JEWS.

Minnie D. Louis, New York.

"Open thy mouth, judge righteously, and plead the cause of the poor and needy."

If I am a part of all nature, if I contain a part of the universal soul, or as Emerson says, if "the soul needed me as an organ to contain it," then am I one with the beautiful golden-tinted clouds that float in such blissful contentment; then am I one with the torturing, crushing, darkening evil that drags down to the depths of nakedness within and without.

Everything in the universe that fulfils its purpose, ultimately reaches upward; even what is matured under the earth's surface has no value till it climbs up into the light; the soul, as part of the universe, partakes of this same upward tendency. If by some chance it should be dragged down, it matters not if it be in my body or in another, it is part of me, and I cannot be relieved from the pain of its dragging, until I lift it up, and gird it with strength that it may freely ascend into the hill of the rejoicing ones of the earth. This is the very essence of mission-work.

Our Jewish history teems with records of such understanding and fulfilment of life's purpose, both through religious propagandism and organized effort for the enlightenment and elevation of a community. The passage in our Bible, "The poor shall never cease out of thy land," is an ever-present mentor, its utterance growing into a louder and louder prophecy that fills men's hearts with fear and trembling, making mission-work tower in men's minds as a barrier of defense.

We lightly say that fashion incites it; that because some known accumulators of wealth bring their trespass-offerings to charity's altar in endowments for her institutions, and contribute toward various modes of relief, and affect a concern about the condition of the poor as officers and patrons of communal societies, a precedent is established for the socially ambitious to follow. But it is something deeper than a mere fad; it is a real concern; there is an actual apprehension that the social body is diseased, and that the virus may be communicated to any spot, and cause destruction; and beside this, there is, in some, an *un*worded, yet sure knowledge, that "if in thy wicked heart, thou sayest, The seventh year, the year of release, is at hand, and thine eye be evil against thy poor brother, and thou givest him naught; he will cry unto the Lord against thee, and it will be sin unto thee."

Like a stream that flows with more volume and swiftness as it approaches its mouth, gathering in its current a constantly accumulating mass of floating matter, so this century is plunging down into the sea of time, whirling along, in its torrent, all the busy, burning thoughts of men; and this hurrying flow draws the people to the shore to anxiously watch it, and snatch therefrom what is valuable, before it is swept into the unsearchable depths of that ever broadening sea. We have come to watch mission-work, and take from it what seems to us best.

See! the claims of the far-away savage heathen that, for so many centuries, monopolized the efforts of the zealous, are no longer paramount. "Borrioboola Gha" has been supplanted by "Whitechapel," "Mulberry

Bend," and the nearest district tenements. Instead of the outward-bound ship with its cargo of beads and trinkets and gay calicoes and missals, unfurling the Constantine banner, see the "People's Palace," the "University Settlement," "Hull House," spread their buoyant pennons at our street corners; instead of the sacrament given to wondering, half-dressed, tawny natives in a distant land, see libraries, club-rooms, lecture-halls, trade-shops, given to wondering, half-dressed, pale-skinned natives in our own towns.

But what have we Jews to do with this? Mission-work has never been with us of such a character that transformations like those must *in rerum natura* occur; what we know of the missions of Abraham, Moses, Samuel and Nehemiah, are to us such ideals of effort in behalf of our suffering brethren that they serve as models for all time. It is true, since our denationalization other peoples have so emphasized the proselytizing motive in mission-work, that we eschewed every consideration of the phrase; now that it has assumed a broader scope, compatible with the Jewish conception of humanitarian endeavor, we no longer hesitate to characterize our own philanthropic work as such, and even follow the trend of popular method.

I do not propose to discourse upon "Mission-work among the Unenlightened Jews" statistically, to give the number of organizations enlisted for it, with the amounts received and expended therefor; but rather to explore the work, dig deep into the soil to discover the accumulated obstructions thrust in by religious and social persecution—of which we Jews share some of the guilt—and venture an opinion as to how they might be removed. And to do this, I trust I may be permitted to cite New York City in illustration of its greatest need and the remedies already applied. We know that throughout southeastern Europe and Syria, the "Alliance Israélite Universelle," within the past thirty-three years, and the "Anglo-Jewish Association," within the past twenty-two years, have established most successfully their secular, religious and industrial schools, which number fifty-eight primary schools, and twenty-seven workshops or industrial schools for both boys and girls; and that the "Anglo-Jewish Association," in connection with the "Jewish Colonization Society," is pursuing a scheme of colonization, whereby indigent Jews from every part of the world may achieve their regeneration mainly through agricultural labors (a scheme much less bruited, less complicated than General Booth's, yet equally comprehensive); and we know that throughout this country, wherever the unfortunate of our people have sought refuge, the most generous assistance has been provided, yet in no place are their needs so great as in New York City.

The Jewish arrivals in that port from 1885 to July 1, 1893, aggregate 285,894, of whom, up to January 1, 1893, 205,416 were exiled Russians.* These people naturally gravitate toward the central body of their compatriots already residing there, chiefly in the Tenth Ward. This ward is the most densely populated area in the world, averaging 25,000 people to the acre. When one hears that one double tenement house contains 297 tenants, one can conceive somewhat of the crowding. In a house in Essex street, which I visited some time ago, the building, front and rear, was occupied by fifty-two families, composed of from three to ten members, besides an almost equal number of lodgers. An ordinance of the Health Board demands that "400 cubic feet of air-space shall be provided or allowed for each bed or lodger," but the rents are so grinding upon these tenants, that the larger the

---

* Statistics furnished by Hon. A. S. Solomons, General Agent of the Baron de Hirsch Fund Committee.

family, the greater the need of the $3.00 or $5.00 per month from the lodger, harbored in defiance of the law.

This overcrowding, humanely, if not wisely winked at by the authorities, who know that enforcement of this law means eviction for non-rent, is the promoter of a greater evil, the immorality of the young. Where, for instance, seven people sleep in a room, say 14 x 14, which is used for all living purposes, there can be no privacy; and where modesty is uncurtained, virtue is in danger. But the real source of this evil is the cupidity of the landlords, which encourages this huddling. Most of them, having been former tenants in that locality, and having made their money through industry and saving, know, from long observation, that the most advantageous investment is a tenement-house, which yields a large and sure and speedy income. Usually domiciling themselves in it, often serving as its housekeepers, they hover hawk-like over their tenants, lest there be tardiness in the payment of the dues; every closet is taxed for its quota of revenue; two of these with one fair-sized room constitute an apartment, and such apartments range in price from $7.50 to $16.00 per month, and are seldom repaired or improved, except under threat of the law. This condition, of course, applies to the older houses, which predominate, though the beguiling exterior of the new ones reveals a still condemnable interior. Very recently, a thrifty woman, with five children, whose husband, a cloak-maker, has been out of employment for months—he is a non-union man—in distress about her rent, came to me. She had recently moved from Ludlow street to Brooklyn, reducing her rent from $13.00 to $7.00. Her former landlord exacted his payment whether or not they had work, or whether or not they had food. She said, if she had to beg, she would not do it for the landlord, so moved where rent was cheaper, but work scarcer. Our "United Hebrew Charities" essays to meet the emergency of dispossessed tenants, but any institution would soon be bankrupt, if acceding to every appeal.

This matter of rent, which absorbs all the energies of the poor working-class, while it fattens the greedy landlords, is an important consideration in mission-work; regarding it, the landlords are the ones to whom reformatory effort should be directed. All laws are made fundamentally for the benefit of all people under their jurisdiction; and while some may object to the so-called "government paternalism" in what I am about to advance, it is, nevertheless, the first duty of a government to protect its people from all manner of oppression.

A law to assess dwelling-house property at its intrinsic value, with a fixed percentage for rent, all demanded above the fixed percentage being made confiscate to the government, would soon regulate the rent scheme to the satisfaction of every one but the owners. The venality that such a measure would induce would be guarded against by the unavoidable requirement that the assessments for taxation and the assessments for rent must tally; each would serve as a balance sheet against the other, and honesty be ensured, *nolens volens*. While the strict construction of our constitutions, both State and federal, would render such a proposition impracticable at present, inasmuch as constitutions have been amended, in .the past, in answer to the louder cry for liberty, so they may be in the future. As mission-work is to-day the greatest factor in the legalized amelioration of social abuses, it is quite within the province of the law to effect this one.

The condition of the houses within the financial range of the poor is a mighty agent in aggravating all the offences of their poverty. The homœopathic supply of air, light and water affords no recuperation to their fatigued bodies, and while we admonish the miserable tenants to keep their apartments clean, we must admit that, with all our philosophy, we would deem the same circumstances for ourselves most extenuating, in case of our derelictions. When the children clamor for food, and there is no prospect of a day's work to furnish the wherewithal, when the father's coat, the feather pillows, the Sabbath-eve brass candlesticks have all been pawned to still the hungry mouths, can we wonder that no ambition is aroused to keep the dismal apartment in proper condition? And while we condemn the filth that gains, we partly condone the negligence of the wretched housewife, to whom life is all a sunless, dingy corner. And here is where the mission-worker must be a law unto him or herself. Encouragement to brace up against misfortune, a loan of money to provide food, the effort to obtain employment for the workers in the family, the supply of a few cleaning implements, with assistance to most pleasingly distribute the sparse furniture, and above all, cheery words of sympathy, and repeated visits,—these make up part of the routine practiced by our "Sisterhoods of Personal Service," the "Volunteer Corps of Friendly Visitors to the Tenth Ward," and the institution with which I am connected, the "Louis Down Town Sabbath and Daily School." The newest organization to undertake this work adds to the above routine daily house-to-house visiting, and nursing of the sick discovered in their rounds. It is known as "Visiting Trained Nurses under the auspices of the Health Board," and all leading Jewish and Christian communal societies have subventioned it; it is supported by a Jewish lady and a Jewish gentleman of New York City,*

* Mrs. Solomon Loeb and the Hon. Jacob H. Schiff. The nurses who have, with beautiful devotion, initiated the work, are Lillian D. Wald and Mary Maud Brewster. The scheme is an outgrowth of the "Louis Down Town Sabbath and Daily School."

but anticipates becoming a municipal institution. But the most strenuous efforts to maintain cleanliness in these rookeries, where "the three D's, Dirt, Discomfort and Disease" hold high carnival, cannot be so effectual as the complete incineration of them. In a report of Sir Moses Montefiore, relative to his visit to the Holy Land in 1866 to apply the "Holy Land Relief Fund," he says: "It seems to have become the settled opinion of those to whom England would point as the men of the highest intellect, and the greatest experience and zeal in the cause of humanity, that the wisest scheme for being at the same time useful and charitable to the poor, is to be found in the erection, maintenance and improvement of dwelling-houses." As early as 1823, he "presented the synagogue with an estate of thirteen houses in Cock Court, Jewry street, on the condition that the rents arising during five years should form a repairing fund, and then the dwellings should be occupied by deserving poor."

The progress, the redemption of man, in every sense, depend upon his education, the standard, self-conceived or inculcated, that he strives to attain; no "trolley" contrivance can accelerate it in its prescribed path; by slow degrees the ideas unfold, the objectionable is abandoned, and the secure causeway laid for further advance. Education to-day is the main instrument of the mission-worker. The last annual report of the "Anglo-Jewish Association" contains the following: "Amid all the ominous sounds of ill-will against the Jews which fill the air at this latter end of the nineteenth century, there is one department of work which offers the best antidote to anti-semitism, viz., the education of Jewish children." The Jewish community of New York City is fully awake to this fact, as is testified by the existence of the following schools, all under charitable maintenance:

Evening classes of the "Young Men's Hebrew Association."

Evening classes of the "Young Women's Hebrew Association."

Evening classes of the "Friendly" and the "Pausey" Club.

"Hebrew Technical Institute," for boys.

Industrial School of the United Hebrew Charities, for girls.

Kindergartens and Industrial Schools of the Hebrew Free School Association, for boys and girls.

Kindergarten and Industrial School of the "Bikur Cholim" Society, for girls.

Kindergartens of the five Sisterhoods of Personal Service.

Kindergarten of the "Shearith Israel" Congregation.

"Louis Down Town Sabbath and Daily Technical School," for girls.

Mrs. Ehrich's kindergarten in Allen street.

Miss Opper's Russian night school, for boys.

Preparatory English Classes, and Evening and Trade Schools of the "Baron de Hirsch Fund" Committee.

The majority of these efforts is directed to the Tenth Ward.

The most recently adopted methods for those above fourteen years of age are weekly entertainments given by ladies and gentlemen of culture, and weekly instructive lectures on the history and government of the United States, which the "Hebrew Institute"—the representative building of the "Hebrew Free School Association," the "Aguilar Free Library," and the "Young Men's Hebrew Association"—provided during the past year; and loan exhibitions of fine art, which the "University Settlement" presented. These are commendable, but they will fail in their purpose, if the people who are to profit by them are to be continually relegated to their original surroundings. Their foreign language and customs are their most flagrant offenses here, and as long as they are permitted to transplant their section of Poland, Russia, or Roumania to a certain area on this soil, it is still the old country, though ostensibly America. Environment is the first educator; and until the legions of the Tenth Ward can be decimated by distribution throughout the city or elsewhere, where their characteristics can become modified by other environment, much of educational effort amongst them will be unresponsive. The "Baron de Hirsch Fund Committee," the "United Hebrew Charities," and the "Volunteer Corps of Friendly Visitors to the Tenth Ward," essay to transport them, the first two to the colonies in New Jersey and Connecticut and to other parts of the United States; the latter society only to the upper parts of the city. But the little thinning out they can do is infinitesimal. Larger organization is necessary. The status of this newly released community here is analogous to that of the returned captives from Babylonia to Judæa; and even at this remote date, the sagacious action of Nehemiah in dividing the area apportioned to them into small districts, and in placing over each a worthy, able and conscientious officer to maintain order and manage their affairs, is most suggestive. Can we not think that similar precautions might have averted the recent outbreaks among our unemployed, easily inflamed brethren, to whom liberty is so new that they do not yet know how to handle it?

To return to the educational processes. Where the tendency is largely toward entertainment specially provided, it is apt to engender a pruriency for culture that can, with circumscribed opportunities, be gratified by only an imitation of it. Mr. Ruskin says: "Sure good is first in feeding people, then in dressing people, then in lodging people, and lastly in rightly pleasing people, with arts, or sciences, or any other subject of thought." He says further, if every effort were made "to enforce the organization of vast activities in agriculture and commerce, for the production of the wholesomest food, and the proper storing and distribution of it, so that no *starving* shall any more be possible among civilized beings," . . . . if every means were tried whereby "the children within your sphere of influence shall no more be brought up with careless habits of person and dress," . . . . if every effort were made to obtain "vigorous legislation and cutting down of vested interests that stand in the way of proper lodgment," and this pursued "till we are breathless, every day, all the fine arts will healthily follow. . . . And out of such exertion in plain duty, all other good will come; you will find nearly every educational problem solved, as soon as you truly want to do something."

Several years of personal knowledge, and concentration of thought on the subject of improving the intellectual condition of our unenlightened Jews have not yet privileged me to affix to the problem, *quod erat demonstrandum.* Every girl who has caught the infection of culture from the grand dames who cater to her amusement rather disdains plain, homely labor; she aspires to nothing less than to be a stenographer or a school teacher. It requires at least four generations of culture to mold the teachers who are to give proper direction to the soul-growth of our young; and certainly the phraseology requisite for a competent stenographer is dependent on the facile use of correct language, which is acquired as much through association as study; this unfitness, although disclaimed, makes the poor Jewish girl a type of unskilled labor. Of course, there are gratifying and noble exceptions to this rule; but I think it is timely to direct the attention of the mission-worker to the inordinate and incongruous aspiration of the young through following many of the present methods. Mr. Zangwill says: "People who have been living in a Ghetto for a couple of centuries, are not able to step outside merely because the gates are thrown down, nor to efface the brands on their souls by putting off the yellow badges." The reaction from the long isolation is visible in every degree of push and ostentation, and is a phase of the injury so long endured, and must be judiciously treated by the mission-worker.

In contradistinction to the indiscretion of elevating the unenlightened Jews too suddenly into an unaccustomed atmosphere of culture—Moses kept them in the wilderness till the older generations had entirely passed away—there is the danger of unwittingly aiding them to keep in the depths of degrading pauperism. Mr. Zangwill says again, in his proem to "The Children of the Ghetto:" "The beggar felt no false shame in his begging. He knew it was the rich man's duty to give him unleavened bread on Passover, and coals in winter, and odd half-crowns at all seasons; and he regarded himself as the Jacob's ladder by which the rich man mounted to Paradise." This class is not yet extinct; it flourishes in the Tenth Ward of New York City, its pathetic woes ever intensified by increasing numbers. The fathers seldom make the appeal; the peddler's box or the push-cart withholds their dignity from such humiliation; but the wives and the children are faithful and energetic ambassadors, whose smiles and tears are ready accessories to their pleading.

In accordance with the growing method of the scientific application of relief, which precludes response to an appeal before official investigation has been made, we are teaching ourselves to deliberate, inducing a scepticism of declared wants that is usually unjust. Very recently, during the struggle for existence occasioned by the present paralysis of labor, a Jewish woman in the Tenth Ward, who for two days was without food, each day placed her cooking vessels filled with only water on her oil stove, to induce the belief that she was preparing her customary meals. And yet various newspaper reporters, even Jewish male investigators, could find no case of starvation. One of the trained nurses discovered this one. We were taught by our pious Jewish mothers, "Cast thy bread upon the waters," and they felt sure that none but the hungry would reach out for it.

It is true that the ceaseless cry for help demands systematic dispensing of charity to avoid confusion and error. But there should be no opportunity to *beg*. "If there be among you a poor man of any of thy brethren, within any of thy gates in thy land which the Lord thy God giveth thee, thou shalt not harden thy heart, nor shut thine hand from thy poor brother. But thou shalt open thy hand wide unto him, and shalt surely *lend* him sufficient for his need, in that which he wanteth." Our bureaus of relief for any kind of assistance, monetary or otherwise, should be abrogated, and superseded by Co-operative Loan Associations, based and conducted on the strictest business principles, their benefits accessible to all, the charges not to exceed, but rather to fall under the legal rate of interest. This would be the surest means to extirpate beggary, yet help a man in his direst need, in a manly way. Such a project is not at all chimerical, as the great "Monts-de-piété" in many cities of Europe testify; and if our men think it too lilliputian for their consideration, I would suggest that our women ponder it, and develop it. Whoever has been besieged by the poor mothers whose families are shuddering under the Damocles' sword of impending destitution that sickness or non-employment of their breadwinners holds over them, will properly estimate the necessity for some honorable means to avert the danger. Certain it is, our present methods are neither adequate nor just. We put humanity at a discount, and then wonder that it becomes depreciated.

But what we want most to do for the material relief of our poor is to busy ourselves with the proper adjustments of labor and capital, the regulation of schools to the equal development of brain and handicraft, and the compulsory attendance of every eligible pupil, which must all be effected through legislative action. And we want for this, legions of mission-workers who can appreciate these needs from personal knowledge of the conditions, and who will not stop till they have razed the obstructions to equal opportunity, which opens the gate to all true progress.

We expect, in the hoped for influence of our most approved philanthropy, to see our unenlightened brethren speedily divest themselves of their persecution-pampered ways, and appear in the pleasing garb of amenity to all the leading demands of our present culture; we do find our foreign unenlightened brethren all too soon becoming Americanized, but in ways we did not calculate upon. We find them entering our prisons to such an extent that necessity has arisen for the latest organization, the "Society for the Aid of Jewish Prisoners." "This fact hath raised up from their thrones all the kings of the nations; they say unto thee, Art thou also become weak as we? Art thou become like unto us?"

We do not want so much to Americanize them as to Judaize them, or rather to help them to know their Judaism. But who amongst us are the enlightened ones to go down to teach them? Are the unenlightened only amongst the poor? And are all the poor unenlightened? Mr. Jacob A. Riis tells us in his "Children of the Poor:" "It happened once that I came in on a Friday evening at the breaking of bread, just as the four candles on the table had been lit, with the Sabbath blessing upon the home and all it sheltered. Their light fell on little else than empty plates and anxious faces; but in the patriarchal host who arose, and bade the guest welcome with a dignity a king might have envied, I recognized with difficulty the humble peddler I had known only from the street." In what of real worth are we wiser or better than they? We glorify the Jew while we almost abandon Judaism. Like Solomon and Hezekiah, we boastfully show our treasures to the world, scarcely guarding the stronghold. We point to Moses as the world's purest type of intellectual and moral grandeur, and yet too many of us deride the work wherein his grandeur lay; we even presume to say that his wonderful code, except the ten commandments, was only for the time in which he lived. Who can disprove that the Sabbatical year was the most far-seeing scheme of humanity that ever occurred to mortal? Do we know whether if, in the seventh year, the needy were entitled to all the overplus in the fields and from every harvest, poverty and discontent would not be reduced to a minimum? We imitate others, and we do not know what powers are in ourselves, and how we may still show mankind the way to happiness. Why shall we not now awe them, and weaken their hands, raised against us, by the overpowering glory of our righteousness, which we must derive from our Law? By our rapid heart-throbs when we hear the Jew spoken of, in praise or censure, by the quickening current of intelligence that flashes through our brain when we hear our God spoken of, by the calm mastery that possesses us when we hear of worldly strifes, and by the glad response in our soul when we hear of the promised universal brotherhood, we feel that we have been chosen to guide God's ark of truth through the shoals of human error; though too often with such unreverential Uzzah hands that we have been smitten down beside it. Our survival is a marvel to man; do we not recognize the will of the Almighty in it? If we were not doomed to perish with the buried nations who have been contemporaneous with us, we must have something to do in the world. Why are we here to-day, strong as ever in our physical and mental strength, our individuality not eliminated? Surely we have a trust; yes, we have the grandest mission ever conceived: "I the Lord have called thee in righteousness, and will hold thine hand, and will keep thee, and give thee for a covenant of the people, for a light of the Gentiles; to open the blind eyes, to bring out the prisoners from the prison, and them that sit in darkness out of the prison-house." But before we can lead other peoples to the pure hill of the Lord, we must ourselves be pure; before we go down to purge the infected quarters, we must first cleanse ourselves. We must put away the stranger's gods—pomp and luxury—that have defiled our sanctuary. Even the "princes of the captivity," those men whose wisdom is an inextinguishable splendor, indulged in the vanities of wealth; and though "absorbed in the task of upholding the Law and Jewish life," took no heed of the Jewish peasants, who drifted into a neglected mental and moral state. Professor Graetz says: "Thus left to themselves and cut off from the higher classes and from all share in communal life, without a leader or adviser, the peasants easily fell under the influence of young Christianity." And when we see to-day Christian missions springing up among our neglected Jews, we have no right to condemn them; it is we who deserve the condemnation for unfaithfulness to our duty.

As the mountains pour down their floods irresistibly into the valleys, impregnating them with new, beautiful life and vigor, so, if we fill our souls from the fountains of Judaism, the spirit will overflow, and descend to the low-lying plains, to refresh and invigorate into new, beautiful life our wounded, weak, languishing brethren.

You Jewish women of Chicago, all Israel honors you! You have inaugurated a new mission of enlightenment! Like unto Samuel, you have gathered us together to unite us, that we may gain strength, to arouse in us a thirst for better knowledge of our people and our trust, with a more loyal allegiance to both, through which we may become invested with that holiness that will make even our enemies wish to worship with us.

Oh! that every voice here might become a prophet's voice to urge us on to the redeeming shore! And every daughter of Israel here become a Miriam to sing the song of triumph:—arrogance and ignorance, vanity and viciousness, unfaithfulness and undoing hath He thrown into the sea! May each lead the forward march, under the cloud-pillar of life's duties and the fire-pillar of God's glory, into the promised land of peace, of plenty and of blessing.

MISSION-WORK AMONG THE UNENLIGHTENED JEWS.

(*Discussion of the foregoing paper.*)

REBEKAH KOHUT, NEW YORK.

The subject so ably treated by my friend, Mrs. Louis, happily fell to her lot, for I doubt whether a Jewess in this broad land can claim that pioneer knowledge and experience which undoubtedly belong to her, whose name is a household word in connection with educational work, and who has rescued families upon families from darkness and despair. In our great city of New York, no practical question concerning the welfare of Judaism is of more vital importance than that of mission-work among the Jews. It will not be my aim to show what mission-work was among our people. Judaism is a stronghold of liberality and independence, in that each of us may worship our one and only God according to the belief that is within him, and yet belong to the grand old faith which inspired Moses to write down the laws of ethics and morality, which have maintained law and order among mankind up to the present date,—the most perfect code of laws conceived by the mind of man of all times and ages, past, present and future. The great every-day phrase, "we are not proselytizers," here changes into the paradox—*Judaize* unenlightened *Jews*. I feel quite sure that at the first view of the subject of our discussion, the question at once presents itself, "Unenlightened Jews?" Our downtown brethren, of course. Friends, a twofold discussion is most necessary. There are two missions incumbent upon each of us. *I plead for Judaism first.* We must

Judaize the brother who, though refined, conscious of his duties toward man, has neglected his great and foremost duty, the salvation of his own soul. It is our earnest and sacred duty, the duty of those of us who have been fortunate in having had parents who have instilled into us a love for our faith, to see that that faith shall not die, but shall live among the sons of men. Our first great need is within ourselves. We who believe, we who are possessed of that great stronghold, faith, who are happy in the consciousness that there is an ever-living, ever-loving one God, the God of our forefathers, must, by the contagious example of heroic self-sacrifice and toiling beneficence, inspire others, less tutored in the ancient creed, and not so susceptible to the heart-throbs of nineteenth century culture.

To strike at the root of all existing evils lurking in the pursuit of genuine missionary work among the uncivilized denizens of the sequestered Ghettos, here and elsewhere, is possible only, allow me to make the startling avowal, by the extermination of corrupt theories and wrong preconceptions in the minds of refined aristocrats, who lay claim to superior fineness, and this course only will pave the way for admitting those deluded and decried co-religionists not basking in the bright sun-gleam of refinement and elevation. "Sin croucheth before the door," is applicable to patrician as well as plebeian life. The lord of the mansion, the purse-proud owner of palatial homes, the full-fledged aristocrat of fortune, disdains to recognize the duty of caring and nurturing his outcast brethren, whom the solace of kindlier, humaner touch, the condolence of tenderer, less brutal persuasion, would mold into rare models of representative Jewish thought, Jewish feeling and endeavors.

The Russian Jew is a pariah in the midst of his confrères. Semitic anti-semitism is the bane of modern

Israel. The opulent members of society, fancying themselves enshrouded in a pleasing halo of centred admiration and universal homage, haughtily lift their heads in the gentle zephyr of prosperity, and, for fear of contracting an inconvenient cold, take scrupulous care not to be ushered into the stiffly blowing gale of neglect and total abandon, where those whose hearts' blood is the law of antiquity, the sublime doctrines of the mother-creed of mankind, and who, above all surviving races, now amalgamated with the jealous, ever-complaining world, possess most eminently the traditional treasure, imparted to posterity by the lightning and thunder of Sinaic admonition. With our Russian brethren, those derided characters on the stage of life's thrilling drama, abides the imperishable impulse of all-permeating and time-transcending faith-lore—a faculty for trust, a gift for comprehending in ethereal conception the import and sublimity of that written heritage which traveled far and wide, and crossed the darkest oceans of Israel's destiny upon the frailest bark of uncertain safety and restless quietude.

In barbaric Russia, where the autocratic Torquemada of tyranny wields the sceptre of oppression with unremitting force, where clerical authority, enveloped in superstitious awe, is the most potent civilizing power of a modern nation, rescued from the tombs of antiquity, the chosen people demonstrated their allegiance to that time-honored standard, and remained to this day the readers of the *Book*. The Bible saved their intellect from the throes of benighted guile, the Bible requited a persecuted herd of nomads with the milk and honey of eternal memories for every momentary agony, for every fleeting pain.

But the Bible is an ancient book. Its code of ethics is not necessarily congruous with modern ideas of conduct and etiquette. The Jews, amid primitive surroundings, devoid of polite arts and refining impetus, preserve intact the seeds of that old-time culture which needed but the fostering care and paternal guidance of a prophetic Moses. They lacked the redeeming Messiah of mercy, fraternity and tolerance to lead them forth out of the house of bondage into the Canaan of enlightenment, which has found its most glorious realization in the United States of America.

Why harp on the deficiencies and glaring faults of these children of the Ghetto, who have but lately crossed the Red Sea of strife, and are as yet deeply intoxicated with the martial ring of victory? Why emphasize so unfeelingly the dearth of refinement, the lack of culture? Who was there in holy Russia—God save the mark!—to release them from the thralldom of uncouth manners or even the valley of sin? None.

And who are there to lend a helping, nay, a saving hand here?

The women of America! The religiously enlightened matrons of our country, delivered from the oppressor's yoke, must dive into the depths of vice to spread culture and enlightenment among our semi-barbaric Russian immigrants, not insusceptible to the keen edge of the civilizers' art. With this prolegomena, let us go into *medias res.*

Friends! Let us now turn to that side of the question which, indeed, is the Gordian knot of our difficulties. I almost fear to touch it when I think how slight results are as compared with the tireless efforts one must expend to attain them. I do not know whether your cities are the haven of so much abject and depraved poverty as we find in New York. I have lived in Baltimore and San Francisco, and can say, from experience, that from the very nature of things, one finds more depravity and greater poverty in the larger city. This, I believe, is a self-evident fact. New York is the dumping ground of the Russian exile, and coming as he does from benighted Russia into the great Ghetto of America, the temptations that are held out to the wanderer are very great. How often have I heard a mother bewail the downfall of a heretofore dutiful son or daughter! How often found the deserted wife with children, or met the husband torn by the pangs of jealousy of the faithless spouse! It is that great serpent which grows by what it feeds upon, which one finds living under the same roof with poverty—vice. The experience of our little band, called the Ahavath Chesed Sisterhood, shows that fully twenty-five per cent of the poor who appeal to us for aid are the unfortunate victims of desertion. O, my sisters! ye who are the mothers of noble sons and fair daughters, ye who are the respected wives of true and noble men, think of the enduring torture that must come of poverty, wretched poverty and shame. When we take the history of one poor heart that has sinned and suffered, and represent to ourselves the struggles and temptations it passed through, the brief pulsations of joy, the tears of regret, the pangs of poverty, the scorn of the world, the feeble cry of the little one for the bread that is not there, health gone, hope gone, happiness gone, when we think of all this, can we sit by, idly by, unmoved? No! "Arise, for the day is calling, and you lie dreaming on." Put on your girdle of charity, light up your lamp of culture and refinement, and go forth into the hovel of your sister, who, without your help and encouragement, will be forever lost.

Some months ago I was invited to a conference with Mrs. J. B. Lowell, one of our most estimable women, and a member of the Charity Organization Society of New York City. Said she, "Have you no missionaries, no King's Daughters among your people? I visit your poor constantly, and have never yet met any of the better class Jewesses in the lower quarter of the city!" The dart went straight home. I knew too well the truth of her statement. We Jewesses are not missionaries; we do not go into the camp of the lowly and oppressed; we await our sisters at our own doors. We do not hunt out the irreligious, and by precepts and suasion teach them how to live, show them how to die! It is by personal contact alone that we can be true missionaries! It is our duty to give, not only materially, but morally as well. We must seek our sister and show her the way. Inspire her with confidence in you that she may feel that in you she has found a friend! This can be done only by entering her home and her home-life. And now that her door is open to you, and you may enter at will, gently but firmly teach her that cleanliness is next to godliness. Make her see that with a pure soul must be a clean body, and that religion not only means blind faith, but is the golden, luminous setting of that jewel called life. If we narrow the sources of internal comfort and internal enjoyment, we lose some of that treasure which God has given us as absolutely our own. Well, then, our next aim is not only to teach morality, but cleanliness as well. Filth and dirt always accompany depravity. Poverty breeds much, and has much to answer for. Dr. Johnson says, "It is the peculiar misfortune of the afflicted poor that the very circumstance which increases their wants cuts off, by disqualifying for labor, the means of their supply." Poor, at best, when seized by sickness, they become utterly destitute.

When I undertook my first rounds among our poor, as a committee of the United Hebrew Charities, the first and greatest discouragement I encountered was the utter lack of cleanliness which prevailed on all sides. When one thinks that the tenants must carry water up three flights of stairs, and there are always the proverbial large families to be provided with this article of luxury; and, furthermore, when we realize that poverty is not usually a great incentive, but rather dulls the senses, it is most natural that when want leads the way, vice follows, and dirt and disease come up in quick succession. A few women, of whom I was one, formed themselves into a broom and pail brigade, and always making reasonable allowances in exceptional cases, we insist upon a clean home before giving material aid. And more than this, we either wait until house-cleaning is over, or call again in a few hours to convince ourselves that it has been done. Instilling habits of cleanliness promotes ideas of economy and exactness in the recipient, awakens dormant ambitions, and instils a feeling of self-respect. It is, indeed, a privilege to give, but it is a greater privilege to see the beneficial results of our gifts. It has never been charged against our people that we do not take care of our poor, but it has been said, and I fear truthfully, that we do not raise them to the standard of an enlightened citizen. Let us not despise the gifts which bring joy and health and comfort into the wretched hovel of the poor, but let us give not only liberally but intelligently, doing the greatest good for the greatest number.

> "Better the blessing of the poor,
> Though I turn me empty from his door:
> That is no true alms which the hand can hold;
> He gives nothing but worthless gold
> Who gives from a sense of duty;
> But he who gives a slender mite,
> And gives to that which is out of sight,
> That thread of the all-sustaining Beauty
> Which runs through all and doth all unite,

> The hand cannot clasp the whole of his alms,
> The heart outstretches its eager palms,
> For a god goes with it and makes it store
> To the soul that was starving in darkness before."

A writer has said: "Every degree of assistance is an act of charity; and there is scarcely any man in such a state of imbecility but that he may on some occasion benefit his neighbor." Our principle in giving should be, as far as possible, to help others to help themselves. This is real and effective charity.

And now, having aided our less fortunate sister morally and materially, let us grasp her by the hand, and show her that religion means, not only the chanting of prayers; it means the practice of goodness and virtue, the living of our faith in our contact with our neighbor. We must not be clannish and narrow-minded. Down with the wall that divides us from our Christian brother! High up with the standard of Judaism in the other camp. Act in every sense of the word as *American Jews.* This is the great lesson we must teach. It is a glorious privilege to be a Jew, but it is also glorious to be an American, and we must appreciate those privileges by acting up to them in the fullest sense of the word. Refined, chaste, quiet in our manners and dress, we must adopt the vernacular of this blessed free country, and perfect ourselves in it. No foreign tongue, no jargon! We are Israelites, but we are Americans as well. The educational aspect of the question presents manifold difficulties, but one with which, I think, we can cope, if we grasp at the root—the children. Save them from other missionaries by doing mission-work yourselves. Form Hebrew free kindergartens, free classes for older children, free Sabbath Schools, free sewing and reading classes, free working girls' clubs, and reading and religious classes for boys and men, and mothers' meetings. It shall not be my aim to go into the detail workings of these classes. Suffice it to say, "Let us each be up and doing." Not all do one thing, nor one everything. The great lesson of the day is, "division of labor." Let us each be a friendly visitor, doing the little we can, inspiring others to do a little too, thereby adding to the glory of Judaism, and placing one more stone upon the structure of our forefathers. Then shall the walls of bigotry and prejudice crumble and decay, and tolerance, liberality, enlightenment, peace and good will reign over all.

HOW CAN NATIONS BE INFLUENCED TO PROTEST OR INTERFERE IN CASES OF PERSECUTION?

LAURA DAVIS JACOBSON, ST. LOUIS, MO.

The consideration of abstract principles becomes of vital interest when necessity of application emphasizes their importance. If this be so, then the theories, by means of which the present question must be answered, should receive eager investigation; for the piteous cry that assails our ears from across the ocean is neither an echo of the past nor the faint muttering of a possible future; it is the agonized wail of the living present. It is because Russia dares offer a living illustration of barbarous persecution that the possible intervention of nations has become a question of burning importance. It is because millions of innocent human beings are daily deprived of the merest rights of living; because a nineteenth century government acquiesces in, yes, encourages the torture that rends heart-strings asunder; because piercing the dawn of universal justice comes the quivering wail of a heavily-yoked people, burdened not only with the load of unjust laws, but harried and stung by an inconceivable swarm of illegal cruelties; for the reason that this persecution is present now, a breathing monstrosity menacing civilization, the world feels the imperative demand of an answer to our question. It is no abstract problem with which we have to deal, but one that has the exigencies of a present situation for its factors. The question demanding a speedy reply, the question that is the present, clamorous phase of the general proposition, the crystallized, material form in which the theoretic problem is presented to our generation, that for which we are really seeking an answer to-day is, "How can nations be influenced to protest or interfere in the Russian persecution of the Jews?"

The *right* to interfere must be plainly demonstrated, ere nations can be spurred to action. No such serious move can be contemplated, for a moment, until that is firmly established. Are we justified, will be the first question. Is the call urgent, the second. Before protest or interference can have a justification, it is necessary to study Russia's methods in her treatment of the Jews, to examine her reasons for the persecution and to decide whether those reasons are either valid or sufficient. To Russia can undoubtedly be given the questionable distinction of producing the most outrageous conditions by which one set of human beings may wantonly harass another. To rehearse the refinements of cruelty perpetrated would require volumes. Yet excuses are advanced, so palpably absurd, that the most cursory investigation discovers their futility. Those complaints that can claim the slightest vesture of truth gather substance from faults that the Russian has forced upon the Jew through centuries of prohibitive legislation and illegal hounding. "All Jews," says Russian law, "are aliens." It is an historic fact that Jews were settled along the Volga, Don and Dnieper, centuries before Rurik founded the first Russian dynasty, since which time they have been obedient subjects, supporting the crown by the payment of heavy taxes, and fighting, when need called, for the country they named home. It is true, a vast number of Jews became Russian subjects through the spoliation of Poland. But if they are classed as aliens, all Poles are entitled to the same distinction, as well as the natives of many other bits of land that Russia has succeeded in grasping. "The Jews form a hostile State within a State," says Madame Ragozin. Emma Lazarus pointed her reply by recalling the injunction of Jeremiah, "And seek the welfare of the city whither I have banished you, and pray in its behalf unto the Lord, for in its welfare shall ye fare well." All students of history know that the Jew has always loved, and served the land in which he was allowed to dwell. When Napoleon called the famous Sanhedrin, one of its first declarations was that the law of the State was binding upon the Jews of the State. It also absolved Jews on the battle-field from the ceremonial observance of their religion that they might be unhampered in their service. Even in Russia, Nicholas declared that his Jewish subjects fought like veritable Maccabees, and it is known that when Alexander I. called upon them to fight against the invader, they responded heartily. Yet libel says that they are hostile to the State.

"But the Jew is not an agriculturist," cries his persecutor. He cultivated the soil successfully in Poland, where laws were moderately lenient. In Russia he can neither own nor lease land. Small wonder that he does not care to till it. By the infamous May-laws the Jews, even within the Pale, the fifteen provinces in which they are permitted to exist, were driven into the towns. Yet the hue and cry goes up that the Jew is not an agriculturist.

"The Jew is a middleman" is another complaint brought to his door. He is not allowed rank in the army, he is limited almost to the extreme in the acquisition of a profession, successful farming is rendered next to impossible, numerous branches of artisanship are closed in his face. He must earn a livelihood; what would you have him be? And this occupation of middleman, viewed by other than Russian eyes, is not the unmixed evil some would have us believe. In a country as large as Russia, where transportation is difficult, middlemen are a necessity. Harold Frederic says that the awful famine in '91 and '92 was largely due to the lack of Jewish middlemen, who usually buy the grain as it stands, and advance money for reaping implements. Whole acres of crops, he says, rotted ungathered in the fields.

We are told that the Jew is a usurer; that he battens on his Christian neighbor. Lanin says that the same economic abuse exists in provinces in Russia in which the Jew never sets foot. Complaints against malefactors of the orthodox Greek Church are rarely heard, for the reason that their voicing would be futile, while the Jew is easily brought to punishment.

Claims are made that he evades military duty. Statistics answer that the Jews constitute 3.95 per cent of the population of European Russia; yet the average proportion of Jewish soldiers for the last twelve years has been 5.97 per cent. That he is not an enthusiastic soldier needs no comment when it is remembered that he cannot rise from the ranks.

It is said that the present administration regards the Jews as advocates of Nihilism. This amazing conclusion was reached because, among the many persons implicated in the assassination of Alexander II., were three people of Jewish birth, one of whom was a Freethinker, another an apostate, and the third a Jew. All three were Nihilists, because they were Russians opposing the government, not because they were Jews.

But, they say, the Jew exploits the peasant. Yet, strange anomaly, the account of the Peasant Land Bank shows the peasants of the fifteen provinces of the Pale to be more prosperous than in districts minus Jews. If any exploiting is done it appears to be accomplished conversely.

The offences gravely laid to their charge by an intelligent Russian statesman in one of the Russian papers— the evils of quick wit, longevity, fecundity, industry, perseverance, and sobriety—these indeed must be admitted. Except these final, sensible (?) objections, all the charges, the miasmal exhalations of Russian hate, are dispelled by the first inquiring ray of reason. Yet these are offered as adequate vindication of the cruelty that taxes the Jews doubly, that denies them land, that brands them as pariahs, and herds them in a lazar house, no other Russian save those of the criminal class being thus restricted in residence. These excuses are offered as reasons why, with a minimum of exceptions, they should be prohibited an education.

These are the bulwarks by which Russia would defend the May laws and innumerable, flagrantly unjust ordinances. And as to the illegal cruelties consistently winked at by the government, nothing, not even the truth of all the charges, could excuse them. The horrors of Mr. Kennan's pictures of Siberia would be fully equaled by the volumes that would relate the sufferings induced by this persecution. The flimsy foundation of justification falls crushed to atoms beneath the weight of facts.

Yet, before international interference can receive the sanction of justice, the question, "Can hope for the rectification of this outrage be looked for from within Russia itself?" must be asked. Russia is a despotic monarchy, her masses are kept in dense ignorance, and their prejudices and superstitions are fostered, the press is manacled, and public expression of adverse opinion is reported and punished with the vigilance that characterized Venice of the Middle Ages. The peasantry of Russia, who compose eighty-five per cent of the population, are uneducated and superstitious. Their extreme aversion to labor and fondness for *vodka* have reduced them to the direst poverty. The Jew, active, alert, abstemious and untiring, thrives in the light of the slightest opportunity. Therefore the peasant needs but a hint from authority to cry out, "Give him no opportunity, as it is he that takes the bread from our mouths. Let us kill him." With such a leader in the highest court circles, under the guidance of Pobiednostsev, who is the real Czar, a bigoted fanatic, and a Torquemada of the nineteenth century, it is not surprising that the peasant, who is a blind follower, should hate the Jew as an unbeliever and the cause of all his troubles.

No change will take place there unless the official attitude is altered, education made general, and liberality supersedes bigotry. The rigid supervision over the press makes these things unlikely. A number of broad-minded editors have disappeared in the wastes of Siberia for public disagreement with government methods. What may we expect from the council of Russian rabbis to be called this autumn in St. Petersburg, when liberal Russian believers are forbidden freedom of expression? What can we hope when rumors are rife that new atrocities are to be perpetrated? The Russians are notorious as liars. Before the May laws were put into operation, floating suggestions of them reached the world, and aroused indignation. The Russian government denied even the thought of issuing such decrees. Shortly after they came like a thunderclap. Is it not likely that this council is to serve as a blind on this occasion? Even petitions of the mildest nature have been followed by disaster. It is known that in May, '91, in Moscow, an old Jewish soldier presented a petition, most humbly worded, to the Czar, begging that those soldiers who had served full time, and whose homes were in Moscow, might be allowed to remain in that city. The petition remained unanswered; the petitioner mysteriously disappeared. Numerous like occurrences admonish the sanguine. The government pursues its course with the dogged persistency that always accompanies fanaticism. Indeed, no chink is left through which the wedge of the liberal few may force a breach. Hope from within is barren.

Unofficial protest has been expressed by almost every civilized nation, either through the medium of the press or of individuals. Russia is deaf. The celebrated protest drawn up at a meeting presided over by the Lord Mayor of London, and sent to the Czar, received no answer. Others enjoyed a similar fate. Governments have at various times instructed their representatives to interpose in behalf of the Jews as far as they could do so in consistence with international relations. Their kindly intervention accomplished nothing. Representations and appeals have been sent to the Czar again and again. They were returned unread or regarded with scorn. The only official utterance that has broken the ominous silence came last February in an article by M. Botkine, Secretary of the Russian Legation at Washington. The weakness and bias of this defence are equal. Since that time no word has appeared. The sentiment of the civilized world, unsupported by official governmental protest, has produced little effect except perhaps to increase the brutality of the persecution.

Since, then, the world must pronounce these Russian persecutions inhuman, since improvement is not to be looked for from within Russia herself, and since enlightened petitions and remonstrances have proved ineffectual, nations may surely consider themselves amply justified in *official* interference. The broad basis of humanity is sufficient support of their right. Vattel, an eminent authority upon the "Law of Nations," says, "If persecution be carried to an intolerable excess, it becomes a case of manifest tyranny, in opposition to which all nations are allowed to assist an unhappy people." But another reason than the ethical furnishes adequate ground for international interference, and urges its expediency. Russia expels great masses of people in such a condition that nations, in protection of their own interests, hesitate to receive them. Although cleaner by far than other Russians of their class, these poor Jews are distantly removed from the ideal. The majority, as we have seen, are ignorant through compulsion. Russian injustice has pauperized them. Even those who, despite all obstacles, have enjoyed comparative comfort in Russia, have been rendered penniless through official robbery and the cruelty that commanded them to quit their homes upon such notice that household effects had to be sacrificed for a trifle. Poverty-stricken and helpless, unacquainted with the language and the mode of thought of Western Europe and America, foreign to our habits, thoroughly Russian, except that they are admittedly superior to other Russians of their class, they come in immense numbers, willing to work for a trifle, and dependent very largely on charity. The industrial army, even in these spacious United States, gives them a most grudging welcome. The European labor market is so crowded, and remuneration so low, that any addition of cheap labor would result most disastrously. Russia is indifferent. Her policy is to make the life of the Jew unbearable in Russia; her law draws its fatal net around hundreds of thousands of these, her subjects, who are compelled to flee *en masse* from its entangling meshes. Now it is a well-recognized principle of international law that nations may rightfully oppose the action of any nation that may be a source of disadvantage to themselves. The two causes, humanity and self-protection, are certainly present to give nations the right in this and like cases, to protest and interfere.

Demonstration having plainly shown the justification of such a course on the part of the united powers, it remains to be seen whether these causes are cogent enough to influence them to act upon their right in the case under consideration. Nations must move with caution, their first duty being the welfare of their own subjects. Fear of provoking hostility and its possible evils acts as a powerful restraint upon impulse. Official protests, to have due force, must be backed by cannon, or supported by commercial action. Such measures are extreme, and a natural hesitation precedes their employment; yet nations have, upon several occasions, been impelled by the mighty power of public opinion and sympathy to array themselves on the side of justice, and to fight for those principles upon whose observance civilization, progress and safety rest. Servia and Bulgaria were dealt with by treaty. Among the other conditions stipulated was one demanding more humane treatment of the Jews and the abrogation of many of the restrictions under whose disadvantages they were laboring. The two principalities depended for their recognition by the powers of Europe upon their assent to these just demands. It is true, the countries in question were the more easily persuaded to justice, because they were weak in military power. But another precedent of international interference in the cause of liberty, though not in behalf of the Jews, interference with a country strong in her army, will be recalled in the struggle of the Greeks against Turkey. In England and France, public sentiment ran sufficiently high to induce those governments to send men-of-war to practically illustrate the sympathy they felt. Russia, perhaps from a complexity of motives, also gave her aid. Cannon backed protest, and supported interference. International law, as interpreted by the well-known authority, Mr. Wheaton, approved the interference, upon the ground that "The general interests of humanity are infringed by the excesses of a barbaric and despotic government." Are we less wise and humane than our fathers in the childhood of the century? Is it impossible for us to be stirred to action by a noble indignation? After every persuasive measure has been uselessly urged, if Russia continues to close her ears to reason and justice, will not nations be influenced by the ties of a common humanity to answer the cries of the six millions of people whom the Czar so recklessly crushes? Civilization should blush to give any reply save one. When to that appeal for aid, motives of self-protection are added, the necessity of intervention gains force. European labor, as has been shown, has just cause for alarm. Europe bids the exiles a hasty adieu, and eagerly hastens their journey to the United States. Suppose, under the strict enforcement of our pauper immigration law, three-fourths of these people were refused entrance at our ports? The steamers would hesitate to take the risk of carrying them from fear of being obliged to give a return passage. Europe would then be forced to maintain them, expel them, or refuse them entrance. The first she cannot do; the second would be expensive, troublesome and cruel; the last course would cause these poor wretches to die in hordes at her very door. She would be left only this choice, murdering the interests of her own people, annihilating the very existence of millions of refugees or taking measures to see that Russia rendered life bearable to her subjects. Is the decision doubtful?

The course of the United States is equally plain. Our country is large, our labor unions are strong, yet constant murmurs are heard against these helpless intruders. Such numbers of indigent people willing to work for any wage to keep body and soul together are a menace to the working classes, at least, until such time when they shall have learned to insist upon the highest market value for their labor. Meanwhile, provision must be made for them by charity, and the best interests of our own wage-workers are being sacrificed. Since between five and six millions of Jews are still in Russia, as each year witnesses new persecutions, and consequently brings its hundred thousand of beneficiaries to our shores, this condition of affairs is apt to continue for years. The menace will become a chronic evil, the appeal, a constant drain. If the comparatively few have cost such expenditures in charity, and are the source of increasing dissatisfaction to the working classes, what may we expect, when the other millions are thrust upon us, equally ignorant, helpless and poverty-stricken? There is no reason why we should suffer the disastrous results of another nation's wrongdoing, when that nation can be compelled to rectify her error.

The wage-workers whose interests are infringed are beginning to see this, and their complaints are becoming louder. They are the power in every free country where public opinion frames and interprets the laws. Their growing dissatisfaction will influence nations to interfere, as a self-protective measure, with Russia's wholesale exile of the Jews, and to insist that she shall maintain a more reasonable attitude toward those members of her empire, so that they may at least fit themselves for emigration. Self-protection and humanity, therefore, urge nations with the ringing call of trumpets to unite in official interference.

But, says M. Anatole Leroy-Beaulieu, "Russia is strong; Europe's protest to have force must be united; united Europe under existing political conditions is impossible." He claims that France looks to Russia as an ally in case of an attack from Germany, and that, much as she deplores Russia's conduct, she will do nothing officially that might alienate her. Germany will not dissipate her forces, when she knows that France is only waiting for a sign of weakness to precipitate a war.

Presuming that this is true, are France and Germany necessary to a successful interference? France would most likely remain neutral, if extreme measures were reached. Germany has no love for Russia, and even if other reasons did not press, would refuse to aid the friend of France. The other European powers, in conjunction with the United States, could easily intimidate Russia, if she were unaided by these great military nations. And should the improbable occur, if either one of these countries could be persuaded to aid Russia, the other would, from motives of long-fostered hatred, ally itself with the opposing forces. M. Beaulieu's apparent obstacles have not sufficient substance to cast a shadow. Fear of failure, therefore, need not prove a deterrent. The certainty of ultimate success, which always acts as an impetus, can, in this case, be assured. But such harsh measures are likely to prove entirely unnecessary. Russia, convinced that the civilized world is intensely in earnest in its protest, will become more amenable to reason. Firmly convinced that a more tangible support than .mere words will be given, if necessary, to just demands, she will yield to the inevitable, and it will be possible to negotiate by means of a treaty. An international congress to consider the amelioration of the condition of the persecuted in Russia could be convened, to which Russia would be invited to send her representative. Arrangements could then be made whereby this evil that touches both the persecuted and the world at large could be mitigated. To the conditions agreed upon by this convention, the Czar should be firmly held. Is it the dream of an idealist to expect nations to endeavor to right a great wrong? If so, then the civil war in which thousands of men fought for the liberation of the negro from slavery was a myth. True, that was a national, not an international correction of an evil. Be it to our everlasting glory that we did not wait for outside pressure, but from the highest of motives undid our own error. It proved at least that the pulsations of a divine sympathy can rouse the soul to fight in behalf of the unjustly oppressed. If international interference be a dream, then the aid that Greece received was a chimera. If nations cannot be stirred to righteous action, civilization is a farce, and the Russian Acksakoff was right, when he said that our boasted progress is but deterioration.

But history assures us that nations can be stirred, and that these things were positive realities. It tells us that great thinkers have swayed the public mind through the press. We know that Horace Greeley and Thurlow Weed aroused the heart of a nation; that Lowell, Whittier and Mrs. Stowe moved thousands to tears and action. We know that in England the eloquence of a Macaulay, a Fox, a Pitt, and a Brougham, drew 97,000,000 dollars from the British treasury to blot out the shame of slavery. Records relate that English and French statesmen championed the cause of Greek liberty in their houses of government, that fervent addresses, in behalf of justice, rang from the lecture platform to be echoed by the masses with ever-increasing volume, that a nation and that nations have been influenced in these ways to champion the cause of the distressed. What has been done, can be done again. Mighty, noble work has been given to our generation. Let those whose interest is moved, the philanthropist, the humanitarian, the statesman, the wage-worker, and the simple lover of justice, form societies throughout the world. Their individual work should be based on carefully prepared plans agreed upon by chosen representatives, who will meet, or communicate, at stated intervals to report progress and consider further measures. Let them procure statistics and reports for publication. Let them persistently and untiringly appeal to the self-interests and the human sympathy of the people by all the arts known to man. Let them gather their resources of finance, of eloquence, and of power that they may employ every channel of communication to gain public attention and enlighten public thought. A part of their work will be to see that their members are sent to Congress, to Parliament, to the Chamber of Deputies, the Reichstag, and to all the bodies that decide the course of nations. They can arouse the voice of labor to vote for those men who will sway the deliberations of legislators to a proper consideration of its interests. Through the efforts of these societies, composed as they will be of the brightest and most liberal minds of the world, let popular literature, the monthly magazine, the rostrum, and above all the daily press be used in the service of the humanitarian and the patriot, and the policy of nations will surely be influenced to a righteous interference with wanton cruelty, a humane defense of the persecuted and a just protection of their own citizens. Then shall justice arise glorified in the dawn of the new century, and vindicate, even for the lowliest among the children of men, the equal rights of men.

HOW CAN NATIONS BE INFLUENCED TO PROTEST OR INTERFERE IN CASES OF PERSECUTION?

(*Discussion of the foregoing paper.*)

LILLIE HIRSHFIELD, NEW YORK.

In our righteous indignation at the ruthless oppression of the Jews in Russia, in our heightened sympathy for the persecuted, and in our burning desire to lighten their burdens, we must not allow ourselves to be swept beyond the confines of common sense. Because this question is one of such vital importance, we must not permit our feelings to usurp our reason. Emotions may excite to action, but action itself must be ruled by sound, practical judgment, if it is to have adequate and lasting results. This question of international protest or interference in behalf of the oppressed subjects of another nation is one of the utmost delicacy.

At the very outset, it clashes with that most precious possession of nations, their sovereignty, their right to be governed as they see fit, which right all other nations are bound to scrupulously respect. On this topic of sovereignty, Vattel says, "Every nation is mistress of her own actions. The sovereign is he to whom the nation has trusted the empire and the care of the government; it has invested him with its rights; it alone is directly interested in the manner in which the conductor it has chosen makes use of his power.

"It does not, then, belong to any foreign power to take cognizance of the administration of this sovereign, to set itself up as a judge of his conduct, and to oblige him to alter it. If he loads his subjects with taxes, and if he treats them with severity, it is a national affair; and no other is called upon to redress it, or to oblige him to follow more wise and equitable maxims."

Hence, the underlying principle of international law, according to all authorities, is non-intervention in a nation's domestic concerns.

No nation has lived up to the letter as well as the spirit of the principle of non-interference so consistently as the United States. Absolute, unswerving neutrality has been the foundation stone upon which it has reared its relations with the other powers of the world. In opposition to the most enthusiastic sympathy of the people, Washington proclaimed, and maintained the strictest neutrality when France, our only ally, demanded our aid against England.

The United States is peculiarly sensitive on this question of international intervention, as witness the Monroe Doctrine. Moreover, did not this government resent, with indignation, Great Britain's interference in favor of the southern Confederacy during our civil war, and did it not make that power pay for its meddling?

On the question of religious persecution, Vattel declares, "When a religion is persecuted in one country, the foreign nations who profess it, may intercede for their brethren: but this is all they can lawfully do, unless the persecution be carried to an intolerable excess; then, indeed, it becomes a case of manifest tyranny, in which all nations are permitted to succor an unhappy people." But in the next breath he qualifies this seeming exception to the principle of non-interference by saying: "If the prince, by attacking the fundamental laws, gives his subjects a legal right to resist him; if tyranny, becoming insupportable, obliges the nation to rise in their defence; every foreign power has a right to succor an oppressed people who implore their assistance." Even in the exceptional circumstances under which interference is allowable, there must first be a rising of the people against the tyrant, and an appeal for aid on the part of the oppressed themselves. However much men, in general, may be affected by sympathy, the deliberations of governments, in matters relating to foreign powers, are swayed by common sense, expediency and diplomatic usage. Hence, all talk about "protest backed by cannon" is manifestly absurd, preposterous. But allowing for the sake of argument that armed interference were possible, who would fight? It is obvious the United States could not, and would not break through its settled principle of neutrality. Now we turn to Europe, and ask what powers there are affected by this expulsion of the Russian Jews. There are really only three vitally interested in this question: Austria and Germany, the highroads along which this outcast people trail their hard and weary way to the seaports, and England, who keeps as many as she passes on. France has no practical concern in this movement. Now is it conceivable that any of these interested powers would further tax its already overburdened people to maintain an army in the field against Russia, would be willing to increase its national debt and to slaughter thousands on thousands of men, thus making countless widows and orphans, and all for a few millions of Russian Jews? In the opinion of the great powers of the world, would the amelioration of the condition of the oppressed Jews justify the expenditure of millions on millions of money and thousands on hundreds of thousands of lives, and would it compensate for the sorrow and desolation that follow in the wake of war? The calm, dispassionate answer is, No.

But cries the idealist, "No cost is too great which procures the emancipation of a people." True, but we must not forget that this people are Jews. And we have not come to the day, no, nor yet to the dawning of that day, when the world will fight for Jews. It is time we openly recognized that fact. It is time we no longer deluded ourselves with the pretty sentimentalities of the brotherhood of man. Chilly toleration and lukewarm patronage are not equality. Humanity is far from being the watchword of the world, else I would not stand here to-night pleading a forlorn cause.

The Greek Revolution has been instanced as a precedent for international interference in a power's domestic concerns, but as an example it does not hold good. In the first place, the Greeks were not wholly under the domination of the Ottoman government, for, according to Finlay, the celebrated historian of Greece, they were in the habit of placing themselves under the protection of some foreign power. Moreover, the Greek Revolution fulfilled the conditions which make international intervention allowable:—the Greeks had risen against insupportable tyranny, and, fighting for their faith and national independence, had called upon the British and the French government for aid. Then again it must not be forgotten that this was a struggle between a Christian people and a Moslem power, and Christendom could not allow its kindred to be crushed. And then what a halo of romance surrounded "Greece, the isles of Greece!" What a debt mankind owes this land, the birthplace of art and letters, of Homer and Plato, and all that radiant, intellectual host! What have the Jews done for art and letters? Compared with Homer and Plato, who are the prophets and Jesus?

Since war is manifestly impossible, what other resources are there to enable foreign powers to influence

Russia in this matter? An international congress has been suggested. But the question at once arises, Who is empowered to convene such a congress? An international tribunal is an impossibility without the concurrence of *all* first-class powers. No nation, or league of nations, dare call another power to account for its domestic affairs. And haughty, autocratic Russia would be the last to submit to such dictation, and no power on earth could compel her. The Berlin treaty is held up as an example of what an international congress can do for the amelioration of the condition of the Jews. It is a misstatement of fact, however, to say that the Balkan Principalities "depended for their recognition by the powers of Europe upon their assent" to the improvement of the condition of the Jews. That was one of the minor conditions of the treaty, and covered the case of the Roman Catholics as well as of the Jews. Even in 1879 the United States government, through its Secretary of State, Mr. Evarts, declared that "the mitigation of the persecution of the Jews in Roumania could not be made a *sine qua non* to the establishment of official relations with that country."

Since an international tribunal is as impracticable as war is absurd, what is to be done? We must arouse public opinion, that "watchdog whose bark sounds an evil omen in the ear of monarchs." The Czar, it is said, feels keenly the imputation that he is a sort of imperial slave-driver, standing, with uplifted lash, to scourge the non-believing Jews into the Orthodox Church, or drive them forth from the homes of their ancestors. It is to this exquisite sensitiveness on the Czar's part that is due the explanation given to the world that the oppression of the Jews is not a religious persecution, but the solution of an economic problem. This explanation was made to Mr. Charles Emory Smith, United States Minister to Russia, in reply to the friendly protests made by Secretary Blaine in 1891. Mr. Blaine put the question on the plane of humanity and economics. In answer to the plea of humanity, the Russian Government, through its foreign minister, M. de Giers, acknowledged that its treatment of the Jews was not in conformity with the enlightened spirit of the age, but that the political conditions in Russia were so different from what they were in the United States that the Americans could not appreciate them. As for the increased immigration of Russian Jews affecting our labor problem, M. de Giers suggested that if the immigrants became good citizens, aiding in the development of the country, the United States government certainly had no cause to complain; and if, as claimed, the refugees were an undesirable element, Russia blandly insinuated that America was not compelled to receive them. An open avowal of mediæval methods and a diplomatic cynicism as to the effect of such Middle Age legislation on our industrial problem were all that the earnest, liberal-minded protests of this government could extract from Russia.

The question is a hopeless one. The Russian government, with arrogant selfishness, refuses to do its share toward solving this problem. It may come to pass eventually that the responsibility of each government for its own people will become a principle of international law, that the expulsion of its undesirable elements by any power will be considered a violation of the law of nations. For the present, however, outside help for the Russian Jews is impossible. But one tiny, feeble ray of light is glimmering within darkest Russia herself, which some day may burst into a devouring blaze to illuminate this desperate state of things. To those who have studied Russian politics, it is well known that both within and without the empire there is a strong and growing revolutionary party, not nihilists or regicides, but men and women who are working for a free, constitutional government. Let this revolutionary party pledge itself to give equal rights to the Jews in case of its success, and there is not a Jew in the world who would not give moral and financial aid to further that cause. This is not the wild chimera it seems at first sight. The spirit of the age has doomed despotisms, and no matter how long the respite may be, the doom will fall. The French Revolution gave to the Jews their first political freedom; the results of the American Revolution have strengthened and augmented that liberty; who can tell but that a Russian revolution may solve the Russo-Jewish problem? But from the radiant dream of the future, we turn to the hopeless, living present, and cry with Isaiah:

"It is a people robbed and spoiled. They are become for a prey, and none delivereth; for a spoil, and none saith, Restore."

The same subject was discussed by others, Mr. Wm. Onahan speaking briefly, and Professor Chas. Zeublin making an earnest plea for the Russian Jews. The Rev. Mr. Jenkins Lloyd Jones brought out the points held in common by the Unitarians and the Jews, and the Rev. Ida G. Hultin bore greetings from the women of the Unitarian Church.

The following letter from George Kennan was then read:

BRETON COTTAGE, BADDECK,
CAPE BRETON ISLAND, NOVA SCOTIA,
August 5, 1893.

MRS. HENRY SOLOMON.

Dear Madam:—Your letter of July 20 is at hand. It would give me great pleasure both to hear, and to take part in, the discussion with regard to the prevention of persecution, if it were possible for me to do so, but I regret to say that my engagements are such that I cannot be in Chicago when the Jewish Women's Religious Congress meets. I fully sympathize with the object that you have in view, and I shall try to do what I can for the abatement of persecution, both religious and political, in all countries, and particularly in Russia.

     Sincerely yours,
       GEORGE KENNAN.

THURSDAY, SEPTEMBER 7, 1893, 9.30 A. M.

ORGANIZATION.

SADIE AMERICAN, CHICAGO.

The foregoing days of this Congress have shown what some Jewish women have been, have done, have thought, and what a few are thinking and planning. This Congress would not be complete without some record of what many Jewish women have done, and are doing. Therefore, an attempt has been made to bring into a short, presentable form, the present work of Jewish women. The present work we say, for though the record be of work past and passing, work which has been good, work which leaves an impress on the world that can never be effaced, is ever present work. It will readily be understood that no attempt could be made to record the names of individual women. There are too many who, in a more limited sphere, have labored as worthily as have such women as Rebecca Gratz, Emma Lazarus, Penina Moise and others, but whose fame has not gone beyond the circle of those among whom they worked, and spread the perfume of their lives. Therefore, this report can contain but an account of work Jewish women have done together in associations or societies, large or small. In order to gain a complete report, requests were sent broadcast over the land for accounts of associations of Jewish women, of whatever kind or nature. We regret that the requests did not meet with more frequent and full response.

The largest cities only replied; their reports must, and may, be taken as typical of what has been done elsewhere. The object of the request sent was to ascertain the nature, field, purpose and success of associated work among Jewish women; not merely to present such a record, but to make it serve as a lesson to teach by the past how to guide the future, to teach what has been accomplished, and what calls for attention, to teach us what paths to avoid and which to follow, to teach us wherein we are able and wherein we lack.

To classify the work was not difficult. In the one great field of Philanthropy was it all embraced—its purpose the bettering of the condition of those unfortunate in the world, its success uniform.

From London comes a most interesting report, which, headed "Philanthropic Work," has been divided into four subdivisions: Religious, Educational, Recreative and Charitable. The first embraces Sabbath afternoon services for working girls, at which are conducted, by volunteers, singing, Bible reading, and a short address; Sabbath classes at the free schools, at which religious instruction is given and prayers are taught in Hebrew and in English, also by volunteers.

Under the head of Educational come the Jewish free schools, infants', primary, high and normal, under the supervision and partial instruction of volunteers; and in connection with these, some cooking and sewing classes. In connection with these schools, are provided penny dinners for the children. Fortunately, in our country, the public school system is such as to offer the chance of acquiring an ordinary education to all, irrespective of race or creed, and to bring together, under one roof, children of all classes and religions. We are thus enabled to throw whatever of force we have into the furthering of the broader training of hand with mind—of schools which, though supported and supervised by Jewish women, are open to all alike.

But for this very reason, our women should give more time and attention to the existing public schools, studying their nature, their defects and their needs, and endeavoring to use all their influence for the bettering of these schools.

The third division, Recreative, presents a record of glorious work—work in which our sisters across the water are in quantity, though not in quality, ahead of us. There are girls' clubs, in which mutual entertainment is encouraged; in which, while some sew, others read, speak, or furnish music, and once a week a concert and dance are given by the ladies interested in the clubs. There are others, at which the ladies from the West End of London entertain the girls at Sunday tea parties, and, with music, stories and pleasant chat, bring a refinement into the lives of the girls, which would reach and influence them in no other way. There are fortnightly free concerts for working men and women, well attended and enjoyed.

There are what are called the Children's Happy Evenings, at which three hundred and fifty children are entertained at fortnightly gatherings, with lively music, by magic lantern exhibitions and conjurers' wonderful tricks, and by dancing, a favorite amusement with all. They are encouraged to sing in chorus and to entertain one another in various ways; and a prize is given for the best performance, the children themselves judging its merit. At some of the Board Schools, also, such "Happy Evenings" are of frequent occurrence.

There are summer country excursions for children, and a Convalescent Home for adults, one for children and a Home for incurables. At all of these, at regular intervals, entertainments, mostly musical, are given, and they are found to be of great assistance in making cheerful and happy their unfortunate inmates. Best of all, several of the ladies who have country homes, entertain poor children there during the summer.

In connection with the synagogues are Women's Guilds, the purpose of some of which is to provide the sacred vestments for the synagogue, and its decoration on festival occasions, and to go among the poor, endeavoring to brighten their lives by social entertainments. Two deserve special mention:

(1) The Hampstead Personal Service Guild. I quote a paragraph concerning it:

"Its duties consist in taking charge of, and befriending one or two or three families residing in any part of London; visiting the sick and suffering at their homes and in hospitals; teaching children who through infirmity are unable to go to school; reading aloud to the sick, the blind, and at various institutions," etc.

The other, worthy of special mention, is the Hammersmith Synagogue Guild, W. E., the only one in which occurs the word mutual—its purpose mutual improvement and recreation and philanthropic work.

The need of more associations for *mutual* improvement among us is very great.

The section of Charitable work consists of various societies for furnishing financial aid and clothing, assisting the sick, for district nursing, visiting hospitals and other institutions; of workrooms where mothers of families are taught to sew, and garments are given out to be made *for the poor*, *by the poor*, at moderate cost. A sale is held in these workrooms once a year, where all garments are sold at cost price. There are workrooms in which girls are taught high-class needlework, embroidering and dressmaking.

There is a society for granting to the poor loans of from one to ten pounds, without interest and payable in weekly installments. A committee visits every applicant for help, and in accordance with its report a loan is made. Last year 330 loans amounting to £1872 ($9360) were made. The society was founded in 1844, and since that time nearly 12,000 loans have been made. Many of its present subscribers were once its beneficiaries. In conjunction with this society is a Relief Society, which gives needed things to those borrowers who are incapacitated from work by illness. There is a labor registry for men and women. There are soup kitchens, a diet kitchen, whence patients (20-30) are supplied with hot dinners at their homes, in accordance with the instructions of the medical attendant; penny dinners for Jewish school children, at which soup, Irish stew and bread are served by five volunteer lady waitresses daily.

There is an association for preventive and rescue work, called Rosaline House, where friendless girls, native or foreign, may find a home till claimed by friends or finding employment. One hundred and seventy girls were taken care of there last year. It also provides board and lodging for working girls at seven shillings per week. Lastly, a Rescue House, accommodating twenty inmates, but fortunately rarely full. Girls are here trained in domestic service and laundry work. Their stay is unlimited. After a year, or at most eighteen months, of the strict but kind discipline of the place, they are found trustworthy, and fit for service. The matron continues her supervision after they are placed in situations; and ladies take a personal interest in these girls. This society acts in conjunction with the Travelers' Aid Society.

In this report there is no mention of kindergartens or crèches, nor of manual training schools; and we have as yet had no reply to the letter, asking information on this point. This report from London is typical of other cities in England.

From the other countries of Europe, we regret to say, we have been unable to secure replies to our requests for reports; but from a hasty glance at some of those gathered in the various bureaus of the Fair, we are justified in saying that the work in these countries is similar to that in London.

Time will not permit, for our own country, more than a report curtailed so as to give merely an idea of the extent and character of what is being done, and the mention of a few societies, whose work especially deserves extension and imitation. The full reports, however, are open to the inspection of any one interested.

In all cities, large and small, exist aid societies, independent or as auxiliaries of institutions or of a central relief society; societies for the distribution of food, clothing, fuel, money and whatever may be needed for immediate relief. There are orphan asylums, hospitals, homes for aged, infirm and incurables—almost as many as are needed—with auxiliary sewing societies, etc., for all. There are societies in plenty, sewing for the very poor; but there are too few societies which teach the very poor and helpless to sew for themselves—the adult poor, I mean. There is in almost every large city a training school for nurses; and the Hebrew charity associations send out one or more district nurses. There are Sabbath Schools to teach the children of the poor something of their religion, and much of the form to which the adherents of orthodoxy cling. These Sabbath Schools are almost exclusively instituted, managed and taught by the orthodox among us, and good work have they accomplished. Yet it is time we of the reform temples should bestir ourselves in this direction, bringing new methods and new ideas to fertilize the old soil. To these Sabbath

Schools are being added classes for teaching industrial branches; but while beneficial in their small way, they cannot benefit the world as they should, so long as they are mere adjuncts to schools started for other purposes. There are a number of industrial schools (the New York Hebrew Charities support one), but there are not enough, nor are those that exist good enough.

I must go on to speak of the charities of New York and a few other cities, because they were the only ones to send a full account of work in time to be incorporated in this report; so that if any of the other cities feel that they are being passed over, they have but themselves to blame.

Almost every feature of the London work has its counterpart in New York, but there are one or two features lacking there and in other cities. I should perhaps modify this by saying that my accounts omit mention of some features, from which I have concluded that they do not exist. There is no loan association, such as there is in London—an institution much needed, and often the means of preventing the first gift of charity, the first step on the road to pauperism. Rosaline House has no counterpart among us, but should have one. For a Rescue Home there is happily little need.

The time and attention given to and for the beneficial results of recreative work among the poor in London are but faintly shadowed forth on this side of the water. The absolute need of the poor for entertainment, for relaxation, is just dawning upon us here. The reports of the various large institutions show that the appreciation of this fact is just beginning; they mention the markedly good results of occasional entertainments, and endeavor to impress upon people the need for multiplying them. The Montefiore Home Auxiliary Association is the only one which gives entertainments at regular intervals. They occur weekly, are small and informal, 'tis true, but visitors and inmates find themselves happier and brighter for them. This branch of philanthropic work in institutions and among the poor and working classes cannot be too much encouraged nor too widely emulated.

There are in existence several working girls' clubs for evening instruction; and one—the Working Girls' Alliance—for mutual improvement and culture. This is a self-supporting institution, and is a pioneer in a field that should be actively and energetically worked.

In New York and in other cities during the past few years have been formed in the various congregations what are known as Sisterhoods. They teach the value of personal service, and practically show it in visiting the sick and poor, in providing and teaching crèches and kindergartens.

Their work is divided into four sections:

(1) Visiting the poor;

(2) Work in Kindergartens, etc.;

(3) Work in Sabbath Schools and sewing classes, combining religious and practical work; and

(4) Work among working girls.

Prevention is their watchword, as it must come to be that of us all. The first three of these sections are in most active operation. Work among working girls is being pushed, but has assumed no such proportions as it should and will.

In addition to these sisterhoods, there exists in Baltimore a society doing much the same work but on a different plan. The organization, known as the Daughters in Israel, is an organization composed of small bands of ten, each doing the special work itself decides upon; its small size insures all workers and no drones.

Among the good things brought into existence through its instrumentality are, visiting among the needy, dressmaking classes, the establishing of a fresh air fund for the care of sick children, the instituting of a temporary home, where Russian immigrants are cared for during a few days till they can find employment; mothers' meetings, at which kindly advice on home matters is given to poor mothers, and at which they are also taught to sew; a small kitchen-garden or household school, and a working girls' club for social approach. This club holds meetings every Saturday evening; often there are informal talks by some outsider on popular subjects, such as physiology, etc. Here, too, their sympathies have been quickened for those *most* unfortunate in this world—the sick and absolutely poor—and they find that out of their small means they still have enough to give something of money, of time, and of friendliness, to help those poorer than themselves. The Daughters seek to procure employment for specially talented girls. They have extended their influence even to children. There is one band that gives such things as children prize—fruit, and flowers, and candies, and good food for the mind in entertaining books. The Daughters in Israel may feel they have indeed deserved to be told, "Well done, thou good and faithful servant."

There are, too, in Baltimore, congregational societies "for promoting the interests of the congregations," furnishing prizes and entertainments for their Sabbath School children and decorations for the synagogue on Holy Days. There is the night school of the Hebrew Literary Society, arranged primarily to meet the needs of adult immigrants, to teach them English and act as an Americanizing influence. For the more advanced pupils here, the history of the United States is taken as a textbook, and some have this year been reading

Lamb's Tales from Shakespeare, with frequent passages from the great bard himself. Sunday evening lectures in winter are a feature of this school; but the best feature is the fact that it is partially supported by the small tuition fee of thirty cents a month, paid by the pupils, and giving them that feeling which is only theirs who know that they are not a burden nor a drag on others.

In Philadelphia, the institutions deserving special mention are, a Wayfarers' Lodge, established by Russian women for the temporary housing and feeding of their persecuted brethren driven to seek new homes; the Household School, providing as an adjunct to itself weekly inspiring entertainments; and the Personal Interest Society, composed of women, each of whom looks after some one family, inculcating principles of thrift, and cleanliness and culture, and seeing that the children get all the benefits of education open to them.

In Rochester, beside the general run of societies, there is one for encouraging and distributing good reading among children, a club giving monthly entertainments, a musical society and a Shakespeare class.

In St. Louis, the Mothers' Club, and the Pioneer Society, a society established for mutual culture and improvement, must be mentioned.

In Detroit stands forth pre-eminent the Woman's Club, established on the fine principle of bringing rich and poor, women of all social conditions together in frequent meetings, that they may learn to know and to help one another. Sewing classes, readings, lectures and general social intercourse are its work; and it has proved its practicability and elevating tendency through the several years of its existence.

These societies, it must be understood, are not worthy above others; but they are on the high road to a nobler manhood and womanhood, and in the van of progress, and therefore it is they that have been selected for special mention.

We could not do without what some are pleased to call more practical work. The time will soon come when all will see that we can still less do without such societies as these, unless we wish to sink back into the mire of pure materialism and toward an animal existence.

There are among the Jewish women various benefit and secret societies, such as the Treue Schwestern, whose purpose is mutual aid in cases of sickness and death, and noble friendship and endeavor, together with some charitable work among the very poor.

There is in existence, too, a society called Sons of Zion, with branches called Daughters of Zion, whose aim is (I read from the report), "To propagate the national idea among the women of Israel, by meetings, lectures on history and literature, and a circulating library.

"Secondly, to assist Jewish colonization in Palestine, with the special aim of colonizing the Russian Jews. These societies, comprising in all about 30,000, exist in Russia, France, Germany, England, and a small number in America, as the Americans think not at all on this subject."

The existence of this society will be a surprise to many of us; yet, while we do not in the least share in the national idea, in fact, scarcely comprehend it and strongly oppose it, we can all see here in the colonization of Palestine another chance of bringing happiness to the persecuted of our religion.

Two institutions mentioned in the London report, and entirely wanting here, are: "The Children's Happy Evenings," and the entertainment of poor children by individuals at their summer homes. Let us hope the mere mention of this fact will bring about the filling of the want, and another year show that in nothing are we behind our co-religionists in England.

Time devoted to rendering childhood happy is well spent; for happy childhood is the gateway to bright and energetic manhood. Children's spirits should be kept high, children's bodies should be well fed—and therefore there should be more penny dinners established; children's minds should be well fed, and their hands well trained—and therefore I beg leave to call your attention to the need for more manual training schools; to the need of emulating that society whose purpose is to aid those children who, through nature or accident, are prevented from availing themselves of the privileges of childhood; "to teach children who through infirmity are incapacitated from going to school; and also to teach or read to the sick or blind at their homes or in institutions."

Individuals can do this; yet associated work in this, as in all things, can do more; and better methods and results can be attained.

To the sewing of garments for the poor, by the poor, I also desire to call attention. In New York there exists a Young Ladies' Society, which gives work to the very poor, to be sewed for distribution by the Hebrew Relief Society. But the like society in London is on a higher round of the ladder, since it arranges that the poor work directly for the poor, and be paid by them. This work should be copied.

There are three institutions in my own city which I must, however, mention. Though not entirely woman's work, women have done more than their one-half share in starting, managing and providing for them, and working in them—and therefore I include them.

In addition to the general run of philanthropic societies in which women are interested, we have the Jewish

Manual Training School—the model of its kind in the United States, and an institution of which we are justly proud. We have the Elise Frank Fund, of which we are equally proud, for its application of funds to the support and bringing up of orphans in private families has proved so successful that it has demonstrated this manner of caring for the parentless to be no longer an experiment, but a finer, a better and, to the practical, a more economical way of solving this great question. In this country, this fine woman, following the plan laid out by the late lamented Dr. Hirsch, of Philadelphia, is the first woman to apply money to this purpose.

In addition to this there is about to be formed a Social Settlement of Jewish Young People. While it will be non-sectarian, welcoming all co-workers, and doing its work among whom it may find, yet its main purpose is the elevation of the Jews, in whose midst the settlement will be situated. Its work will not be charitable, but philanthropic. The distinction between these terms should always be carefully noted. The raising of the people from their outward and inward degradation, the helping of working men and women, girls and boys, to learn, to cultivate themselves—to play and relaxation and recreation—that is their mission—to inculcate the principles of independence, of self-dependence, of self-reliance; by living and working directly among them to become their friends, not their benefactors nor patrons, and thus to teach and to influence them, as only personal contact can teach and influence.

Time will not permit me to go more into detail. I repeat—whatever reports are in our hands are at the disposal of anyone interested. There is also a possibility that they may be printed.

These organizations are Jewish women's organizations, doing work almost exclusively among Jewish people.

Yet it must not be judged from this that Jewish women are engaged in exclusively Jewish charity (there is scarcely a charity in which our Jewish women are not represented), nor that Christians take no interest in them. While the management is Jewish, and the great majority of cases assisted are Jewish, many of these societies, notably the hospitals, are non-sectarian. While the larger part of the money expended is from Jewish purses, Christians almost invariably extend a helping purse when called upon. And I believe that to-morrow, if the very desirable abrogation of ALL sectarian charity could be effected, and all join hands in helping the poor—our poor—the Jewish poor could be quite as well taken care of as they are now.

While many of the associations are dignified by the name of organizations, they scarcely deserve it. They are merely associations; for work done with willing heart and hand may yet not be done in the best way, nor so as to do the most good—present good often leading to future ill. There is too much and too little in these associations—too much unjust distribution, too much consideration of the present; too little real justice, too little thoughtful consideration of the past and for the future. There are too few ounces of prevention, too many pounds of so-called cure. The wound is but lightly covered, and again and again breaks open.

While there is need of more and greater organization, there is need of more and greater personal service; and while personality and its expression in action accompanies organization, yet, with greater organization, there is always danger that too much dependence may be placed on the work of the organization as a whole and too little on that of its individual members. To-day, the growing understanding of the importance of each is counteracting this danger. In various societies of personal service, but especially in the social settlement idea, is this service being trained to perfect work. It is the personal service which does not go and give, but goes and gets; which finds what there is, and strives to lead it forth—whether it be ability to work, to act, to think, to speak, to smile, or what not. That is personal service in a twofold sense, the service to the served and to the server.

This has been a record of organized work, so called. There is to follow this a paper on organization. Why devote time to the consideration of this subject? Do we need to study the matter more closely? Are we Jewish women particularly interested, and if so, why? Are we organized? and if not, should we be? and why?

If you will give me your indulgent attention for some minutes longer, I will endeavor, with your kind permission, to answer these questions.

The reports just read sufficiently indicate the extent and the limits, the breadth and the narrowness of organizations of Jewish women. There naturally arise in the mind the questions: Do these reports contain anything new? Have they any value? Their value lies in the light they cast on past and future. Every report of work done is like the two-faced god of the Romans: One face looking down the vista of the past, the other turned to the vision of the future. Above the face of the past is written in clear, white light, " Follow—Follow—Lead ! " Above the face of the future stand forth in changing roseate hues, the words, " Lead—Lead—Follow ! " But to him of clear sight appears high above both a vision of one young, and straight, and strong, with forward, upward gaze, leading, on a steep, precipitous slope, a man, bent by the weight of years, with glance restlessly wandering to and fro, whose guiding finger points the way between the threatening obstacles his eye discerns.

A purpose of this paper is to bring prominently forward the work and power of organization. Why emphasize the work of organization rather than that of the individual? To emphasize one is to emphasize both. Let us try to see this clearly.

There are some words and ideas which are part and parcel of a time or era, words that are constantly on the lip—ideas that consciously or unconsciously are embodied in almost every speech. So common become their use and abuse, that for the general public, the average person, their meaning is entirely lost. Instead of being alive with vitality and force, conveying in one word what would before have required sentences to explain, they are mere empty phrases rousing no thought, not understood, rousing no desire to understand. Among such words in our own day, are organization, individuality, independence—terms often used together, paradoxically it may seem at first view, but intimately connected as hand and brain. To recall the real meaning of these terms, to look into them and bare to the light the truths covered by the cobwebs of time and use, is to bring back for us their original force.

What is organization?

An organ is an instrument through which some important end is accomplished, a medium through which the functions of life are carried on.

An organization is the differentiating, or grouping together of capacities for performing the functions necessary to one end, the act of endowing with organs or the state of being so endowed, *i. e.*, of having various powers so co-ordinated, as by united action to render possible the accomplishment of one great purpose, of having that which we call Life.

Association and organization are often used interchangeably, and it therefore becomes necessary for us to bear in mind the distinction between the two. An association is a number of persons banded together in pursuit of one end, each of whom may be doing the same thing. An organization is such an association of units, in which the work necessary to the attainment of an end is ordered, divided, apportioned among its members, so that each becomes an organ through which a special part, and that part only, of its work is to be done.

Primal nature was unorganized. The *Fiat Lux* of the Eternal Spirit, which separated light from darkness, and made visible the surrounding chaos, was the first step toward organization; the separation of the warring elements of chaos, that each might bring forth or support after its kind, made possible all subsequent life. When from the first simple forms of life, organless, in which all parts equally and alike performed the functions necessary to existence, was differentiated the first apparatus for digestion and circulation, primitive organization came into being.

As differentiation increased, co-ordination accompanied it, and organization became higher in proportion to the number and dissimilarity of parts, until, in the rise of the scale of life was reached the wonderful complexity of man with his nature physical, mental, spiritual.

Man, in his social development, followed in the footsteps of nature. When he formed the first group for defence against wild beasts, for protection against the wilder elements, when some watched, while others worked, man made the first movement on the road toward the magnificent complexity of modern organizations and social relations.

In the realm of man as in that of nature, differentiation is the law of progress; in proportion to the unity and diversity, the number and complexity of its parts, organization became great and perfect. Perfect subordination of its units to one supreme purpose, perfect co-ordination of dissimilar parts, perfect performance of diverse functions with one underlying intention, are the essence of a great and powerful organization, and alone make possible the carrying out of its design.

The principles that underlay the first simple organizations are the principles that underlie the complex organizations of our day.

The necessity of satisfying man's nature, of satisfying his needs, physical, mental, moral, called into action his diverse endowments. Man's increasing needs and wants brought about the appreciation and application of his various faculties and varying capacities. The strong were called on to defend, the wise to counsel, the able to lead or to do; as association increased, latent ability was made patent, was called on and developed, work and play were divided and apportioned, all worked for each, and each worked for all, under the guiding light of one common inspiration. Because men saw that what one can do with utmost difficulty another can do with utmost ease; because they recognized that what is impossible to one becomes possible to many acting as one; because they recognized that division is multiplication, that many, each of whom is doing a part, can bring about results more quickly and better than can one who does all, therefore did they organize.

Organization has been likened to the human body with its various members. Organizations among primitive peoples and in primitive civilizations may be likened to a body with head commanding and members obeying, the head alone recognized as of importance or value, the members counted as mere tools. Absolutism, subordination, strength, are its underlying principles, offence and defence its purpose. In the Middle Ages the head was still supreme, but the body was recognized in its entirety, and was given a higher place than in time before. Some of its members, having proved their importance, were regarded as of value to the whole; the ideas of might and subordination still underlay its development, but slowly and surely the ideas of the individual and independence were forcing their way to the light of day, even though as yet it was but the independence of the few powerful individuals which was maintained, even though it was the privilege of the few, not the right of all. The growth of these ideas caused the development of the conservatism and the exclusion of the Middle Ages—the desire to keep things in *statu quo*, to retain the power and privilege gained; and the endeavor to keep down and out the struggling, striving, awakening mass of humankind, until from the very nature of the case, the lines, drawn closer and more close, tighter and more tight, could no longer stand the strain from within, the pressure from without, the energy of the one and the force of the other. They broke, and after an interval of turmoil and mingling and striving for place, arose the bright form of modern organization, with its far-reaching arms, its body healthy and strong and beautiful, because at last head and members were seen to be of equal value and import. It is a body with a soul animating, directing, the head no longer commanding, but guiding, co-ordinating, answering only to the impulses sent from the members; the members no longer obeying, but co-operating. From the heart through each member pulses its life, while the animating soul determines the nature and quality of its work. It is no longer individual and independence which hold its underlying ideas, but these have overflowed from the narrow limits of those words into the larger compass of Individuality and Interdependence. It is no longer conservatism, exclusion, stand-still, which are the watchwords of the time, but liberalism, advancement, inclusion, growth and progress, not in straight and narrow lines, but in ever widening circles, extending the bounds of their influence, their usefulness, their power.

Individuality and interdependence, individual and independence—they sound alike. Are they not so? No, and again, no. Individual is simply that which is indivisible—one—a unit. Individuality is that quality by which a man—a unit—is distinguished from every other unit, that which is inseparable from him, which belongs to him and to him alone among the millions of men about him. Independence is the negative of dependence, and is but a relative term—some object or force of which one is independent is always understood. Absolute independence cannot exist in the universe, for if a man were independent of all other men, he would still be dependent on Nature, on the Higher Power immanent in every object of which his senses give him cognizance.

Interdependence is the expression of an absolute truth—the highest knowledge to which we can attain; for the recognition of absolute truth, and the endeavor to make it live, are knowledge no longer, but wisdom. Interdependence acknowledges that every being, every thing, is dependent on every other being or thing, that which affects one affects all, that we are simply parts of that great organization which we call the world.

Independence separates; interdependence joins. Independence, individualism, selfishness, tyranny co-exist; interdependence, individuality, altruism, freedom live together.

Men's awakening to the knowledge of their mutual need of one another has been a bond to hold them close. It has become crystal clear to men that association is a necessity, a law of man's existence; that only by and in association can he develop his faculties—the faculties by whose possession he is distinguished from the brute, the faculties which distinguish him from every other man. Men have come to know that no individual, however small or insignificant he may seem in himself, is small or insignificant for good or for ill, as a part of a great whole; men have learned that only by exchange of services does it become possible for each to develop his particular aptitude to the utmost point of perfection, that by mutual exchange of knowledge and the lessons of experience are men saved from the sadness of wasted energy and effort and of useless repetition. Men have found that mutual easing of burdens is increase of strength and power, raises and widens the field of vision, induces true fellowship and happiness; and men have learned that association without organization means failure—while association with organization means success. For these reasons has organization become the bidding of the *Zeitgeist*, and individuality and interdependence a cry of the time. For these reasons are they connected close as brain and hand. Because men know these things, do we find organizations in every field of human endeavor, in every department of human thought and activity. It is needless to weary you with a rehearsal of them in detail; the records are daily before you in reports, newspapers and periodicals. It is needless to repeat their success. To speak of the power of organization to-day is almost to perpetrate a truism. Yet it is a fact on which we cannot place too much insistence, and therefore, even at the risk of some wearying repetition, let us attempt a short analysis of this power in order that we may see clearly wherein it lies.

Its power lies (1) in its association, centralization and concentration, like a lens focusing the scattered rays of light and heat upon one point, thus piercing the shell of difficulty surrounding any problem. Our most familiar stories hold embodied the great truths which men need to know. This truth was long ago set forth in the fable of the bundle of sticks a father gave his sons to break. The bundle, held together by a stout cord, resisted all the strength of each of the sons to break it. But the father, loosening the cord and taking one stick from the bundle, broke that with ease, and all the others quite as readily. Thus was brought home to the sons and all who know the tale, the truth that in a union bound together by the cord of a strong purpose, is strength unconquerable, the strength of the living oak; but the bond of union once loosed, the strength becomes but as the strength of the dead branch.

Its power lies (2) in its division of labor, entailing a smaller amount of work on each; its consequent development of special functions, and the uncovering of hidden energies and capacities. It is a magic wand striking the sparkling waters from the rock.

(3) In its economy of force and work, of time and attention. It opens wide the gates of opportunity, and thus throws into work itself, energy which would otherwise be dissipated in the possibly fruitless search for an opening. This and its division of labor enable a man to put his whole force into what he desires to do, and in consequence of the skill attained in the practice of his specialty, multiplies production by turning out better work in shorter time. It facilitates communication, since by its close connection any information, any plan or purpose, demand or idea given the head, thrills like an electric current instantly through every part.

The rushlight in the hand of the individual searching for the way to an end, passing through the transforming medium of its crystallized knowledge and experience, becomes a searchlight making clear and bright the way to means and to ends.

Its power lies (4) in the inter-relation of its parts, their order and discipline, and the relation to a head, without which each is powerless, but which itself is powerless without the parts. Through it are effected combinations of force, disentangling of knotted threads, solving of weighty problems; through it is secured balance of parts, which insures full and rounded growth, the one indispensable condition of success, of attainment of the highest.

Its power lies (5) in the activity it induces among its members, the fire of interest and investigation it lights by contact of mind with mind, in the *esprit de corps* it rouses, calling forth the best that is in one; in the common thought, idea or principle which holds it together, insuring mutual comprehension and harmony; laying constant stress on the fact that each is a part and but a part of one great whole, working in different ways to one great end, it makes prominent the ideas of interdependence and unity, unity and interdependence—as the one great principle of growth, of progress, of success.

It is not the purpose of this paper to attempt a history of organization, yet some preliminary remarks were necessary to its design—the bringing home to the Jews the value and the necessity of Organization.

The Jews have had many of the benefits, and suffered many of the disadvantages of organization.

The average Jew has had certain outward characteristics, and has been known by them. Repression and oppression made more intense his native intensity, and at the same time prevented normal growth, normal differentiation of work and character. He came to be known by the qualities which the world about him called into action and notice, by the qualities in defence, in *opposition*, if I may coin the phrase; his qualities in *conjunction*, his feelings and actions for and with his fellow-beings, Jew or Gentile, were lost sight of, or deliberately hidden by men's prejudgment. In spite of and through the covering of likeness with every other Jew which custom and law threw over him, his versatility and adaptability have shown themselves. He has adopted the ways of the people in whose midst he settled; their virtues and vices he has added to his own. He has reflected the ideas of his time, even if on account of his distance from the world's head and heart—only when they have become a part of it, and not at their birth.

The Jew is an idealist. He has been guided through Egyptian gloom and darkness by the light that never was on land or sea. But he combines with the ideal the practical. He has seen the stars reflected from the well-springs on the earth about him; and so, though he gazed at the stars, he has fallen into no waterpit by the wayside, nor into the abyss of loss of faith and trust in the eventual triumph of right and justice.

And because he combines in himself the practical with the ideal, having adopted an idea he studies it, watches closely its development and influence; but he himself does not apply it till he is certain of success. For this reason the modern Jew, while identified with all the movements of his time, has yet been slow to apply the principle of organization to his own concerns. He has not properly understood, nor appreciated the great and growing power of organization. He has not fully realized its importance to himself and his history. He is beginning to do so now. Heretofore, he has needed no formal organization, for the enforced closeness of relation in his restricted life, his peaceful nature, his feeling of brotherhood have led him unconsciously into means and ways that an organization would consciously adopt. Yet he has done less organized than associated work; he has done much and great individual work, with but little individualization. Indeed, the greatest work among and for the Jews has been done by individuals who, like Moses Mendelssohn, were gifted above their fellowmen, felt within them the strain and stress of the spirit of liberty, and had the courage of their convictions. But individual work is no longer adequate; the work that is to be done requires the power of a great, well-disciplined army, not individual prowess.

The Jews needed no formal organization. They need it now—times have changed. In the larger, freer life which has been opened to them, the closeness of their union has been broken; their restraining fetters loosed, the spirit of organization no longer animates their doings; in the reaction from the close band of a common fear, there is danger that their interdependence will be forgotten, that in the spirit of *sauve qui peut*, which the law of self-preservation causes to show itself, some may forget that each is his brother's keeper, that every act done by any Jew casts its light or shade on every other Jew; there is danger of forgetting that so long as one Jew is oppressed or suffers because he is a Jew, so long are Jews bound together by chains of adamant, which no straining can break, which none can escape—so long must they unite under one banner to break those chains, opposing might with might, until the full triumph of truth and justice shall break them with a touch.

The Jew has been a Goth rather than a Greek, if I may commit the Irish bull. He has seen the details rather than the whole, the present rather than the future. His environment compelled him to do this; for the present moment was the only one he could call his own. Now that restraining laws and bars are down, he can and must look at the whole equally with the details, he must look to the future more than to the present. Now for the first time, the future is his to make of it what he will. Let him understand and rise to his opportunity and its responsibility, let him know and understand his duty, and fulfil it through light and darkness, as in past ages, to the glorious end. From the past and present, let him build a mould for the future. Through organized and united endeavor can he alone fulfil this, his duty.

The Jewish woman has shared the ideas and thoughts of the man. She has aided with heart and hand in his work; the assistance of her head has rarely been asked. Her real work has been confined to the home. There it is she has made her influence felt. Though the Jew daily thanked God that he had not been born a woman, it was not because she was degraded far below him, as was the case with other peoples, but because she was prohibited from the observance of certain religious rites; and he considered himself much more fortunate than she was since in the performance of these rites he was allowed to show his worship and devotion to his Maker. For this it was that he daily thanked his God. To the Jew, the mother was and is the highest, noblest type of womanhood. In the home, the Jewish woman reigned as queen; to her were left the performance of religious rites in the household, the important preparation of food, etc. There she was looked up to and regarded. She was adequately protected by law; her position was assured, her influence very great. As the Jew has reflected the ideas of his time, she has reflected them through him. She needed to make no movement for herself, she has made no movement for others, but has been content through her influence to impel him to move. Because her work has been done largely in the home, because the man has been the medium of communication, the Jewish woman has been a little slower to feel the heart-beats of her time than have other women.

For this reason, we find no trace of organization among Jewish women until we come to modern associations for charity—associations often independent of man in work, but not in purse nor direction.

Indeed, woman is only just awakened to the realization of her true part and function in the economy of the universe, she has only begun to feel her real power and to exert it for the progress of her fellow creatures. She has been a passive agent, like the child that follows the path laid out for it with no responsibility, no duty but obedience, but which, when the time comes for it to throw off this yoke of obedience, and act for itself, becomes a responsible agent with duties to fulfil, with the duty paramount to properly exercise its newly gained freedom and power. Individual Jewish women have understood the meaning of the new, bright star in the galaxy of heaven. Individual Jewish women have been in the van of every movement of the time; but as a body, Jewish women are behind the times, and have done nothing.

Is there any reason why they should do anything?

Jewish women have been accused of being bound down to the narrow limits of their own homes, of having no interest outside of them, of having no interest in the interests of women as women, of not being in sympathy with their time. No greater mistake was ever made. The Jewish woman—every Jewish woman—is interested in all that interests woman, is in perfect sympathy with the time; but custom and tradition, and the misunderstanding, misconception and excluding prejudice of the world have militated against her showing this publicly.

It is the bounden duty of the Jewish woman, on account of this misunderstanding of her true nature and interests, to make these manifest; it is her duty, as it is that of all Jews, to make prominent her qualities in conjunction, that they may cast in the shade her qualities in opposition. It is not enough that she be in sympathy with her time, she must be running hand and hand with it.

The question whether Jewish women should have an organization cannot be answered in a word, and I beg leave to present certain matter for your consideration.

This Congress has a unique place among the various congresses. Never before have Jews been given a place on a plane with other men, not to defend themselves and their doctrines, but to present them. This Congress holds a unique place among Jewish congresses. Never before in the history of Judaism has a body of Jewish women come together for the purpose of presenting their views, nor for any purpose but that of charity or mutual aid; never before have Jewish women been called upon to take any place in the representation of Judaism. When work was begun toward bringing together a body of Jewish women which should represent Judaism as exemplified by its women, Judaism in its various phases, religious, philanthropic, educational, in its different shades of opinion, under varying influences and environments, no path to its accomplishment was visible; the field had to be surveyed and a way found through virgin ground filled with the boulders of custom and tradition, of indifference and opposition even. No law existed against such a convention, but the step was a new one, and the difficulties in its way seemed insurmountable. It required long continued and untiring effort first to arouse interest, then to rouse to action. Woman took no part in religious matters outside the home and Sabbath Schools—what could she have to say in a religious congress other than what men would say better than she could? Jewish women had never before held a congress;—why should they do so now? Was the matter so important that custom should be disregarded and a precedent established? The chairman and the ladies of the committee, realizing the possibilities, the responsibility and duty of this great opportunity, deemed the matter was important, knew that the women had something to say worth saying. They determined not only that a precedent should be established, but followed. They set to work with a will, determined that success must crown their efforts. Practical questions were to be answered, high ideals to be realized! How was this to be done? Where were the women who could best represent Judaism, and in representing Judaism represent the Jews? That there were many who could do so, no one for a moment doubted, but how to reach them was the question. Had there been a central body to which to refer, much, very much wasted time and useless effort might have been saved. However, no stone was left unturned, no avenue untried, in the search to find the proper representative women and to interest them in the project.

But it required untiring energy, earnest zeal and enormous labor. Their efforts were rewarded by hearty response and sympathy from a few, and a growing interest from many, which showed that they were but embodying in concrete form a latent feeling and want. In view of the last three days, I venture to say a glorious success *has* crowned their efforts. But I repeat, it took almost a year of continued, repeated, unceasing and untiring, determined and disinterested hard work to bring about this success. The interest and enthusiasm shown the past days has caused all, everything to be forgotten but the joy in this magnificent realization of their almost utopian desires and dreams. The economy of time, of toil, of energy, which would have resulted from the existence of an organization reaching in all directions is, I am sure, sufficiently manifest to you and needs no insistence.

In the course of its work, the lack of many things impressed itself on the Committee.

The lack of a proper understanding of our position, our responsibility, our duty and our time, the lack of widespread knowledge of our history, and even of our ethics, of those things wherein we differ from other religions, of the difference that the broken gates of the Ghetto have made, and of the specter of indifference that, like a worm in the bud, is sapping our vitality, and which, unless stamped out, will, by the inertia it induces, sink us through the quicksands of apathy to death.

Then it was that the Committee determined that the Congress should flash a light into the darkness, that it should be a voice to proclaim our needs, our wants, our difficulties, our facilities, telling our women wherein we lack, calling to them in clarion tones: "Awake! arise! A new house is to be built in Israel, which shall be the home of all that is fine, and true, and pure, and beautiful. From it shall go forth an influence and power which shall uplift men, its atmosphere shall be sweetness and purity and light; it shall be builded on the firm rock of principle and unselfish love and enthusiasm. It shall be a vehicle by which shall be conducted to the top the forces accumulated and accumulating in hidden reservoirs beneath the surface, and only waiting for an outlet to rush and mingle with the upper air, for a kiss of fire to burst into a flame aspiring to the stars, a beacon of pure light scattering the darkness like the rays of the morning sun, sending its messengers of life-giving warmth and brightness, of hope, and love, and beauty into every tiniest hidden nook and cranny of the earth."

It was determined that the Congress should not be a mere ephemeral success, but that its memory should live in a lasting monument—a National Jewish Woman's Organization; an organization which shall unite in true fellowship and noblest endeavor all thinking Jewish women, which shall be a means and medium of interchange of ideas and thoughts, and projects and services; which shall encourage jousts and tournaments of mind on ground where she o'erthrown shall rise like Antæus, with strength renewed from touch of mother earth; which through knowledge and experience shall beget wisdom, and from whose head shall spring Minerva-like a free and fiery spirit, animating, actuating, directing to all things good and true and beautiful.

We need a wider organization. We have some organizations 'tis true, but you have seen that they are all confined to charity, they do for others—we need to be taught our duty to ourselves; they go and give—we need to be taught that to go and get is of equal importance, we need to be taught the value of the word *mutual*. The extremes of society receive more than their share of the world's attention. For the poor in pocket, in mind, in spirit, much is done; the rich in purse and intellect do much for themselves; the average woman is neglected. Her we desire and aim to reach. It is the average woman whose time is occupied in household duties, who needs an outside force to pull her out of her rut on the broader way of life. She has never done anything outside of her home, not because she did not want to do anything; but because she had not time to do much, she has done nothing. Prove to her the possibilities for happiness to herself and others of her wasted half hours, and one round has been climbed on Jacob's ladder. Show to the individual the resources within himself. Wake what lies dormant. Rouse the desire to do. Provide an outlet for the new-born energy. Then through the individual, you have leavened the mass.

It is not easy to overcome the obstacles which custom puts in the way of any new movement; it is well to parry her weapons in advance. Therefore, it is well to answer in advance some questions of protest: (1) Is organization necessary at all? (2) Cannot, are not individuals doing as well? It is a narrow and uninformed mind that asks these questions. I have tried to prove that it is more than justified; that it is demanded for man's prorgess. Individuals, individual societies are doing good work, a larger organization can do more work, better work, quicker work.

Again, we are in a time of transition and turmoil, new forces have been awakened, and are boiling beneath the surface. Among these is Woman. And the question arises: Will wider organization not take her away from her place in the home? Is not the separation of women from men in work a disorganizing tendency? Is it not a step on the return to chaos and night, instead of toward harmony and light? Should not this great danger be stamped out in its incipiency? Is it not separation instead of union? Are not men's interests and women's alike? Are not the interests of Jewish men and women alike, and the same as those of other men and women? Why, then, if they organize at all, should they organize separately?

Certainly their interests are alike. No Jewish woman has any interest apart from any Jewish man, no man from any woman, no human being from any other human being. But the recognition and understanding of these interests are not always equally clear to both; sometimes it is the man who sees the way more clearly, sometimes it is the woman whose spiritual eye discerns through the mist and cloud the steep and narrow path which must be followed. Whichever thus discerns and *acts* is doing the right; thought and discernment alone never accomplished much in this world, but thought and action together, whether combined in one or many. I repeat, whichever discerns and acts, takes the first step, is justified by the purpose in the step—nay more—should and must take that step, and go on until the correctness of vision is proved or disproved.

It will not take her away from the home. That place will and must remain first and most sacred to her. When, in the economy of the globe, an allwise Creator made male and female, and assigned them varied functions and duties, this variety of function and duty became a law of being, and no advance of civilization can change these functions nor abrogate these duties. The lines of their duties may, nay, do run parallel, but can never converge. No two beings are constituted exactly alike, their tendencies are different; similarly, men and women differ, only in greater degree. This fact must never be lost from sight. Circumstances may so modify these tendencies and aptitudes, heredity, training, and what not, may so modify them, that the work produced by individual men and women may be the same, but for the majority, the fields of labor will always be separated. Open wide as you will the door into these fields, the law of nature will keep each in his just and proper sphere, and will no more allow men and women to rush into them equally, than it will ever allow individuals or men and women to become mere interchangeable units in the mass of humankind. Granting, then, that their lines of work and duty run parallel, the goal they are trying to reach is not a point, but a broad, high plane. The lines run so close together that they influence each other's motion, sometimes faster, sometimes slower, each responds to each. What does it matter which changes place or direction so long as it leads to the goal, and the movement of one means the speedy answering movement of the other—means soon a joint movement of both? It is differentiation for the sake of a higher union. Therefore are women justified in organizing separately. They act with men where men's insight and justice allow them so to act. But where they are excluded from regions whither the law of their nature sends them, they are banding together in solid phalanx to conquer what is refused their necessity; they are but hastening the time when men and women will know that before they are men and women they are human beings, and as such, each will follow the special law of his being first—then speak and act and work together where they may. But are Jews justified in acting separately?

Jews are justified in organizing because environment, heredity, social conditions and prejudice within as much as without their ranks sweep before their doors an accumulation of material, through which it is their duty to cut a way to the great green common and the invigorating air of the eternal heights of true freedom; free and healthy development and intercourse of head, hand and heart, of mind and soul.

As men and women we should and must and do take interest and action in all that concerns men and women; but as Jews, holding fast to one great faith, certain problems are forced upon us to be solved which present themselves to no one else—certain circumstances and conditions, certain privileges and duties, certain aptitudes and powers are ours, and therefore certain work lies before us, peculiarly our own, demanding our first attention. Do you still ask, Are Jewish women justified in acting separately? Does it need additional proof? We all grant that there is work to do. Do Jewish men see it and refuse or neglect to act, or do they not see the great needs of the times? Do women see them? Then let them act at once. The men will soon follow and join us.

Do some claim that organization will separate us more from the world? I answer, It will not. We must look facts in the face. We *are* separated from the rest of mankind by barriers which must be broken down, broken by forces from within and forces from without. An organization can and will but hasten and help to raze this wall about us. It will separate us no more than heart and hand are separated because they are not doing the same thing. We are all members of that great organization of which the all-pervading Spirit of the universe is head, which works for truth and justice and righteousness. And we, by working under its guidance, not for the Jews alone, but for the elevation and progress of mankind, will join hands with those outside the wall, whose end and aim are one with ours, and through our combined efforts the wall will be undermined, and must fall.

It is maintained that an organization must have a definite purpose. I can see looming up in the distance purposes in plenty, beckoning with fingers of golden light.

First and foremost, let one purpose be, to study the causes and conditions of this so-called separation; let us learn to know ourselves; then to knowledge let us add discernment and disinterestedness that we may find the best and quickest way to obliterate dividing lines. Let us study our history and our literature, and their bearing on our character and position. Religion, true religion, with which every thought and action are connected, is in woman's hand, because the inward life, the home, is what she makes it; therefore, it is eminently fit that from her should come the impulse to study more closely the underlying principles of her religion. Let us look into their very heart in order that we may know exactly where we stand, that we may know them in every phase of their development. Let each and every one among us know that they make us one with all the world, that they hold the springs of all moral life, the living germ of all morality. Let us learn, that all may judge intelligently, that we may cling to the old faith, not because we were born into it, but because we are convinced that for us it is the only possible belief or act. Let us encourage a deeper study of that book, our book, which has been the bread of life to half the civilized world, because it contained the story of the eternal springs of action of men, the records of nobility of soul and character, of faith and patience, integrity and bravery and high truth, those things which command men's admiration and emulation through all time.

The Jew of the Ghetto was cut off from almost everything but his religion; he made of that, almost exclusively, his study, his inspiration, his joy. The high walls of the Ghetto thrown down, the burst of sunlight proved too much for his unaccustomed eyes. His sight was dazzled, blurred. In the endeavor to reach the many enticing objects disclosed to his view, he lost his hold on the old joys; they looked different to him now from what they had looked in the dim Ghetto light. His well-known love of learning caused him to rush to the new founts to drink and to neglect the old springs of inspiration. Two things have resulted—the one a party clinging to the old forms, many now grown meaningless, lest in losing the form, the spirit too should escape; the other sinking slowly but surely from indifference through apathy into a heavy sleep, akin to death. Let us blow the trumpet whose magnetic tones shall waken to new life and joy and gladness the beautiful, slumbering spirit of Judaism. Let us prove that ours is a progressive religion, whose liquid character molds itself to every form that time or change can produce. Jews associated in bondage have carried their principle high and unsullied through Cimmerian gloom; now let us show what Jews associated in freedom will do.

Having studied our history, our literature, our religion, let us apply our knowledge for the progress of the world. Our Sabbath Schools need attention. Let us make of them not mere religious schools for children, but schools for the study of religion in its broadest sense. Let the magic armor of knowledge there gained shield our faith against the sword strokes of secular learning.

A second purpose shall be the study of our social conditions and relations, to study our own needs and the needs of those less fortunate than ourselves; and having studied, to supply them. Let us grind the ax which shall free those bound by the shackles of ignorance and circumstance.

A wide territory lies before us in the immigrants whom Russian persecution is forcing to our shores. So accustomed are we to our freedom that we scarcely realize the shock, which contact with our own free air must be to them. It dazes or intoxicates them. These people brought up where every man's hand is against them, and therefore theirs against every man, need our help to keep them sane. We and we alone can raise them, because experience has taught them to distrust all who do not hold to their faith, causes them often to refuse aid proffered with the noblest intention, because they fear the iron hand in the velvet glove. To bend every effort to lift them out of their slough of suspicion and prejudice and meanness should be our desire, *is* our duty. Freedom, possession, carries with it obligations; if we do not fulfil these obligations, the penalty will come upon us none the less because our sins are sins of omission, not of commission. In order to fulfil our duty to these unfortunates who suffer torture, exile, death for their convictions, we must understand them. Their standards are not our standards, their ways are not our ways, and only by close contact, study and attention, can we get that insight into the "not our own," which is the condition of useful and effectual work.

If our watchword be not charity, which has come to be almost synonymous with alms, and leaves a sting behind, but Philanthropy—love of our fellows, the sympathy which holds healing balm for all our wounds, and in whose wake follows a doubled happiness, numerous luminous ways to do our duty will open to us.

It shall be our purpose, not to increase the number of existing institutions to their detriment, drawing nourishment from the old and worthy to the new, thus crippling both, but to concentrate, organize and aid those deserving with our might, to plant new ideas in them, and to start new institutions where there is a crying need for them. In doing this, it shall be our business to further and emphasize so-called preventive work, it shall be ours to proclaim to all, the truth which the popular mind has crystallized into the homely proverb, "An ounce of prevention is worth a pound of cure."

Do we need a Jewish organization for this? No; and yes. No, for there are chances plenty for us to study this fine ship moving in the social horizon. Yes, because we and we alone can show it to many whose line of vision is too short or too narrow to behold it.

It shall be our purpose and our pleasure to preach the gospel of recreation—re-creation to all who need to hear; to the unenlightened of every age and condition, that they may know that all work and no play makes Jack a dull boy, but worse, that all play and no work makes Jack an evil boy; that each may know the meaning of rest—not sleep, which induces heaviness and dullness, but change of occupation, which brings into play the faculties that have lain idle, which induces rounded growth, adds skill and quickness to mind and hand, raises the tide of life, keeps the spirits high, brings brightness to the eye, smiles to the face and lightness to the soul.

"Man cannot live by bread alone." The toiler needs to be led to the enjoyment of his mental faculties; he whose life is spent amid the practical, the material, the sordid, must have his thoughts turned to the ideal—music, reading, pleasant converse should be brought to the doors of all workers. But quite as needful is it for the idler to know that only by contact with the worker, for the dreamer to know that only by grasping the real, can full happiness or rounded character be attained.

We cannot too much or too deeply contemplate the ideal, for only the marriage of the ideal with the practical, produces the wealth of the world and adds to it. From the perfect blending of the two, results the noblest character; while according as one or the other prevails, it is great or little. To begin to satisfy ideal wants tends to their realization; for it is a law of nature that they propagate themselves; they hold within themselves an inexhaustible fount of reproduction, while sensual wants cloy with satisfaction, and feed on their own energy to annihilation.

It shall be our purpose to do the work of education in its broadest sense—to lead forth to the day and to activity whatever of ability we in our search can find; to make it like the wind carrying the germs of growth and beautiful blossoming where'er it touches; to teach the obligation of possession, the duty and value of personal service. Bring forth those who have energy or talent or enthusiasm or power of expression to move men's souls, and a new force which will eternally persist for good has been quickened into life.

It shall be first and above all our purpose to create an exchange, where all thinking women in Israel, standing on the common ground of their religious convictions, shall meet and enjoy each other's uncommon ideas and aims and plans, whence such ideas and plans and projects may be sent on a journey of success, impelled by the unfailing force of thinking, active women banded together to forward the cause of progress and social reform. Its meetings shall give free scope to the power that lies in the human voice and countenance, to the free and full personal contact which generates the electric spark of interest, of enthusiasm, of accomplishment; shall make place for and give free play to the exercise of that potent quality which we call personal magnetism, which draws adherents for a cause as the magnet does iron; shall encourage and sow the seed of that noble friendship and fellowship which will be a potent factor to obliterate all trace of the ignoble prejudice of class and caste which, we must sadly admit, exists even among ourselves. Such meetings can accomplish more in one day than can be done in months of work apart; can make of an idea a propaganda, which any amount of writing or reading might be powerless to do.

Friends, a great opportunity is ours. Let us understand it. Let us live up to it. Others have died for Judaism; let us live for it—a harder task. There is indifference in our ranks, there is narrowness, there is ignorance within and without them. Let us apply the torch of knowledge and enthusiasm to them. We may encounter opposition, tradition will plant itself in our path, apathy will drag our feet. Let them be burned away by our ardor. On the wings of a mighty purpose let us soar above and beyond them all and every obstacle. This Congress has given us pleasure, has given us mental and spiritual profit, has cemented friendships, has opened our hearts to new joys—let them live again and yet again, gathering beauty as they grow, leaving beauty and perfume and efflorescence in their path. The Congress has clarified for us things that were dull or blurred. Let it not be like a meteor in the sky, leaving no trace behind. We are in the labyrinth of a transition period. Let the Congress be the thread to lead us out of it. We are in the throes of doubt. Let us prove they are not the precursors of disintegration but of re-adaptation, of a new birth. On the bridge of the Congress, let us walk from the dead level of growing apathy to the beautiful rising slope, to sunlit heights of fire and activity. The time no longer shouts in the ear of the Jew, "Thou shalt not!" but "Thou shalt!" Let us be the first to obey its thundering summons. Let us be the first to do and to dare. Let us understand and fulfil our duty, our responsibility. By organized work alone can we do this. Our individual efforts are but as tiny rivulets making oases in the desert, then losing themselves in the sand; they can be, if we will, a mighty river, to make the desert rejoice and blossom as the rose, transforming the wilderness into a garden of delight. Not again may we have together so many women from all parts of our country, drawn hither for the purpose of representing Judaism at its best. Let us strike while the iron is hot. Let us form an organization whose object shall be the spreading the understanding of and devotion to the highest type of Judaism, in whose service shall be put every faculty of our being. Let us prove that it is synonymous with the highest type of man; that in serving Judaism, we are but doing our part with system, sense and insight toward bringing about that religion which shall be neither Jewish nor Christian, but human, humane, divine, which shall be known by no name but that of the Religion of Humanity, God's own religion. It behooves us above all others to teach the beautiful and eternal truth of interdependence and unity, to teach that not the smallest act or thought of one of us, a drop in the ocean of humanity, but the waves carry to every other drop, to every grain of sand that touches on its shores. Let our actions cover its surface with a glowing phosphorescence surrounding the ship of life.

Our heritage is a vineyard, a royal vintage lies buried there. With the spade of organization let us stir the earth, and put new mould to the roots, that it may bring forth an hundredfold.

We need united effort, mutual approach, extension of intercourse—let us form an organization which shall make this possible; an organization whose platform shall be so broad, that all, of whatever age or condition, of whatever shade of belief, or opinion, can walk thereon in noble fellowship; whose purpose shall be a stimulus and stimulant, a constant source of heat and motion and activity; whose meetings shall give full and free expression to the thoughts, desires, needs and plans of our age; its bond of union shall annihilate space and time, shall create a sentiment to be contented only by the best there is, a sentiment which will bring in its train demand and satisfaction. It shall concentrate our energies, make our strength as the strength of the oak to stand and the willow to bend before the storm; it shall make way for hidden talents, and apply them, shall insure full and rounded growth, shall turn the light of truth into the darkness, and prove that we are one with the aims and ideals of the world, that the exceptional among us is but the stronger expression of the average. Let us be pioneers, working with hand and heart and head and voice and purse, unfurling to the wind the banner on which is graven: "Know thyself—learn and propagate the best there is." But let there be no misunderstanding. It is not learning we must seek for its own sake, erudition in and for itself we are not seeking, but knowledge which shall enable us to satisfy those higher needs, which transform life from mere existence to joy and gladness and beauty. It is not our intention to rush into wild projects of reform. No utopian schemes of immediate regeneration are seething in our brains. But only to do what we feel our force, our capacity, our principles make possible for us to do; only to place within the grasp of those who may be tied to the treadmill of daily work those highest ideals toward which, from the best that is in us, there is a constant stream.

But it is the nature of ideals never to be reached. They are the stars in the nightly firmament. Yet, "Hitch your wagon to a star;" not that you may lie down in listless inactivity—if you do, the star will take you to the zenith, 'tis true, but only to plunge you on its downward course into darkness and night. No; hitch your wagon to a star that your eyes and hands and mind may be left free to gather energy in your flight through time, that when you reach the zenith you may have force to leave the star behind, and continue on your upward journey to heights no star can reach, which can be attained only by the human soul striving for the highest.

Then let us marry the practical with the ideal, that it may produce wealth, mental, moral, spiritual. Let our ambition be unlimited, our enthusiasm infinite; when it comes to practical work, let no prospect of trouble or sacrifice make our hands fall in despair, but let us remember that in union is strength to do and to bear. Let us not dissipate our forces by overtaxing individual effort, but shoulder to shoulder let us climb one step at a time, slowly and surely. The time is ripe; isolated movements show it; but it is not isolated acts, it is their combined and blended effect which tells for eternity.

Therefore, oh, friends, let not this plea be in vain. Let none think himself small or insignificant. Let none wait, but each help to give momentum to this impetus of the Congress. Let none forget that we may be a power for good, and we will. There is ignorance, there is prejudice outside our ranks—no words can conquer them. We must conquer them by our deeds. To you who are apathetic I say, "Awake from your lethargy." To you who are interested, enthusiastic, I say, "There is work to do; there are others whom you must interest." Remember, "There never was a great or commanding movement in the annals of the world but is the triumph of enthusiasm." Let us realize the vision of past and future. The Congress has launched this ship of organization; it is yours to propel her on the river of life. Equip her with enthusiasm, like the grand ship of the Republic in the MacMonnies fountain at our great World's Fair. Let zeal, earnestness, courage and perseverance, knowledge, work, faith and love be the rowers to send her on her way—high to the fore seat the radiant young form of your purpose, with her straight, strong back of an iron determination, her head proudly erect, in her hand the staff of dignity and power. Place the past at the rudder; from the prow let the spirit of the future trumpet forth the glad tidings of the coming of this new splendid beauty into the world. High above all let shine the sun of your union. Individual efforts are like the elemental colors of the dawn, serving to make the darkness visible. Let your organization be the prism to convert them into that pure, brilliant, piercing white light whose shafts alone can penetrate and divide the gloom of ignorance and apathy and hostility, like the staff of Moses at the Red Sea, an undying light and glory, which shall persist for truth and beauty and goodness even through all time.

REPORT OF THE BUSINESS MEETING.

After the reading of the paper on Organization by Miss Sadie American, the chairman called a business meeting to consider the advisability of forming a permanent organization, and to transact such other business as might be necessary.

The following resolutions were presented by Miss Julia Richman, of New York, and were unanimously adopted. To wit:

Whereas, The officers and members of the general committee of the Jewish Women's Religious Congress have, by their earnest and untiring efforts, made this convention so brilliantly successful, and

Whereas, These same officers and members have so generously extended the hand of friendship as well as that of courteous hospitality to the visiting essayists and delegates, and

Whereas, These visiting essayists and delegates recognize, and thoroughly and gratefully appreciate the heartiness of their welcome and entertainment, therefore be it

Resolved, That the visiting essayists and delegates offer a cordial vote of thanks to the chairman and the members of the general committee for their zeal and labor in organizing the Congress, and for the warm-hearted reception tendered to those invited to participate in the Congress; and be it furthermore

Resolved, That, in recognition of this and other obligations, the visiting essayists and delegates pledge themselves to the support of any permanent organization, which shall be the outgrowth of this Congress.

Upon motion it was unanimously decided to publish the entire proceedings of the Congress.

The chairman appointed as the committee on publication:

Miss Richman, of New York, chairman.
Mrs. H. Frank, of Chicago.
Mrs. C. S. Benjamin, of Denver
Miss Cohen, of Philadelphia.
Miss Szold, of Baltimore.

Miss Richman then offered the following resolution, which was seconded:

Whereas, It is desirable that the zeal, energy, and loyalty to the cause of Judaism which have been evinced by the Jewish women of America in the preparations for and the discharge of the duties connected with this Congress be turned to permanent good; and

Whereas, This is an opportune time to establish closer bonds to draw together the Jewish women of America; therefore be it

Resolved, That this Congress resolve itself into a permanent organization to be known as the Jewish Women's Union, for the purpose of teaching all Jewish women their obligations to the Jewish religion.

Mrs. Rosenberg, of Allegheny, offered an amendment changing the name to "Columbian Union." Seconded; lost.

The original resolution was then presented, and after the expression of opinion that the platform outlined therein was too narrow, it was lost.

Miss American, of Chicago, then presented the following resolution:

Resolved, That we, Jewish women, sincerely believing that a closer fellowship will be encouraged, a closer unity of thought and sympathy and purpose, and a nobler accomplishment will result from a widespread organization, do therefore band ourselves together in a union of workers to further the best and highest interests of Judaism and humanity, and do call ourselves the "National Council of Jewish Women."

Seconded and adopted.

It was then moved and seconded that the chairman appoint a committee to draw up resolutions defining the objects of the new organization. Carried.

The chairman thereupon appointed:
Mrs. Minnie D. Louis, of New York;
Mrs. Henrietta G. Frank, of Chicago;
Miss Witkowsky, of Chicago;
Miss American, of Chicago.

The committee retired to deliberate, and during its absence letters of encouragement were read from Dr. S. Morais, of Philadelphia; Mrs. Nina Morais Cohen, of Minneapolis; Mrs. J. Steinem, of Toledo, Ohio, and the following from Mrs. Palmer:

My Dear Madam:—I beg to express to the Jewish Women's Congress my sincere appreciation of their great kindness in presenting me with the beautiful souvenir, recently received through your committee.

I also desire to extend my cordial thanks for their words of appreciation and interest in our work, and to assure you that it is very pleasing to receive this evidence of approval from the women of our country.

I beg you will express to your committee and to the women of your Congress my renewed thanks for their kindness, and with best wishes for the success of your Congress and kind regards to yourself, I am,

Very sincerely yours,
BERTHA HONORÉ PALMER,
Pres't., B. L. M.

MRS. HENRY SOLOMON,
Chairman Committee of Jewish Women's Congress.

Dr. E. G. Hirsh spoke urging the women on to active work.

Mrs. Harris moved a unanimous vote of thanks to the ladies of the Jewish Women's Committee. Seconded and carried.

It was moved and seconded that the full proceedings of this Congress be published in pamphlet form. Carried.

Mrs. Moyer, of Buffalo, moved that a committee be appointed to draft resolutions of gratitude and appreciation to be presented to Mrs. H. Solomon, Chairman of the Committee.

(Mrs. Fanny Adler was called to the chair during the consideration of this motion.) The motion was seconded and carried, and the following committee appointed:

Mrs. Moyer, Buffalo.
Mrs. Barbe, Chicago.
Mrs. Wolf, Chicago.

Mrs. Solomon thanked the women of Chicago for their hearty co-operation in making the Jewish Women's Congress a success.

Mrs. Seelig expressed gratitude to the essayists for their work, and moved a vote of thanks to them. Seconded and carried.

It was moved and seconded that a vote of thanks be tendered Mrs. Chas. Henrotin, Vice-President of the Auxiliary, for the interest shown in the work. Carried.

The committee appointed to draft resolutions setting forth the objects of the National Council of Jewish Women, then reported, through its chairman, Mrs. Louis.

The following resolution was presented and adopted:

Resolved, That the National Council of Jewish Women shall (1) seek to unite in closer relation women interested in the work of Religion, Philanthropy and Education and shall consider practical means of solving problems in these fields; shall (2) organize and encourage the study of the underlying principles of Judaism; the history, literature and customs of the Jews, and their bearing on their own and the world's history; shall (3) apply knowledge gained in this study to the improvement of the Sabbath Schools, and in the work of social reform; shall (4) secure the interest and aid of influential persons in arousing the general sentiment against religious persecutions, wherever, whenever, and against whomever shown, and in finding means to prevent such persecutions.

A motion was then made, seconded and carried, that the meeting proceed to the election of officers.

Mrs. H. Solomon was nominated for President, and elected by acclamation in a rising vote.

It was moved and seconded that there be one Vice-President for each State in the Union. Carried.

The following ladies were then nominated and elected:
Mrs. Babette Mandel for Illinois.
Mrs. Julia K. Simpson for New York.
Mrs. Carrie S. Benjamin for Colorado.
Miss Goldie Bamber for Massachusetts.
Mrs. Pauline H. Rosenberg for Pennsylvania.

It was moved and seconded that the President be empowered to appoint the other Vice-Presidents. Carried.

Miss Sadie American was nominated as Corresponding Secretary, and elected by acclamation.

Mrs. Sadie Leopold, Miss Felsenthal, and Mrs. L. J. Wolf were nominated for Recording Secretary. Mrs. Leopold and Miss Felsenthal withdrew in favor of Mrs. Wolf, who was then elected unanimously.

Mrs. J. Harry Seelig was nominated and elected as Treasurer.

It was moved and seconded that a Board of Directors be appointed by the President. Carried.

It was moved and seconded that, as soon as may be, a Constitution be drafted, and that a copy, with a circular setting forth the desirability of organizing, be sent through the land. Carried.

It was moved and seconded that the proceedings of Wednesday evening be printed, and sent to Secretary of State Gresham. Carried.

Miss Ray Frank, of Oakland, then offered a prayer, after which the Chairman declared the Congress adjourned.

CONTENTS.

	PAGE
Introduction by the Chairman. *Hannah G. Solomon*	3
Programme of the Congress	6
Prayer. *Ray Frank*	8
Address. *Ellen M. Henrotin*	9
Address by the Chairman. *Hannah G. Solomon*	10
White Day of Peace. *Miriam del Banco*	13
Jewish Women of Biblical and of Mediæval Times. *Louise Mannheimer*	15
Jewish Women of Modern Days. *Helen Kahn Weil*	26
Discussion by *Henrietta G. Frank*	43
Woman in the Synagogue. *Ray Frank*	52
Influence of the Discovery of America on the Jews. *Pauline H. Rosenberg*	66
Discussion by *Esther Witkowsky*	74
by *Mary Newbury Adams*	77
Women Wage-Workers: with Reference to Directing Immigrants. *Julia Richman*	91
Discussion by *Sadie G. Leopold*	108
The Influence of the Jewish Religion on the Home. *Mary M. Cohen*	115
Discussion by *Julia I. Felsenthal*	122
Israel to the World in Greeting. *Cora Wilburn*	129
Charity as Taught by the Mosaic Law. *Eva L. Stern*	133
Woman's Place in Charitable Work: What it is and what it should be. *Carrie Shevelson Benjamin*	145
Discussion by *Goldie Bamber*	157
by *R. W. Navra*	163

CONTENTS.

	PAGE
Address by the Chairman. *Hannah G. Solomon*	166
Presentation of Hymn Book. *E. Frank*	168
Mission Work among the Unenlightened Jews. *Minnie D. Louis*	170
Discussion by *Rebekah Kohut*	187
How can Nations be Influenced to Protest or Interfere in Cases of Persecution? *Laura Davis Jacobson*	196
Discussion by *Lillie Hirshfield*	210
Letter by *George Kennan*	216
Organization. *Sadie American*	218
Report of the Business Meeting	263

www.ingramcontent.com/pod-product-compliance
Lightning Source LLC
Chambersburg PA
CBHW032132230426
43672CB00011B/2307